3765378
943.603

C

# THE REVOLUTIONARY
## EMPEROR:
## JOSEPH II OF AUSTRIA

Joseph II when Emperor

# The Revolutionary Emperor: Joseph II of Austria

SAUL K. PADOVER

EYRE & SPOTTISWOODE
LONDON

First published *1934*
Second edition, revised and reset, *1967*
Second edition © Saul K. Padover *1967*
Published by Eyre & Spottiswoode (Publishers) Ltd
*11* New Fetter Lane London EC4
Printed in Great Britain by
T. H. Brickell & Son Ltd
Gillingham, Dorset

# Contents

# Illustrations

ACKNOWLEDGMENTS

The author and publishers are grateful to the
following for permission to reproduce copyright
material: The Mansell Collection for frontis-
piece and plates 2, 3, 4, 5, 6, 7; Mansell-
Wolfrum for plate 1.

# Introduction

This is a new and completely revised edition of the book first published in 1934. It was then, as it still is today, the only full-length biography of Joseph II in the English language. Its relevance has not changed with the years.

Joseph II was the eighteenth century's epitome of political reform. In view of the scope of his operations and the size of the territories under his imperial control, he was perhaps the most significant of the Enlightened Despots of his time.

No ruler of his day was more passionately eager for reform than was Joseph. He battled to destroy the entrenched feudal iniquities, to provide the overburdened peasantry with a chance for justice, to establish schools for the common people, and to institute religious liberty in his vast and polyglot dominions. He did not live long enough to see his efforts crowned with success.

Joseph's war against feudal privileges should mark him as one of the liberators of humanity. Despite fierce opposition, this Habsburg emperor was the first great ruler in Christendom to grant freedom of speech and conscience to his subjects. He also modernized the age-encrusted administration and instituted a system of compulsory public education. These were memorable achievements. But even his failures – due largely to impatience, tactlessness, and needless military adventures – were on a grand scale. They left an imprint on history.

His story is one of high drama and personal tragedy. He is a man who cannot be forgotten.

SAUL K. PADOVER

New York City
June, 1967

PART ONE

# The Crown Prince

12

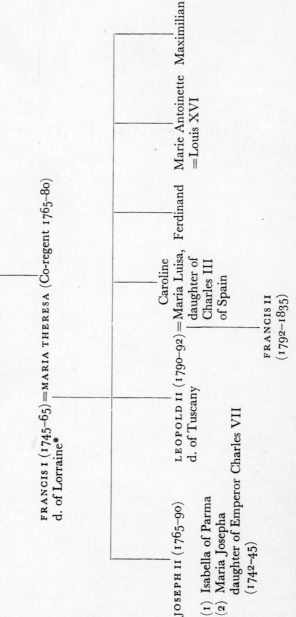

The Immediate Family of Joseph II

CHARLES VI (1711–40)†

FRANCIS I (1745–65)＝MARIA THERESA (Co-regent 1765–80)
d. of Lorraine*

JOSEPH II (1765–90)

(1) Isabella of Parma
(2) Maria Josepha
daughter of Emperor Charles VII
(1742–45)

LEOPOLD II (1790–92)＝Maria Luisa,
d. of Tuscany          daughter of
                       Charles III
                       of Spain

FRANCIS II
(1792–1835)

Caroline   Ferdinand   Marie Antoinette   Maximilian
                       ＝Louis XVI

*  *Note:* Francis I exchanged the dukedom of Lorraine for Tuscany, which on his death was inherited by his second son, Leopold.
†  Dates in brackets refer to reign as Emperor.

# CHAPTER I

# Youth

On March 13, 1741, Empress Maria Theresa of Austria gave birth to a long-awaited heir and having often commended herself to St Joseph, she had the boy named after the saint. Couriers were sent to all the courts of Europe except that of the hostile Frederick the Great of Prussia, to announce the happy event. Maria Theresa, grateful to God for this second child [the first was a girl], sent a silver statuette weighing over sixteen pounds to the Mariazell church.

She was a woman of imperious temper, dominating all around her. The absolute ruler of the empire, she was also the autocrat of her immediate household. Emperor Francis I was merely the husband of Maria Theresa and the father of her children. 'The empress and my children,' he said, 'compose the imperial family. I am but a private individual.'

He had been Duke of Lorraine, a great-nephew of Louis XIV, when he married Maria Theresa, the greatest heiress in Europe, in 1736. Later she had him crowned Emperor of the Holy Roman Empire, but it was an act more of uxorial affection than of political power.

Emperor Francis I loved his children, especially Joseph, but he could only exert limited influence on them. Not being permitted to rule or to assert himself otherwise, he devoted himself to making money and, as a good Frenchman, he succeeded in his aim. Frederick the Great referred to him mockingly as 'the banker of the court'.

Young Archduke Joseph was an observant boy and the position of his father at court did not escape him. He considered his father's place humiliating, without understanding that to Francis the imperial crown was light in comparison with the compensating pleasures, of which there were four – money-making, the theatre, the chase, and women. Young Joseph thought his father 'an idler surrounded by flatterers'.

Joseph possessed some of the characteristics of both parents. He had his mother's harshness and despotic inclinations, and his father's simplicity and common sense. They did not blend well. When Joseph was four years old his mother said of him: 'My Joseph cannot obey.' He was a haughty and domineering little boy. 'He thee-thous everybody,' reported Count Heinrich von Podewils, the Prussian envoy in Vienna, 'his aspect is fierce and haughty . . . It is only people of rank and ladies whom he honours with his attention. He has already a very high conception of his station.'

When Joseph was eight years old his mother created a separate court for him. At the same time she placed him in the charge of two men, a general and a priest, to direct his education. These two, Field Marshal Count Carl Batthyany and Franz Joseph Weger, were asked by Maria Theresa to help discipline the wilful heir, who had, she said, a 'violent desire to carry out his will in all . . . his demands'. She instructed them to try to win his confidence; to be strict; to execute what they promised or threatened; to make him admit his mistakes; and to change his habit of ridiculing people. Count Batthyany, Maria Theresa instructed, should:

> censure vice and evil in general . . . , but should not speak harshly of anyone, not even of enemy nations . . . , and should make the Archduke understand that those who underestimate or criticize other princes, do so in order to tempt and flatter, and that neither the one nor the other should be listened to by a good Christian and a good soul.

In addition, the empress commanded that her son should be taught not to exaggerate his own importance, to learn to esteem each man according to his merits, to be friendly and cordial, and to try to earn the love of his parents by diligence and good conduct. The chamberlains, of whom there were six, were forbidden any kind of gossip and levity in the archduke's presence. Above all, the instructions emphasized, Joseph was to be treated with candour and sincerity, so that the same qualities be aroused in him.

Joseph was put under a rigorous schedule. He had to rise at 6.45 in the morning for prayer. From 8 to 9 he studied Latin, and from 9.45 to 10.30 history. German and calligraphy took up the next hour. After lunch, one hour was devoted to geography and another to religion, the latter taught by a Jesuit, Father Höller. The young archduke had to hear Mass daily, say his prayers every morning and evening for half an hour each, and attend church during the innumerable holidays. Once, in 1752, when Joseph was eleven, his father took him on a visit to sepulchres in eighteen different churches in one week.

To the surprise of the relentlessly pious Maria Theresa, Joseph came to develop an aversion for churchly and clerical matters. As emperor, he was to carry out a drastic anti-ecclesiastical programme.

In other ways, too, Joseph reacted negatively to his curriculum and tutors. He was taught music, dancing, riding, and hunting. Later in life he occasionally played the violoncello, but he never had any understanding or sympathy for music. In his mature years he rarely danced. As for hunting, possibly as a reaction to his father's known passion for the chase, Joseph came to loathe it. On his trip to France in 1777, he said he detested hunting because it 'distracts the mind and serves as an excuse to neglect serious occupations'.

He was interested in mathematics and natural science. But his curriculum provided little of either. He knew so little of natural history that in 1787, when his vice-chancellor, Philipp Cobenzl, asked him to buy a zebra for the Schönbrunn Zoo, he replied 'I am not sure I know what a zebra is, but I find 800 ducats too much for it'.

His curriculum was loaded with history. Its purpose was utility, as Emperor Francis I stressed when he ordered State Secretary Christoph von Bartenstein to draw up a programme for the archduke's historical education.

History should be so transcribed for my son Joseph that neither the mistakes and evil deeds of the rulers, nor their virtues be

glossed over. It should be presented before my son in such a way
that by and by he should learn to notice the good and to acquire
sound *principia*, which would have the effect of teaching him early
to avoid the mistakes of preceding rulers.

Bartenstein produced a stupendous compilation in fifteen
folios, which is still gathering dust in manuscript form in the
vaults of the Vienna archives. The history, with its emphasis on
Austria and the Habsburgs, dealt with natural, civil, international, and canon law. This was weighted with laborious
reflections, verbose circumlocutions and long-winded comments. The boy of eleven was asked to memorize such passages
as:

> Question: What lands did Charles V possess at the time of his
> accession to the throne?
> Answer: He possessed all of Spain, except Navarre, both Sicilies,
> the hereditary Austrian lands, and the Netherlands, which he in-
> creased by the addition of West Frisia, this having been redeemed
> before the election of both Dukes of Saxony, George and Henry.
> To administer so many far-flung great kingdoms and lands, differ-
> ing totally in their constitutions, and whose inhabitants likewise
> differed in customs and languages, was exceedingly difficult. Im-
> possible it is for one man to be up to the task involved in the
> administration . . . , etc.

Joseph had to memorize his lessons, recite them, and the following day write them out from memory. Examinations were held
every two months, attended by the parents and some specially
honoured visitors. Prince Johann Josef Khevenhüller's diary,
particularly for the years 1758 and 1759, contains such references as:

> On the 2 [January 2, 1758] I had the honour of attending an
> *Examini historici* of the Archduke Joseph;
> the 16 [January 16, 1758] I attended an *Examini feudali* of the
> Archduke Joseph. The Empress also came;
> the 27 [February 27, 1758] I assisted in the last *Examini* of the
> Archduke Joseph ex *jure feudali*, whereupon he began the *Collegia
> juris publici*.

Father Weger, who taught Joseph languages and literature,
was perhaps the most successful of his teachers. 'Herr Weger,'

Maria Theresa said, 'did everything possible to make the lessons agreeable . . . Sensitive to the taste and moods of the Archduke, he knew how to employ a thousand little artful methods to achieve his aim, so that the lessons seemed to the Archduke more of an amusement than a serious occupation.' The young heir to the throne, as required by the Golden Bull, had to learn 'the Italian and Slavic tongues'; he was made to read Corneille, Racine, Crébillon, the *Satires* of Boileau, and Voltaire's *Henriade*. Considering Maria Theresa's piety, it is doubtful whether Joseph read anything else by Voltaire at this period. Italian, the archduke learned readily, and so he did French. He read the Italian historian, Ludovico Antonio Muratori, Cardinal Guido Bentivoglio's *Lettere diplomatichse*, and Enrico Caterino Davila's *Istoria delle guerre civili di Francia*. It is a commentary on German culture of the time that a Teutonic prince was brought up on French and Italian writings.

Perhaps the greatest influence on Joseph, in the light of his future reforms, was Professor Anton von Martini of the University of Vienna, one of the scholars of the Austrian eighteenth-century Enlightenment, who taught the young prince natural and international law. From Martini, Joseph seems to have imbibed theoretical arguments for his dislike of the Church, especially the Jesuits, for whom he had a special antipathy. As he pointed out in a letter to the French statesman, the Duc de Choiseul, some years later, Joseph resented the Jesuits because for a long time the Habsburgs – including his mother – had been the tools and slaves of the Society of Jesus.

At the age of fourteen, Joseph was granted a few small privileges. He was permitted to dine at the imperial table with his parents, to go driving with them, and to be more often in their company. When he was eighteen, reports the gossipy Khevenhüller, he was given 'permission for the first time . . . to escort his own lady' to a ball at court.

He now emerged as a serious young man, lonely and introspected. Batthyany said of him: 'He is not what he seems.' There was no gaiety in him. He neither flirted nor played games, but read serious works, mainly on military, political, and

B

economic subjects. Among his favourite authors were the French Encyclopedists and Physiocrats, including Voltaire.

As he grew into manhood, he kept more and more aloof from the amusements and personalities of the court, nursing a particular antipathy for the courtiers who flattered his mother's vanity. Toward his mother his feelings were ambivalent, an unstable mixture of love and resentment. He was jealous of all possible rivals for his mother's affections and was particularly cold to his many brothers and sisters, including Marie Antoinette whom he was later to treat as a political tool, considering them 'useless ballast'. But he was resentful of his mother's pedantic attitude toward him. She was in the habit of correcting his manners, especially when he was sarcastic toward his siblings, even in the presence of strangers.

# CHAPTER 2

# Manhood

Joseph's marriage, which took place when he was nineteen, was an unavoidable political arrangement, which, while it lasted, turned out to be a happy one.

The marital union was connected with the Austro-French Alliance of 1756, known as the Diplomatic Revolution. It was the joint work of the Austrian chancellor, Prince Wenzel Anton von Kaunitz, and the mistress of Louis XV, the beautiful Madame de Pompadour. To cement this union of Habsburg and Bourbon, Louis XV suggested that Joseph, the young heir to the Austrian throne, marry his niece, Isabel of Parma. Maria Theresa was pleased, and so was Joseph, who liked Isabel's looks when he was shown her picture.

The wedding was celebrated, in June 1760, in splendour. The papal legate, Borromeo, performed the ceremony in the Augustinian church. Afterwards a magnificent feast was held at the *Redouten Saal* in the Hofburg, and was followed by several days of festivities. It was a moment when Frederick of Prussia inflicted a severe defeat on the Austrian armies at Torgau, but the Viennese celebrated their prince's marriage as if there were no war *'come se guerra non essistese'*, in the words of Ruzzini, an Italian visitor.

Perhaps for the first time in his life, Joseph was happy. He loved his wife, and now his mother also softened and began to bring him into the Administration. She invited him to attend the meetings of the *Staatsrath* (Council of State) and to participate in some governmental affairs.

The *Staatsrath*, consisting of dignified Councillors addicted to leisurely speeches, was a disillusionment to the impatient young archduke. The elderly gentlemen stirred him to sarcasm:

A young man without experience . . . , I hoped to find myself among Solons and Lycurguses and to listen only to oracles. . . .

The long palavers were so sublime to me, that I, understanding
neither their import nor their relevance . . . , was badly enough
advised to think of other matters, when no doubt I should have
imbibed all those artful contortions which were supposed to serve
in place of reason and common sense.

In a long memoir, entitled 'Reveries', Joseph developed two
fundamental ideas that were to guide him the rest of his life:
the absolutism of the government, and the policy of not relying
on foreign assistance – *'le pouvoir absolu de . . . l'Etat, et le moyen
de soutenir cet Etat sans secours étranger'*. The underlying principles
were those of Enlightened Despotism. 'I believe,' he wrote,
'that it is necessary to reform the separate states and make them
realize how necessary for them would be the despotism which
I propose.'

One of the means of strengthening the central government in
Vienna, Joseph pointed out, was to tax the hitherto exempt
nobility. He sharply criticized the idle and sumptuous existence
of the aristocracy. It was unjust, he argued, that those who
worked had to pay the taxes, while aristocratic idlers, loaded
with privileges, contributed nothing but their personal extravagance.

The inner strength of the State [he wrote], good laws, and a just
execution of them, well ordered finances, a respect-inspiring
army, and a flourishing industry are more beautiful ornaments
. . . than splendid festivities, gala holidays, magnificent salons,
golden treasures, rich fabrics, and precious jewels.

Such ideas were heresy to Maria Theresa. She sensed their
deeper meaning, a challenge to her own person and position,
and strongly rejected her son's views. The archduke was kept
at arm's length from real power.

He tried to forget his political frustrations and anxieties in
the company of his wife. Isabel was accomplished in the genteel
arts, played the violin, sang, and painted. But she continued to
be melancholy and introspected. Joseph did not understand her
and was not aware of her obsession with the idea of an early
death, which a gipsy had prophesied. Despite her husband's
devotion to her, she was not happy in the court of the Habsburgs.

A princess [she wrote], cannot, like the poorest woman in a hut, relax in the midst of her family. In the high society in which she is forced to live, she has neither acquaintances nor friends. It is for this that she has to leave her family, her home. And why? To belong to a man whose character she does not know, to enter into a family where she is received with jealousy.

She courted death. Life was nothing but misery, sorrow, distress. The soul is shackled to the body, cruelly delaying its ascent to the 'heavenly home'. In the third year of her marriage, Isabel wrote to her sister-in-law Marie Christine:

Death is beneficent. Never have I thought of it more than now. Everything arouses in me the desire to die soon. God knows my wish to desert a life which insults Him every day . . . What business have I in this world? I am good for nothing . . . If it were permitted to kill one's self, I would have already done it.

Joseph had no suspicion of his beloved wife's suicidal impulses. But a sharp-eyed contemporary observer, the famous Italian amorist Jacques Casanova, saw something similar in the archduke's face. To Casanova, who had made a career of meeting the famous and the great, young Joseph's countenance expressed 'conceit and suicide'.

After three years of married life, Isabel had her deepest wish granted. She died – of smallpox. It was a shattering blow to her twenty-two year old husband. 'I have lost all,' he wrote to his brother Leopold. 'I wish you from all my heart as good a wife as mine was, but may the Lord protect you from a similar misfortune.' The embittered Joseph was never to love another woman.

His position did not permit him to isolate himself in private grief. Four months after the death of Isabel, in March 1764, he went to Frankfürt-am-Main to be crowned King of the Romans. This honorific position, hereditary in the Habsburg dynasty, was, according to the Golden Bull of 1356, a requirement for the succession to his father's position of Emperor of the Holy Roman Empire.

For the grieving Joseph, the trip to Frankfürt, in the company of his father, two brothers and an assortment of nobles, was an ordeal. He was haunted by the memory of his wife. 'I am like a man dazed,' he wrote to his mother in one of his daily letters to her. 'My heart is cruelly torn; the loss of my darling wife is still buried so deeply in my heart that it comes back to me every moment . . . I cannot restrain my tears.'

At Frankfürt, the bustle, intrigues, petty squabbles, and social manoeuvrings connected with the coronation repelled the young archduke. He confided to his mother, 'With my heart full of pain, I must pretend that I am enraptured with a dignity of which I know only the burdens but not the pleasures. I love solitude . . . and yet I have to chatter all day and say meaningless nothings.' He complained to her of the 'trash and idiocies' to which he had to listen all day. The assembled noblesse and the eight hereditary Electors[1] and their pompous retinues would have been shocked had they known their king-elect's opinion of them.

> It costs me great efforts [he wrote to his mother], to restrain myself from telling these gentlemen to their faces how idiotically they act and talk. I have controlled myself so far, but I cannot guarantee what will happen later, for even an angel would lose his patience.

It was all a species of historically established comedy. Three days before the coronation, the deputies from Nuremberg brought to Frankfürt the ancient 'imperial ornaments', as Joseph called the crown and vestments. The burgher who headed the Nuremberg delegation aroused the mirth of Joseph's clever young brother Leopold, who confided to a friend:

> Imagine a big fat man, with a fat head enveloped by a pigtail hanging down to the middle of his belly, and covering his chest, his back, his shoulders and his loins. You can judge the size of this enormous pigtail by the quantity of ringlets, for from the chin down one could count forty-eight in a row, thick as a fist. I did

[1] There were originally eight hereditary Electors, three ecclesiastical and five secular: the Archbishops of Cologne, Trier, and Mainz; and the Count Palatine of the Rhine, the Elector of Saxony, the Elector of Hanover, the Margrave of Brandenburg (Prussia), and the King of Bohemia (whose crown, and Electoral vote, were held by the Habsburgs). A ninth Elector, the Bavarian, was added in 1648.

not laugh, however, for he harangued me, and I kept a straight face.

To Joseph the whole thing was not funny at all. He tried on the coronation robes and found them heavy, clumsy and, as he said bitterly, preposterous. 'Their weight is terrible,' he complained, 'and I am afraid I shall be sick.' He noted that the crown weighed fourteen pounds and 'the whole outfit more than one hundred and thirty pounds'. It was, he said sarcastically, 'a pretty burden to carry on one's body all day'.

The coronation was a glittering event. For the last time before the French Revolution, European royalty gathered in all its pomp to celebrate the perpetuation of an ancient myth. Colourful parades started at the city gates and wound their way to the *Roemer*, where the coronation was to take place. Even the lackeys sparkled with colour. So did the caparisoned animals. The mules of the Archbishop of Mainz were decked with precious lace; his horses were decorated with gold and silver ornaments. The archiepiscopal retinue followed their lord in fourteen resplendent carriages.

It was, climatically, a cold day. The Frankfürt garrison and the bourgeois guard stood shivering at attention, achieving an occasional measure of warmth by a round of saluting, presenting arms, and lowering and raising flags. The drummers drummed, the trumpeters trumpeted, the buglers bugled, the horses neighed steamingly, and the ordinary poor shivered in their unheated homes; for as the city magistrate pointed out in his appeal to the emperor, there was little fuel in Frankfürt.

Among the spectators was a fifteen-year-old boy, destined to become Germany's greatest poet. Years later, in his autobiographic *Dichtung und Wahrheit*, Johann Wolfgang Goethe recalled the picture:

> The eye was tired from the richly dressed servants and attendants, and the majestically moving nobility. And when at last the emperor in romantic dress, and somewhat behind him, his son in Spanish costume, came riding slowly on magnificently ornamented horses . . . , the dazzled eye could stand it no longer. . . .
> Finally both majesties made their appearance . . . The

emperor's vestments of purple silk, richly adorned with pearls and precious stones, as well as the crown, sceptre, and imperial orb, struck the eye, for everything was novel, and the imitation of antiquity tastefully carried out. So he moved comfortably in his robes, and his loyal, dignified face proclaimed both the emperor and the father. The young king, however, dragged himself in his monstrous raiments, so that he himself, glancing at his father from time to time, could hardly restrain a smile. The crown . . . hung on his head like projecting roof.

What was a magnificent spectacle to Goethe was a painful ordeal for Joseph. He could not forget Isabel. 'The image of my dear wife,' he wrote to his mother, 'is always before my eyes.' When at last he left Frankfürt, six days after the coronation, on April 9, he exclaimed 'Today is the happy day'.

A royal title was not enough. The heir to the Habsburg dominions had to perpetuate the dynasty. But the thought of remarriage nauseated Joseph. Pitilessly, but with a show of ever ready tears and affection, Maria Theresa went at the task of breaking her son's aversion to taking another wife. He told his mother: 'The memory of my adorable wife is so deeply graven in my heart that I consider marrying again as the crown of all misfortunes.' He wanted, he said to her, to remain a widower or, better still, be 'for ever united with my beautiful angel in heaven'. In the end, however, he yielded to his mother's persuasions, telling her bitterly: 'I am ready to sacrifice myself for you.'

Forced to choose, Joseph decided upon Louise of Parma, his dead wife's sister. Marrying Louise, he said, was the 'last duty I owe the memory of my adorable wife'. To humour him, Maria Theresa asked the consent of Charles III of Spain, the head of the Bourbon family. A union between Habsburg and Bourbon, the letter pointed out, was 'necessary for our holy religion and the maintenance of both our Houses'. Charles III's reply was a polite refusal: the Princess of Parma was already engaged to his own son.

The choice of available princesses was then limited to three: the Princess of Portugal, the Princess of Saxony, and the Princess of Bavaria. Chancellor Kaunitz opposed any alliance

with Portgual because, he pointed out practically, in view o
that country's firm ties with England it would be of no use
whatever to Austria. As for the other two, there was no objection, and Joseph himself was completely indifferent in the
matter. Since he was not emotionally involved, he would be
guided by purely political considerations, as calculated by his
mother's astute chancellor.

In the autumn of 1764, Joseph went to look over the two
princesses. He inclined towards the Saxon heiress, as the less
ugly of the two. 'Princess Cunigunde of Saxony,' he wrote of
her, 'has . . . a solid character. She is virtuous, but of course
also . . . without spirit . . . She possesses common sense, and is
unusually tender.' Her exterior, however, repelled. She was so
bulky and hideous that Joseph recoiled when he first saw her.
He might have sacrificed himself by marrying her anyhow, but
the court in Vienna decided that an alliance with Bavaria
would be more profitable for Austria. Joseph fatalistically
agreed to marry Josepha of Bavaria, of whom he wrote brutally:
'She is twenty-six years old; a small squat figure, without
youthful charm, pimples and red spots on the face, repulsive
teeth. . . .'

Even Maria Theresa was sorry for her son. 'The most bitter
thing of all,' she confided to her daughter Marie Christine,
'is that we have to pretend that we are happy and delighted.'
A story circulated at the court that the empress asked a courtier
which of the two princesses – both notorious for their ugliness
– he would select if he had to do so. The courtier replied:
'Madame, if I were master of my actions I would take neither;
but, with a dagger at my gullet, I would choose the Bavarian,
for at least she has a bosom.' Maria Theresa burst into laughter.

The wedding took place at Schönbrunn early in 1765.
Joseph was almost mad with despair. He told a friend that he
found himself in a 'hopeless situation'. His bride, he said, was
'irreproachable', but he had no feelings for her, except loathing.
The 'scorbutic eruptions' on Josepha's body filled him with
disgust. Joseph publicly showed his implacable aversion for his
wife by partitioning off the balcony which connected their

apartments. With his mother's streak of cruelty in him, he did not hesitate to speak contemptuously of his wife in the presence of other ladies. 'My wife,' he said, 'has become insupportable to me . . . They want me to have children. How can I have them? If I could put the tip of my finger on the tiniest part of her body that is not covered with boils, I would try to have children.' He was so openly cruel to Josepha that his sister Marie Christine remarked: 'I believe that if I were his wife and so mistreated, I would escape and hang myself on a tree at Schöenbrunn.'

Josepha, an object of scorn, suffered in silence. Two and a half years after the marriage, on May 28, 1767, the smallpox finally freed her from her earthly burdens and humiliations.

Joseph never remarried. Ambition took the place of love; war replaced affection.

PART TWO

# The Co-Regent

(1765–1780)

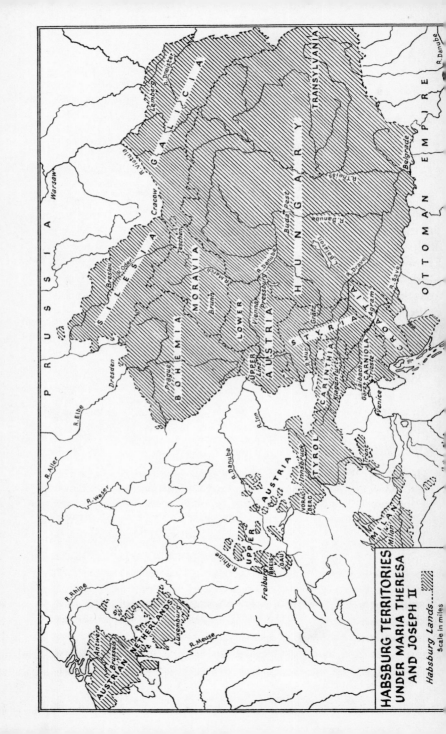

HABSBURG TERRITORIES
UNDER MARIA THERESA
AND JOSEPH II

Habsburg Lands......

Scale in miles

CHAPTER 3

# Conflict

*If I did not have a little philosophy to sustain me I would go
mad.* Joseph to Leopold

In the summer of 1765, the court went to Innsbruck to celebrate
the marriage of Joseph's young brother Leopold to the Infanta
of Spain. On the night of August 18, Joseph's father, Emperor
Francis, who had been suffering from apopleptic fits, had a
sudden seizure as he was leaving the ballroom to go to his
apartments. Joseph, who had followed his father from a distance,
rushed forward, caught him in his arms and carried him to bed.
'Father confessors, doctors and surgeons were summoned,' an
eyewitness writes, 'they opened the veins in his arm and in one
temple, but he gave no sign of life.'

'We have lost,' Joseph wrote to one of his sisters, 'the best of
fathers and the best of friends.'

In a letter to his former tutor Batthyany, Joseph – now auto-
matically becoming emperor – expressed sorrow and self-pity
at the death of his father.

He was my teacher, my friend . . . I am now twenty-four years of
age. Providence has given me the cup of sorrow in my early days.
I lost my wife after having possessed her scarcely three years.
Dear Isabel! thou wilt never be forgotten by me! You, my prince,
were the guide of my youth; under your direction I became a
man. Do now support me also as a monarch in the important
duties which destiny imposes upon me, and preserve your heart
for your friend.

Maria Theresa's grief was deeper. Francis had been the first
and only love of her life. Now she wished to retire from the
world, to spend the rest of her days in a convent there to com-
mune with God and the spirit of her Franzl. Upon her return
to Vienna, she locked herself in her rooms, wept and lamented.

She cut her own hair, dressed in black, decorated her apartments in grey, and expected everybody at court to be in gloom. The court ladies were forbidden to wear rouge. All of this sombrousness stirred Joseph to risibility. He wrote sarcastically to his brother Leopold that the tears did no harm to the pretty eyes of the pretty ladies at court, but, in trickling down their surreptitiously rouged cheecks they made the ladies look like ghosts.

The trouble was Maria Theresa could not make up her mind as to what to do. If she could be sure that Chancellor Kaunitz would remain at his post, she might definitely retire. In the wily chancellor with his superb imperturbability she had infinite confidence. 'I count upon you,' she wrote him, 'and will do nothing without your advice . . . I will leave the care of my family to you as gladly as I will entrust the government.'

Kaunitz, whom the ever suspicious Joseph also trusted, was one of the great personalities of the age.

Prince Wenzel Anton von Kaunitz-Rittberg (or Rietberg), Maria Theresa's *alter ego* for twenty-seven years, was born in 1711, scion of eight centuries of nobility. After a brief ecclesiastical career (as canon of Münster), he chose diplomacy. He served in Turin, where he learned the diplomatic craft from the crafty Italians ('dangerous people', he called them), then in Brussels, and finally in Paris as Austrian ambassador. It was in Paris that the slender, blond, blue-eyed Kaunitz prepared the ground for his great diplomatic triumph – the Austro-French alliance – that won him the undying trust of Maria Theresa.

As Austrian ambassador to Paris, Kaunitz moved adroitly to lay the foundations for the shift in the great-power alliances that came to be known as the Diplomatic Revolution. He impressed the gay French capital with his magnificence and calculated eccentricities, having at his disposal one hundred thousand florins to spend as he saw fit. Realizing that the power behind the Bourbon throne was the Marquise de Pompadour, Kaunitz – 'of medium size . . . very muscular and slender,

blond, of white complexion' – lost no time in ingratiating himself with that unreluctant lady. The crafty diplomat and the
king's mistress became great friends. 'My dear Marmontel,'
Kaunitz said to the French writer, 'I am here for only two
things: for the interests of my queen, and these I serve well; for
my pleasures, and on this score I need consult nobody but
myself . . . I have two persons to manage, the king and his
mistress. I am getting along well with both of them.'

Three years later Kaunitz returned to Vienna and was made
chancellor, with almost absolute powers. By 1756, the 'coach-
man of Europe', as he loved to call himself, reaped the fruit of
his work in Paris by effecting the Diplomatic Revolution – an
alliance between those traditional enemies, Habsburgs and
Bourbons. This Austro-French alliance, aimed against Prussia,
estranged England and led to the Seven Years' War (1756–63).
This was truly a global war, fought on land and on sea, in
Europe and America, in India and the West Indies. In the end
only England emerged a world empire. Austria gained nothing
(neither did Russia). Maria Theresa had learned her lesson,
but not so Kaunitz. He never gave up his addiction to planning
and scheming for Austrian expansion.

The guiding principle of this *homo politicus* was the supremacy
of the 'August House of Austria', as he loved to phrase it. To
this end he fought Frederick of Prussia for thirty years, planned
to dismember Turkey, partitioned Poland, placated Russia,
allied Austria with France. For the aggrandizement of the Habsburg monarchy Kaunitz devoted his whole life and his cold,
calculating mind. In internal affairs he was, like Richelieu
whom he so much resembled, a believer in absolute monarchy.
Under Kaunitz's leadership, Austria was powerful and respected as she had never been before and was never to be again,
except under his kinsman Metternich.

Maria Theresa adored her chancellor. To her he was the
greatest statesman in the world, the profoundest thinker, the
purest character. She consulted him as if he were an oracle.
Their relations were a mixture of confidence and finesse, affection and shrewdness. He flattered her subtly, never obtruded

himself, never antagonized her. He knew how to conceal the most unpalatable truths and the most disagreeable suggestions in a phraseology so complicated, sinuous and polite that Maria Theresa generally accepted his ideas. Even when she knew better, she yielded to this superior dialectical skill.

The chancellor managed the empress with matchless skill, something he never succeeded in doing with Joseph. Every act, from the spending of a few florins to the making of a treaty, was respectfully submitted to Maria Theresa for consideration. Upon the margins of his memoranda she would write *Placet*, or, in case of rejection, would scribble in her impossible hand the reasons for her disapproval. Kaunitz would ostensibly bow to the all-wise and all-powerful will of the 'All-Highest', as he addressed her. Then, if the matter was important, he would return to the attack with new arguments, new tactics, new subtleties, purring like a cat and hiding his sharp claws.

Maria Theresa's trust in him was as complete as her admiration. 'Everything great in the monarchy,' she once told him, 'and everything good in my family I have you to thank for. My gratitude and genuine friendship will cease only when my long and sad days will have come to an end.' On another occasion she confessed to him :'You have always been right in your explanations and I wrong.' Nothing caused her greater misery than a threat of his resignation. He did, indeed, resign a number of times during his career – generally when his vanity was hurt – and was always persuaded to come back. Like Bismarck, he invariably gave weak health as the cause for his withdrawing from office. Weak health, real or imagined, was one of Kaunitz's assets. It served to arouse compassion in the empress, to give him an excuse for withdrawing from boring court activities, and to make people including the highest personages – once even Pope Pius VI – come to him.

Kaunitz's eccentricities were notorious. Fearing fresh air as if it were the dreaded smallpox, he rarely exercised outdoors. In the hottest days he would take a short walk from the ministry to the *Burg*, a distance of a few yards, holding a perfumed handkerchief to his mouth and nose in order not to be contaminated.

When he was seen coming to the palace, everyone, including Maria Theresa, hastened to shut all doors and windows. In his own rooms there was a thermometre and barometre; the heating had to be precisely regulated. A confirmed hypochondriac, and one who wisely distrusted doctors, Kaunitz lived on a careful diet. He spent from two to three hours a day upon his toilet, sometimes changing his clothes twenty or thirty times. In his impeccably powdered wig (and powdering the wig was a solemn ceremony), black hose, black breeches, and black coat, Kaunitz looked like an immaculate, sombre actor, which, indeed, he was. He pretended to be indifferent to everybody, never making any effort to meet people, not even the emperor. Often Joseph had to go out of his way to see the chancellor, for the latter would never dream of visiting even a monarch. Kaunitz's rare public appearances shocked conventional souls. Not only was he habitually late, even for High Mass, but often singularly dressed.

> His dinner hours [writes Ségur, the French diplomat who knew Kaunitz well], were never regulated, and his guests were exposed to the double risk, either of arriving late, or of being obliged to wait several hours . . . At the dessert, a mirror, a basin, a sponge, and tooth picks were brought in, and without embarrassment he began slowly to cleanse his mouth and teeth, without anyone wishing or daring to leave the table.

The chancellor began work at noon and continued until evening, dictating systematically, precisely, clearly. He rarely used a quill himself, except to sign his name. Every document that left the chancery bearing his signature – and there were thousands of them – was read and corrected by him. His love of order was almost a mania: even the quills, inkbottles, erasers, and bric-à-brac on his desk had to be laid out symmetrically. 'I was born,' he said, 'with the spirit of order.'

Every evening he made out an agenda for the next day. His readers and secretaries were given written instructions never to mention death and smallpox in his presence. His orders were obeyed to such an extent that when Maria Theresa died, no one dared tell him the news, except his disciple Philipp Cobenzl who

c

did so merely with a nod. This was the only occasion any one
ever saw him shed a tear.

Kaunitz's weakness as a statesman lay in his incurable tendency to theorize. He had a theory for every fact and a fact for
every theory, without being a slave to either. He could always
invent new hypotheses to suit every occasion. 'A statesman
without principles,' he used to say, 'is like an architect without
blue prints'; and, 'Nothing great can be achieved without
system.' He was perhaps the most cool-headed politician in
Europe, as completely lacking in passion as in scruples. He
worked well with the cautious Maria Theresa; but the impetuous Joseph he almost drove to distraction when he murmured
with exasperating coolness, 'All in good time'.

Kaunitz agreed to remain at his post and the lamenting widow,
after delegating all authority to Joseph, retired to her cell.
Joseph was now master of all the Habsburg dominions and
thought himself at liberty to clean the Augean stables. He
plunged into work with all the ardour of an impetuous reformer.
'I am overwhelmed with business and conferences,' he wrote to
Leopold, 'I rise at six-thirty, go to Mass, and am at my desk at
eight.'

The first task was to establish economies in the Administration. Emperor Francis' will left 10,000 florins to pay for Masses
for his sinful soul, 1,000 florins for his domestics, and 50,000 for
the poor; the rest of the emperor's private fortune, about
22 million gulden in cash, was bequeathed to Joseph. Instead
of appropriating the money for himself, Joseph used it to reduce
the interest on the 300 million state debt from 5 and 6 per cent
to 4 per cent. He thus saved the state 870,000 florins in interest
annually, but the Austrian poor, overburdened with taxes as
they were, did not appreciate Joseph's selfless act; they had
hoped that their monarch would use his private wealth to lower
their taxes.

Joseph, however, could not have been expected to be more
generous to his subjects than he was to his favourite brother.
About 2 million gulden of Francis' money was tied up in

uscany, where Leopold was the grand duke. Joseph wrote to
is brother that 'having made a cession of my whole inherit-
nce to the state, without leaving anything for myself', he
ished that Leopold would return their father's money. The
rand duke thought the demand outrageous. The emperor in-
sted upon the money, saying drily that 'the state has great
eed of the cash, and therefore I must remind you to send it
nmediately'. Leopold temporized; Joseph sent peremptory
rders. The grand duke finally promised to obey.

There was great need to retrench financially, for the state
as deeply in debt and Maria Theresa had been reckless in her
xpenditures; but in Joseph the motive force was the urge to
act from a father's generosity and a mother's extravagance.
he twenty-four-year-old emperor began a ruthless elimination
f useless court expenses. He abolished the separate tables for
e imperial family, making all the brothers and sisters suffer
ach other by dining together; he did away with the system of
eding the court officials, ordering the chamberlains and
unkeys to compliment their wives by dining at home; he re-
uced the number of gala days to one: New Year's day; he
ismissed many superfluous officials, hoping thereby to make
em useful subjects.

Then began a reform in styles. Joseph ordered that no one at
urt should appear in the ugly black Spanish robes, nor any
nger continue to be slaves to Spanish ceremonial, especially
the bending of the knee in greeting. For public dress,
llowing the novel Prussian custom, Joseph preferred a
ilitary uniform. This Prussian habit he introduced in all his
nds, Austria, Hungary, Poland, Czechoslovakia, and the
alkans.

Nor were the animals left unmolested. Joseph cut down the
umber of court horses from twelve hundred to seven hundred
nd fifty. His most savage, and most thorough, attack centred
n his father's favourite beasts, wild boars. Francis had been
enamoured of hunting that he filled the environs of Vienna –
ineyards and woods – with boars, which, piglike, caused un-
ld damage to trees and crops. His son now issued a decree for

all wild boars to be exterminated. There began a blood-bat
the like of which Vienna had never seen. The imperial family
including the dainty archduchesses, helped in the crusad
against the boars. On December 19, 1765, Joseph, who dislike
hunting, wrote to Leopold that the delicate ladies alone ha
killed over fourteen hundred of the beasts.

Now Joseph decided to do something to be remembered b
the Viennese. On the outskirts of the capital there was
meadowy preserve which in the summers had been used by th
court nobility. It was, and still is, known as the *Prater*, one
the great parks in Vienna today. Joseph, possibly to show h
contempt for the nobility, opened the *Prater* to the public. Th
aristocracy, outraged in having to rub shoulders with plebeian
vehemently protested. This gave the sardonic emperor a
occasion to make one of his famous remarks: 'If I were t
associate only with my equals, I would have to descend to th
vaults of the Capuchin church [where the Habsburgs are buried
and there spend my days.' Joseph himself made frequent appea
ances in the *Prater*, and he issued a decree that no one shoul
pay any attention to him or to any member of the roy
family. A few years later the emperor opened another park, th
*Augarten*, to the public and inscribed on the gate: 'This amus
ment place is dedicated to all people by their well-wisher.' Th
words can still be read there.

'Love for the fatherland,' Joseph wrote to his brother, 'th
well-being of the monarchy, these, in truth, are my sole pa
sions . . . Nothing appears petty or trifling to me; all thin
interest me equally.'

The zealous emperor had far-reaching plans. His work ha
just begun, but already it threatened the entrenched interes
in the empire. Appeals were made to Maria Theresa to con
out of her retirement and save the state from the recklessness
her son; friends pressed upon her from all sides, pointing o
her indispensability to the government and the need for sel
sacrifice. Maria Theresa heeded the call and returned to th
throne, especially as Kaunitz – immersed in the *Grosse Politik*
had shown himself unable or unwilling to restrain the empero

he privileged classes – nobles and courtiers, clergy and pro-
teers – breathed with relief. The old order had returned!

But Maria Theresa now felt herself incapable of carrying on
he administration single-handed and decided upon the un-
precedented step of making her son co-regent. Joseph was
mperor, that is only titular head of a venerable but lifeless
nstitution known as the Holy Roman Empire of the German
Nation; while Maria Theresa, as the ruler of the Austrian
hereditary dominions, had the real power. During his mother's
fe Joseph could have only as much authority as Maria Theresa,
n her capacity of Archduchess of Austria and Queen of
Bohemia and of Hungary, cared to delegate to him.

After long consultations with statesmen and jurists the
fficial declaration of the co-regency was signed, on November
7, 1765, by Maria Theresa, Joseph and Kaunitz. 'We have
decided . . .' the empress publicly stated, 'for a co-regency of
ur entire hereditary kingdoms and lands, without, however,
elinquishing the original control over our inseparable states,
nd, consequently, without the slightest apparent violation of
he Pragmatic Sanction.' In less diplomatic words, Maria
Theresa declared that although she was taking in a junior
partner, she had no intention of giving him any legal rights to
he partnership. If Joseph had any illusions about the extent of
his powers as co-regent, he was soon to realize his error. Only
n court administration, finance, and the army did the co-regent
have any authority. This, however, was limited, for the final
decision on all important matters rested with his mother.
oseph had somewhat more power in military affairs, but know-
ng his mother's temper he wisely refrained from using his
authority and always deferred to his maternal superior.

If the co-regent had small powers, he had large ideas, and
hese he set forth in a document immediately after his appoint-
ment. It was a manifesto of radical reform:

> Instead of twelve ministers and councillors, one man should be
> at the head of the internal administration. Instead of limiting and
> checking zeal and activity, rewards and punishments should be
> meted out. . . .

Studies are to be improved, universities founded in the pro
vinces where there is little room for diversion, and the professor
to be encouraged in their zeal by receiving part of the lectur
honoraria. No one should enter a clerical order or be consecrate
under the age of twenty-five. The pious foundations are to be re
organized for the public welfare. Young nobles, having finishe
their education at the age of eighteen, should serve in the arm
for three years to improve their characters. The regiments, where
ever possible, are to remain in their places of recruitment, whic
should enable a larger furloughing and facilitate their marriage
Recruiting abroad should continue unabatedly; the army is to b
used for public works, to be trained in camps, and its emulatio
aroused by just promotions. The officials, especially the highe
ones, are to be spurred to greater zeal, the presidents to train can
didates for state service, and the regent should frequently trave
through his lands, inconspicuously and without retinue. Religiou
toleration, a mild censorship, no prosecution for morals, and n
espionage in private affairs should be the maxims of the goverr
ment. Industry and commerce are to be promoted through th
prohibition of all foreign goods, except spices, through the abol
tion of monopolies, the establishment of commercial schools, an
the destruction of the principle that the pursuit of business
incompatible with aristocracy. The idea of misalliance shoul
cease. For the sake of economy, the officers should appear at th
court in their uniforms, and the officials in simple black garment:
All this must take place not piecemeal, but as a whole.

The co-regent further proposed that the privileges of th
nobility be drastically reduced, the third estate be raised t
greater power, all talents be gathered around the throne, th
administration unified, the government practice rigid economy
and that the interest on state bonds be lowered to 3 per cent.

In this bold programme Joseph went far beyond any of th
eighteenth-century 'enlightened despots', and perhaps eve
beyond the French *philosophes*. Unlike the latter, he was n
theorist or dilettante; he meant every word he wrote, and late
as absolute ruler, he staked his empire and his reputation t
carry out his ideas. At the moment it was too much for Mari
Theresa to swallow; practically all the Josephan proposition
violated her deepest convictions. Until her death in 178c
mother and son were in an almost continuous struggle.

The clash between mother and son extended to all fields of
thought and action. It was a conflict of opposing temperaments,
philosophies, aims – a reflection of the intellectual struggle that
went on everywhere in Europe.

When Joseph became co-regent, the states of western Europe
were taking steps to destroy the all-powerful Jesuits. The Society
of Jesus, founded by Ignatius Loyola, a Spaniard who gave
up chivalry for sainthood, had become in the course of time the
most feared and hated organization in both Protestant and
Catholic lands, a dreaded Black International.

> The originators of all the evils [the Styrian Estates wrote to the
> emperor as early as 1618], are the Jesuits, whose main thought is
> how to strengthen the Roman See and how to bring all kingdoms
> and lands under their power, and they are unscrupulous as to
> means. They incited regent against regent; provoked revolt and
> insurrection among the Estates of every land . . . instigated rulers
> against subjects . . . armed friends against friends; discovered all
> secrets by means of the confessional; coerced the conscience of all
> people . . . and introduced the principle that one need not trust
> or believe those who were not of the Catholic religion.

The Jesuits, satiated with power, had long strayed from the
narrow path of chastity, poverty, and piety. 'I noticed,' Archbishop Migazzi of Vienna wrote to the pope, 'that there was no
longer any discipline among the Jesuits, that they neglected the
Scriptures and church usage, and that they cared neither for
morals nor for honesty.' In France the Society of Jesus had
powerful enemies in the person of the Duke of Choiseul, the
foreign minister, and Madame de Pompadour, the king's
mistress. Louis XV, following the precedent of Pombal in
Portugal, suppressed the Jesuits, and his example was soon
imitated by the other Bourbon courts, Spain, Naples, and
Parma.

The Jesuits, however, had a mighty protector in the pious
Maria Theresa; under the empress the Society of Jesus had a
stranglehold on Austria's educational and intellectual life.
Unfortunately for the Jesuits, Kaunitz was their silent and
implacable enemy, and like an indefatigable spider, the

chancellor – whose espionage system spread over all the courts of Europe – worked for decades to destroy them.

Joseph, who sympathized with Kaunitz, pretended to be neutral. 'So far as we are concerned,' he confided to Leopold, 'we do not want to interfere, as we have no cause to wish for their dissolution, nor do we consider their existence necessary enough to give them protection.' Then Pope Clement XII died of apoplexy, on February 2, 1769, and Kaunitz, upon receiving the news from his Roman agent, hastened to scribble a note in his own unsteady hand to Maria Theresa. Not only the chancellor and the emperor, but the whole Catholic world was interested in the event, for everyone knew that the fate of the Jesuits would be decided by the new pope.

Joseph prepared to leave for Rome where the College of Cardinals was deliberating about a new pope. What was in his mind? He revealed it in a jest. Bidding farewell to his old teacher, the Jesuit Höller, the co-regent smilingly told the anxious man he would have to change his dress with the new pontificate.

In the morning of March 15, Joseph accompanied by Leopold, appeared in Rome, unrecognized by anyone. Two days later the brothers, to the astonishment of the cardinals, entered the Vatican. Cardinal Albani, the leader of the pro-Jesuit faction, took the emperor's hand and led him into the conclave. Joseph, in military uniform, made a gesture as if to remove his sword. A cardinal told him that as the *Defense Ecclesiae* he had the privilege of entering the conclave armed. The emperor showed himself very gracious. When the cardinals asked him to protect the future pope, Joseph answered in fluent Italian: 'You can do more about that than I, if you choose a pope who takes the words *Ne quid nimis* to heart, and who does not drive things to an extreme.' What the emperor whispered to the anti-Jesuit faction has not been recorded.

Two months later Lorenzo Ganganelli was chosen pope; he took the name of Clement XIV. Maria Theresa did not know what to think of this Ganganelli, an unknown man of sixty-four. Joseph, not without malice, enlightened her:

This new pope, who is of the lowest origin, whose brother is still a cabinetmaker and whose nephew is a violin player in taverns, will thoroughly displease the whole Roman nobility, especially the Jesuits, whose sworn enemy he has always been. He is a man of spirit and a great casuist. His Secretary of State, Cardinal Pallavicini, is likewise a man of spirit, who has travelled much, in Germany, France and Spain. Let us hope that he will be more moderate than his predecessor.

The contest over the Jesuits raged for four years after Ganganelli's election. The pope had little sympathy for the Society of Jesus, and he was under constant pressure from the Bourbons. To Clement XIV, a Franciscan and a Thomist, the Jesuits were 'those men abandoned by God, who are about to undergo the consequences of their obstinacy'. But the moderate pope hesitated taking the final step. He knew of the sympathy the powerful Maria Theresa entertained for the Jesuits, and was not at all sure of Joseph. The emperor, like Kaunitz, played an inscrutable game.

Had the pope known of the vitriolic letter which Joseph wrote to the Duke of Choiseul in January, 1770, he might have acted sooner, 'Sir,' the emperor wrote to the French statesman,

I thank you for your confidence. If I were regent, you might boast of my support. With respect to the Jesuits, and your plan for their suppression, you have my perfect approbation. You must not reckon much on my mother; attachment to this Order has become hereditary in the family of the House of Habsburg. Clement XIV has proofs of it. However, Kaunitz is your friend; he can effect everything with the empress. With regard to their suppression, he is of your and the Marquis Pombal's [the Portuguese minister] party; and he is a man who leaves nothing half done. Choiseul, I know these people as well as any man; I know all the plans which they have executed; their endeavours to spread darkness over the earth, and to govern and confuse Europe from Cape Finisterre to the North Sea. In Germany they were mandarins, in France academicians, courtiers and confessors, in Spain and Portugal the grandees of the nation, and in Paraguay kings . . . So it was once, Choiseul! But I foresee that things must change.

Things did change. The Jesuits intrigued and bullied, and in the end antagonized even their friends at Rome. Early in 1773, the pope drew up a tentative bull, but later revised it to suit Maria Theresa's scruples. Apparently Clement XIV was secretly encouraged by Kaunitz and Joseph, for he informed Maria Theresa of his intention to suppress the Society of Jesus, asking for the empress's protection and suggesting that she use the Jesuits' property for the best interest of church and state. About two weeks later, on July 21, 1773, Clement XIV issued the famous bull *Dominus ac Redemptor*, abolishing the Jesuit Order.

The news of the bull filled Joseph with delight. As soon as he heard of it he wrote one of his Swiftian letters to Count Aranda, the Spanish Ambassador in France.

Clement XIV has acquired eternal glory by suppressing the Jesuits. He has annihilated these apostolic sybils from the earth . . . Before they were known in Germany, religion was a doctrine of happiness to the nations; but they have converted it into a revolting image; they have degraded it by using it as an instrument to promote their designs . . . The principal object of the Loyalists was to acquire glory, to extend their power, and to spread darkness over the rest of the world. Their intolerance caused Germany to go through the horrors of a thirty years' war. Their principles cost the lives of the Henrys of France; they were the originators of the loathsome Edict of Nantes. The powerful influence which they had over the princes of the House of Habsburg is too well known. Ferdinand II and Leopold I were their patrons to their last breath. The education of youth, literature, rewards, the distribution of the first dignities of the state, the ear of kings, and the hearts of queens, all were confined to their *wise* counsels. We know too well what use they made of their power, what plans they executed, and what fetters they imposed on the nations. I am not unaware that besides the great Clement, the ministers of the Bourbon courts and Pombal worked for their dissolution. Posterity will do justice to these ministers' efforts and will build them altars in the Temple of Fame. If I were at all capable of hatred, I should hate a race of men who persecuted a Fénelon.

When the Bull *Dominus ac Redemptor* reached Vienna, Maria Theresa, despite high papal sanction, was loath to publish it. Joseph was then away on one of his customary trips, and the mother wished to consult him first. The news of the suppression of the hated Jesuits spread far and wide, however, and the empress could no longer delay executing the bull. She finally proclaimed the decree, but generously offered the Jesuits her protection. The empress confided to a friend, 'The fate of the Jesuits is decided. They have my deepest sympathies, but there is no way of saving them'. To another friend she wrote, 'I am disconsolate and in despair about the Jesuits. I have loved and honoured them all my life, and never say anything of them but what was edifying'. In such a mood she could not be expected to execute the bull. Taking refuge in a threadbare political subterfuge she appointed a commission. When Joseph returned in September and found the dilatory commission doing nothing, he became enraged.

> Jesuit affairs [he stormed], are entrusted to an idle commission. The gentlemen take comfortable vacations on their estates . . . I have read the whole bull . . . I wrote, I pleaded that preparations for its execution be made . . . Do you believe that anything was done. . . ? Not a thing! It is three weeks now since the Jesuits were suppressed, and yet they still function in Pressburg, Prague, Brünn, and in Neustadt, and God knows how much longer they will exist, for, I see, nobody bothers about it.

Joseph galvanized the commission into action. But in the meantime the Jesuits had time to remove most of their cash, valuables, and papers from Austria. Driven from Catholic Europe, the Jesuits found refuge in Protestant Prussia, where they were welcomed by the Voltairean Frederick the Great, who, having no religious prejudices, appreciated their learning and intelligence. In Austria, despite Joseph's ruthlessness, Maria Theresa was powerful enough to have the Society of Jesus treated gently. Jesuit property was confiscated, but the members received money, pensions, clothes, and other gifts. The value of the estates taken from the order was estimated at 15,415,220 florins. The state used the property for educational purposes.

At every step Joseph stumbled over the conservatism of his mother. The ageing empress fought desperately to preserve the old feudal institutions and the Church from the onslaughts of the heir to the throne who represented the new Europe, the Europe of Voltaire, of Turgot, of Beccaria, the Europe that was yet to be born in the blood of the French Revolution.

Maria Theresa was growing old and her world, even her immediate world, was dead and dying. By 1771 the statesmen who had served her in her youth – Ulfeldt, Carl Cobenzl, Liechtenstein, Starhemberg, Taroucca, Chotek – were dead. The embittered woman felt herself alone, deserted, unable to cope with her revolutionary son and the eager young men who were clustering around him.

The empress took refuge in God the Father and Franzl the husband; the one she had never neglected and the other she had never forgotten. She spent many hours brooding over her deceased husband and counting the fractions of time he had lived.

> Emperor Francis, my husband [she wrote in her prayer-book], lived 56 years, 8 months, 10 days; he died on August 18, 1765, at half-past nine in the evening. This means he lived 680 months, 2,958 weeks, 20,778 days, and 496,992 hours. My happy marital life lasted 29 years, 6 months, and 6 days; this makes 29 years, 335 months, 1,540 weeks, 10,781 days, and 258,744 hours . . . Widowhood is a penance, a preparation for death. Four things should occupy it; more frequent use of the holy sacraments; prayer; reading of spiritual works; charity, and penance. The Old and New Testaments should be read; also the works of the Holy Fathers, histories of the Church, and lives of saints. A widow should especially concentrate on the Psalms, the Songs of Solomon who teaches to despise the world, and Job from whom one learns patience.

At this moment her son and successor was planning to abolish superstition, destroy the power of the clergy, and establish schools for all the people.

In the struggle between Maria Theresa and Joseph two parties inevitably developed.

> The first and strongest party [a French traveller in Vienna observed], is that of the empress. It consists of Cardinal Migazzi, some monks . . . and a few pious old dames. This party is always full of schemes for chastity-commissions, prohibition of books,

exile of dangerous teachers and preachers, maintenance of papal absolutism, and the persecution of the so-called new philosophy. A large part of the nobility, whose rights are tied up with those of the parsons, supports this group.

The second party is that of the emperor, constantly at war with the other. It stands for the reform of justice, the promotion of agriculture, commerce and industry, the undermining of the power of bigotry and its satellites, the diffusion of the new philosophy, the reduction of the unfounded rights of the nobility, and the protection of the weak against the strong . . . These two hostile groups are in constant communication with each other by means of a third, the chief of which is Prince Kaunitz. In his heart Kaunitz probably leans to the emperor's side . . . but the latter wishes him to be a mediator. Kaunitz has influence with the empress, and he knows how to conceal his philosophical ideas with a religious tint . . . He masks the emperor's advances . . . so well that Cardinal Migazzi, despite all his excellent spies, is often forced to capitulate before he even knows that the enemy has stolen a march on him.

As Joseph's power increased, the enlightened group became bolder. Radical centres were formed in many cities, watching and spying on those who were generally dubbed 'aristocrats', 'secret Jesuits', 'darklings', and 'obscurantists'. It became dangerous for any man, no matter what his position, to be known as a 'darkling'. A deep-rooted class struggle developed throughout the Habsburg dominions, especially in the cities. It was the reverberation of the clash of modern ideas in France. The democratic and enlightened Josephan groups stood in sharp and bitter opposition to the aristocratic and papal fanatics, the supporters of the old regime. In many cities the educated and professional classes, including a number of cultured aristocrats, formed secret Masonic societies.

When I am dead [the empress once lashed out at her son in despair], I flatter myself that I will live on in your heart so that the family and the states will not lose by my death . . . Your imitation is not flattering. This hero [Frederick the Great] who has caused so much talk about himself, this conqueror – does he have a single friend? Is he not forced to distrust the whole world? What a life, when there is no humanity! No matter what your talents may be, it is not possible that you have already experienced everything. Beware of falling into spitefulness! Your heart is not yet evil, but it will become so. It is time no longer to take pleasure in all these *bon mots*, these clever conversations whose only aim is to ridicule others . . . You are an intellectual coquet. You are only a thoughtless imitator where you think to be an independent thinker. A *bon mot*, a felicitous turn of phrase, whether in a book or elsewhere, captivates you, and you use it at the first opportunity, whether it is appropriate or not.

Such outbursts were not uncommon. In 1769 mother and son clashed over signatures on official documents. As co-regent Joseph had to co-sign all public decrees; but since he disagreed with many governmental actions he demanded that he be excused from signing documents whose contents he could not approve. 'My peace, my happiness, nay, even my future reputation are at stake,' Joseph pleaded. Maria Theresa appealed to his filial love, begging him not to be obstinate. Joseph answered that he did not wish to hurt his mother to whom he owed all. 'But, dear mother,' he asked, 'is it possible that you will demand a sacrifice which is not important to you, but is of the greatest consequences to me?' The mother's argument was that his refusal to sign official documents would cause a public scandal. For the sake of the good name of the monarchy, the co-regent was forced to yield.

As the years passed Maria Theresa's opposition to her son's ideas was becoming perceptibly weaker; this accounts for many reforms instituted under the co-regency. One of Joseph's most humane acts was to annul from the statute books the crime of heresy which had been in force for over two centuries; at the same time the Church was deprived of its right to condemn heretics. When the Council of State could not make up its mind on the question of abolishing torture, the harassed empress left the decision to Joseph. The co-regent overruled the Council and forbade torture in all the courts of the empire. He also made a vain attempt to abolish the death penalty.

Under the proddings of her son, Maria Theresa took the first step in establishing secular schools. In 1770 a model Normal School was founded; it was to teach 'religion, reading, writing, and arithmetic, as well as the elements of the German mother tongue'. Geography, history, and ethics were likewise to be taught by clerical and lay instructors. Despite the empress's intense Catholicism, she officially declared the then-revolutionary doctrine that 'the school system is and will always be a political institution'. Count Pergen, Dr van Swieten, Professor Martini and others, urged that the whole school system be reorganized and secularized: but the empress refused to remove the clergy from their ancient pedagogical positions. At any rate, there was a lack of trained lay teachers. In 1774 Privy Councillor von Kressel, a member of the enlightened party, drew up a new educational plan and created a Study Commission. At the end of the year Joseph and the Commission set up a universal public educational system.

According to this *Allgemeine Schülordnung* (December 6, 1774), there were to be three types of schools: Normal, Main, and Elementary. The winter term was to begin on November 3rd in the cities, and on December 1st in the country; summer sessions were to start after Easter: 'The school should be attended by children from the ages of six to eight, although the parents are at liberty to send younger ones to the winter school and older ones to the summer school.' Children from the ages of nine to thirteen were compelled to attend the winter sessions.

The co-regent could make his mother carry out some of his ideas, but in one important respect he was helpless; he could not make her economize. The Austrian lands contained over 25 million people – about 8 million Germans, 4 million Belgians, 5 million Hungarians, 8 million Slavs – with an income (from 1773 to 1777) of 53,876,000 gulden and an expenditure of 55,650,000. The army consumed 31 per cent; the administration, including pensions, 32 per cent; interest on the debt amounted to 27 per cent; the remaining 10 per cent was swallowed up by the court.

In an unindustrial country like Austria the huge burden of supporting the ponderous administration and the lavish court fell on the lower classes, chiefly the peasantry. There was no end to the taxes, direct and indirect. A secret report of von

Echt, the Danish ambassador in Vienna, tells some of the story.

> All the impositions created during the last war [von Echt wrote in 1770], still subsist in their entirety; ordinary and extraordinary contributions, capitation tax, imposts on houses, on industry, on food, drink, salt, tobacco, capital, inheritance, bonds, lotteries of all kinds, etc.; none of these taxes has been abolished or diminished, and many have been increased.

The debt in 1770 was about 400 million gulden and kept on growing. Maria Theresa did not mind. She squandered the revenues with royal generosity. 'There is little economy in any of the departments,' von Echt observed, 'except in that of war.' The War Department was under Joseph's direction. Foreign trade was crippled and shackled; with Germany it almost ceased entirely, and the balance with Turkey was unfavourable.

This did not trouble the empress. Joseph vehemently urged economies; careful expenditure was his continuous refrain. The mother went on spending, considering it beneath royal dignity to occupy herself with such trifles as financial retrenchments. She bought diamond-encrusted toys for her grandchildren. As a reaction, Joseph's efforts to save expenses became petty. He became more and more miserly. While his mother was growing daily more corpulent from good living, Joseph slept on straw, ate only beef, and drank nothing but water. When Maria Theresa wanted to invite Leopold's family to Vienna, the co-regent insisted that the state could not afford money for such luxuries. But it was like trying to stop a sieve with a pin point.

The co-regent loved his mother but could not work with her. He could not remain idle and he could not act independently. In December, 1773, he wrote his mother a long and touching letter, begging her to release him from his duties as co-regent. She answered him with tears. She was ready, she wrote, to resign her own position and leave the government to him, but she could not do it because she knew he would object and because conditions in the land were such that she was afraid to give up.

1. Maria Theresa, Joseph's Mother

2. Francis I (1708-65) Joseph's father

I must admit [she confessed], that my abilities, face, hearing, and skill are rapidly declining, and that the weakness which I have dreaded all my life is indecision, accompanied by discouragement and lack of faithful servants. The loss of you, of Kaunitz, the death of all my faithful advisors, the irreligion, the deterioration of morals, the jargon which everybody uses and which I do not understand, all this is enough to overwhelm me. I offer you my whole confidence, and ask you to call my attention to any mistakes I might make ... You love the state ... Help a mother who for thirty-three years has had only you, a mother who lives in loneliness, and who will die when she sees all her efforts and sorrows gone to waste. Tell me what you wish and I will do it.

The emotional appeal was irresistible.

There was much to be done. The cancer that was devouring Austria and the rest of Europe was serfdom. The situation of the peasants, especially in Bohemia and Silesia, was so pitiful that a hardened privy councillor like Borié, when visiting Bohemia, exclaimed, 'But this is even worse than Hungary!'

The province of Bohemia, ravaged by numerous wars, was dying from famines, epidemics, and mismanagement. At Joseph's insistent urgings, a number of steps were taken to eliminate the worst abuses. In 1768 the manorial lords were forbidden to take away the serfs' victuals; next year the *tenth* from the fodder on the fallow lands was abolished; soon after, the lords were forced to feed the serfs they had imprisoned in the workhouse. In 1771 the government appointed an Urbarial Commission to settle disputes between lords and serfs. It was not until the great famine of 1771 that Joseph began to take more desperate measures.

1770 was a bad year for Central Europe, particularly for Bohemia where the harvest was unusually poor. In 1771 the rains destroyed the young crops in the fields, and the population was faced with imminent extinction. The Austrian state machine was never famous for efficiency, but in 1771 it became paralyzed altogether. Chotek, the aged Chancellor of Bohemia, was sick; Kolowrat, the governor at Prague, was eighty years old and he could not have been expected to realize

D

that a few million wretches had no food. When things were at a breaking point, the two venerable gentlemen were politely asked to resign, and two other gentlemen took their place. The government issued a decree prohibiting the export of grain. Maria Theresa ordered that three million guldens worth of grain be bought in Hungary and transported to Bohemia.

Driven by impatience and pity, Joseph decided to leave the comforts of Vienna and go to Bohemia. Maria Theresa protested; it was too dangerous for the heir to the throne to expose himself in a famine-ridden and disease-stricken country. But to Joseph, as he told a friend, 'Kingship is a profession', and it was his duty to be where he was needed. He packed a few belongings and mounted his horse, entering Bohemia like a common traveller. He visited Brünn, Olmütz, Troppau, Iglau, conferring with officials everywhere. The situation was appalling; the dismayed monarch began to search for fundamental causes. Everywhere he went he heard heart-rending tales of brutality on the part of nobles. The famine itself, he was sure, could not cause so much misery. Something deeper, as he wrote to the Bohemian officials, was at the root of the evil.

After a more than three weeks' trip through the country, Joseph arrived at Prague. 'Incapable sufficiently to describe the misery,' the emperor wrote a report to his mother. For the moment, he admitted, nothing could be done except immediate relief; but the next step must be thorough.

When he returned to Vienna, he found there the same dilatoriness and incompetence. 'Nobody takes a step without bickering, scribbling, and preaching for hours,' he complained bitterly. 'Petty reforms will not do; the whole must be transformed. What good does an occasional reform of the clergy achieve? . . . What matters it whether or not there is a holiday or a nun more or less? It is the foundation, the inner spirit and constitution, that must be changed.'

The emperor proposed that all the ecclesiastical property in Bohemia be consolidated. The Church possessed more than one-seventh of the land in Bohemia, and much more in Moravia.

The ecclesiastical land, he pointed out, would be a 'rich source for the establishment of beneficial foundations, for the increase of parishes, schoolmasters . . . asylums for foundlings and orphans, educational institutions, houses of correction, poor houses, hospitals'. The item about increasing parishes he added to please his mother.

Joseph also proposed the establishment of a complete system of education, both for the nobility and the common people. To him ignorance and bigotry were the cardinal sins. He knew that the position and privileges of the nobility and clergy depended entirely upon the ignorance and superstition of the masses.

Galled by what he had seen in Bohemia, Joseph made a savage attack on the nobility and bureaucracy.

> What prospects does a young man have after he has finished his education? If he is a cavalier, he loafs idly, and easily learns his luck in pleasures, horses, operas, and comedies . . . If he dances and gambles, he is much sought after and honoured by society . . . A position with the government is the least that can be done for his beautiful name and ancestors . . . If he has means, every family tries to capture him and uses its influence at court to create a position for him, regardless of his abilities, in order that he could marry somebody's daughter or niece. The title of Privy Councillor, may he be ever such a fool, cannot be denied him, simply because once upon a time there was a sensible and honest man in his family . . . And then salary, position, rank . . . ; yes, such a sixty-year-old do-nothing is entitled to all the privileges even for his family.

He concluded vehemently, 'If the court and ministers would not only refuse to honour all these vacuous and useless members, but also look upon them with contempt, there would soon be a change'.

There were more reports, debates, arguments, and sessions of the Council. The year 1772 was still bad, the crops suffering from lack of rain. 'The cruel drought,' Joseph told Leopold,

> produced innumerable worms and mice which devour the seed, and I fear even greater misery than last year; and nothing is done about it, which drives me to despair. One must have patience;

apparently God does not intend it otherwise. When they ask me about the 150,000 trivialities with which the Council of State is killing itself annually, I always answer that all non-essentials are useless so long as the fundamentals are not changed. When I am asked for advice . . . I always answer that so long as the foundation is not changed, everything is futile. If a pagan were to ask me whether Jupiter, Juno, or Fitzliputzli should be worshipped for the salvation of his soul, my answer would be that since he is no Christian he cannot save his soul, and as things are it makes no difference anyway.

He exclaimed bitterly, 'Poor Bohemia is groaning and all she gets for aid is words.'

Joseph's invective finally moved the Council of State to take up the question of serfdom. A vigorous debate developed as to the meaning and legal status of villeinage. Feudalism, the social and economic basis of the Austrian state, had been so thoroughly taken for granted that no responsible person in Vienna knew its real nature. Was serf labour personal or was it real property? Was it compensation for the lord's protection, or was it inherent in feudal property? Even Joseph was not clear on the subject and asked Kaunitz's advice. The old chancellor had a retentive memory wherein were stored many scraps of recondite information. Kaunitz's opinion was that there were so many kinds of feudal tenure it was not possible to pass a uniform regulatory law. To make matters worse, the local Estates, controlled by the propertied classes, opposed governmental intervention. Their cry was modern: Governmental protection for their privileges, yes; but Government in business – their business – never!

The Bohemian serfs had no appreciation for legal quibbles; unlike their masters, they did know the real meaning of serfdom and villeinage. They had to support the provincial administration, to pay indirect taxes to the state and direct dues to the manor, taxes to the Church and parish, alms, offerings to the local church, contributions for pilgrimages, brotherhoods, foundations, saints and all other inventions designed for the welfare of the peasants' souls. There was little left to support the body. Bohemia rose in rebellion.

Things looked so serious that even the leisurely Council of State began to stir; it decreed that serf labour (Robots) be left to the voluntary adjustment between lords and serfs, an act which meant precisely nothing. The Council then adopted a half-measure, specifying the amount of labour the serfs owed their masters. This Urbarial Law of 1774 gave the lords six months in which to make the necessary adjustments with their peasants.

The aristocratic Estates, threatened in their privileges, opposed even this innocuous law. The Hungarian Parliament, possessing more power than any other Habsburg province, refused to accept the Urbarium (Hungary did not accept it until 1791). The Bohemian Estates finally offered the government what they called a compromise, among others, to transmute some labour dues into fixed cash payments (twenty-one Kreuzer for a working day with two horses, fifteen Kreuzer for two oxen's work, and six Kreuzer for hand labour). To the penniless serfs this was no relief.

Joseph then decided to break the deadlock. By virtue of his power as emperor, he issued a decree making the Urbarial law obligatory (August, 1775). This law provided for a graduated scale of days of labour, depending upon the amount of taxes the serf paid. The minimum established was thirteen days of labour annually, and the maximum three days weekly. Extraordinary labour dues in harvest time were also regulated. In the winter a day's work was to be only eight hours, with one hour off for rest; from April 1st to September, twelve hours, with two hours off. There was to be no Robot on Sundays and holidays.

This was the best that could be done at the moment. Joseph himself did not believe the Robot could be entirely abolished by decree, but hoped the serfs would be ultimately freed by the voluntary action of the nobles. He had occasion to change his mind – and to liberate the serfs himself – before half a dozen years had passed.

The Urbarium, which was pompously promulgated in the provinces by an imperial commissioner travelling from county to county, helped matters very little. It brought the peasants neither more food nor more land. What was worse, the nobles simply refused to obey the law. The desperate peasants, encouraged by the emperor's promises on the one hand, and faced by a cynical and recalcitrant nobility on the other, rose in revolt in Bohemia. Peasant bands overran the country, sweeping along with them those who remained passive, pillaging and burning. The government called out the army.

> The repression [a contempory reports], was severe: military commissions were set up in each district, and a certain number of leaders were executed on the spot. The less guilty ones underwent corporal punishment, while the peasants who had been forcibly dragged into the affair were conducted back to their villages by military escort.

The Bohemian revolt put Joseph in a dreadful position. His sympathies were with the peasants, but as a ruler he could not openly favour rebellion. Nor, considering that his liberal ideas were widely known, could he support violent repression. Maria Theresa vindictively blamed him for all the troubles. He would talk about liberty to *canaille*, would he! Hitherto everything had been peaceful: the nobles had luxuriously enjoyed their privileges in undisturbed serenity: the serfs had been contented in their slavery. The empress was very bitter. 'The emperor, who pushes his popularity too far,' she confided to her friend Mercy-Argenteau,

> on his various trips has talked too much to these people [the Bohemians], both about religious liberty and their emancipation from their lords . . . All this has caused confusion in all our German provinces . . . It is not only the Bohemian peasant that is to be feared, but also the Moravian, the Styrian, the Austrian; even in our section they dare indulge in the greatest impertinences.

Mother and son fell to quarrelling again. Joseph complained of Maria Theresa's fits of temper, of her dilatoriness, of her lamentations. She made everybody miserable, constantly bewailing her unhappy fate; she became hysterical whenever there was the slightest trouble in the empire. 'I have reasoned with her,' the unhappy Joseph told Leopold, 'I have analyzed words and phrases; in vain. It is like washing a Negro white.'

In the heat of emotion the varnish cracked and peeled off both sovereigns. Maria Theresa emerged as a bigoted and fanatical reactionary. She was galled by the feeling that her son represented a world to which she was a stranger, a world which she violently hated without understanding it. Joseph, on the other hand, was forced to be a reformer; for, he confessed, the internal situation was 'incredible and inexpressible; . . . the heart bleeds to see it all'.

The class conflict in Bohemia was mirrored at the court of Vienna. 'Among the many fundamental principles,' the empress wrote to her son,

> the three most important are: Free exercise of religion, which no Catholic prince can permit without heavy responsibility; the destruction of the nobility . . . for which I see neither the necessity nor the justice; and the so frequently repeated liberty in every-thing . . . I am too old to accommodate myself to such ideas, and only pray to God that my successor will never try them.

To this Joseph's answer was to resign. If his principles were so dreadful, he pointed out, why keep him in the government?

> Of what use to Your Majesty is a man . . . whose ideas are inflammatory, hasty, prejudiced, full of false notions. . . ? In short, let Your Majesty relieve me from the cruel burden of a co-regent . . . Then everything would be better and simpler, and I would be happier, more at peace, and perhaps more useful than I am now. While I have the will and the strength to obey, I find it impossible to change my principles and convictions.

Maria Theresa answered:

> It is a great misfortune that, with the best intentions, we do not understand each other. Perhaps my anger is due to the fact that I get neither the confidence nor the frankness which I had hoped to deserve. For thirty-six years I have occupied myself only with you; twenty-six of these have been happy, but I cannot say that now, for I can never agree to such lax principles in religion and manners. You show too much antipathy for the old, especially for all the clergy, and all-too-libertarian principles in questions of morals and conduct. This justly alarms my heart for your position and makes me tremble for the future.

In the summer of 1777 while Joseph was on a visit in France, conversing with scholars and thinkers about toleration, about ten thousand Moravians left the Catholic fold and turned Protestant. Maria Theresa was outraged to the depths of her soul. The Bohemian rebellion was still fresh in her mind; the recent famines had not only depleted the Bohemian and Moravian population to the extent of about 14 per cent, but also left great bitterness behind. Dangerous as the situation was, Maria Theresa could not and would not let such a thing occur in the shadow of her Catholic throne. She sent two emissaries to Moravia to found forty new parishes, for she believed the conversions to Protestantism to be due to lack of Catholic ministration. Then she consulted Joseph by letter.

The emperor's answer was galling. He urged the revolutionary step of complete religious liberty. 'Things cannot be done by halves,' he told his mother.

> Either complete freedom of religion, or you must drive out of your lands everybody who does not believe as you do . . . But you will not do that . . . if you wish to retain excellent workers and good subjects . . . Has any one a right to abuse his power to such an extent . . . as to save people's souls in spite of them, to coerce their conscience? So long as men serve the state, obey the laws of nature and society, and do not defame Your Majesty – what right have you temporal rulers to interfere in other things. . . ? This is my conviction, and your Majesty knows it; and I hope I will never be forced to change my mind.

The angry Maria Theresa wrote her son a letter which deserves to become famous:

> This letter will find you in Switzerland; those people do not appreciate the value of your presence. The country is an asylum for dissolutes and criminals. [Switzerland was the home of Calvinism and republicanism] . . . There can be nothing more ruinous than your persistence in religious toleration . . . But I still hope, and will not cease to pray and let more worthy persons pray, that God will preserve you from such a misfortune, the greatest disaster that ever afflicted the monarchy. In your striving to save useful workers you will destroy the state, and will cause the damnation of innumerable souls. What good will it do you to have the true religion when you love and respect it so little . . . ?

I do not see such indifference among the Protestants; on the contrary, I wish we would imitate them, for no state can permit religious indifference. You will see this in that evil Switzerland. Look at England, Saxony, Baden, Holland and finally Prussia. Is that land any happier? There are few more unfortunate and backward countries than those. What is necessary is a good religion and unalterable laws.

Joseph, from Freiburg, defended his position. He pointed out the inefficacy of religious coercion. 'To me tolerance means that in purely secular things I would leave everybody free to pursue his work and profession, without regard to religion.'

Maria Theresa replied:

What, without a dominant religion? Toleration, indifferentism, are exactly the right means to undermine everything . . . What other restraint is there? None. Neither the gallows nor the wheel . . . I speak politically, not as a Christian. Nothing is so necessary and beneficial as religion. Would you permit that everybody should act according to his fantasy? If there were no fixed cult, no subjection to the Church, where would we be? Fist-law (*Faustrecht*) would be the result . . . Ideas such as yours could cause the greatest misfortune and make you responsible for thousands of lost souls . . . Consider what I have to suffer to see you in your erroneous ways . . . It is not so much the state or you that I am concerned about, but your salvation . . . I only wish that when I die I can join my ancestors with the consolation that my son will be as great, as religious as his forefathers, and that he will give up his false arguments, the evil books, and the contact with those who have seduced his spirit at the expense of everything that is worthwhile and sacred in order to establish an imaginary freedom which could never exist and which would only lead to universal destruction.

Having put her son in his place, the empress proceeded to deal with the Moravian heretics in the time-honoured fashion. She sent out troops to persuade the Protestants that it was best for their souls to remain in the true faith. Protestant meetings were suppressed, emigration was prevented, and the leaders were arrested. Those who persisted in the error of their ways were taken to the army and forced to do hard labour; the heretic women were sent to the workhouse. The more obstinate converts were torn from their families and exiled to the wildest

Hungarian mountains. Heretics under fifteen were taken over by the priests to have their souls saved in good time. From Rome came an emissary to congratulate the empress.

Joseph returned to Vienna, rested a few days, and again left the capital for a military inspection of Moravia. There the furious emperor found out about the decree against the Moravians. He wrote his mother a protest that burned with indignation.

> To convert those people, you make soldiers out of them, send them to the mines, or use them for public works; such a thing has not been seen even during the persecutions in the beginning of Lutheranism, and it will have dangerous consequences. I find myself forced positively to declare . . . that whoever is responsible for this order is the most infamous of your servants, and a man who deserves only my contempt, for he is both a fool and short-sighted . . . I humbly beg you if such things are to take place during my co-regency, to permit me to withdraw, to detach myself from everything, and to let all the world know that I had nothing to do with all this. My conscience, my duty, and my reputation demand it.

Maria Theresa immediately wrote an apology. It was the Council of State, she defended herself, that was responsible for the Moravian decree. She then reproached Joseph for his threat to resign.

> I do not believe [she added], that my actions and ordinances cause you shame. You go a little too far in your ideas. In a private person such activity is admirable, but he who commands must reflect and act according to the laws of the land . . . We have to render account to no one, except to Him who has put us in this place in order to govern His people according to His sacred laws, which we must cherish and sustain against everybody.

But Emperor Joseph cared nothing for His sacred laws. Such arguments were specious to an eighteenth-century libertarian.

> I was mistaken, I thought that this decree was not approved by you, and still less ordered by you . . . There is then nothing left for me to do but keep quiet and . . . ask you to excuse me. You have issued an order which I consider unjust and harmful . . . and with my convictions, even if they be erroneous, I cannot tolerate it.

He then asked again to be permitted to resign.

> I protested vigorously [he confided to Leopold], but the only result was that the more harsh penal laws against those who would not promptly declare themselves Catholic and at least ostensibly go to confession, were halted. But I will remain steadfast in so important an affair; even if I am forced to surrender, I will do so by declaring to the whole world that these things were done against my will.

Maria Theresa was already half beaten when a delegation of Moravian Protestants came to see Joseph in Vienna, pleading for liberty of conscience. The empress promptly arrested the deputies. But now Kaunitz intervened. A few subtle phrases of the chancellor succeeded where Joseph's impassioned pleas had failed. Slyly Kaunitz pointed out that, after all, the true faith was a gift of God and that it was not right to impose it by force. The persecutions were stopped and the Protestants were permitted to worship quietly in their houses.

# CHAPTER 4

# Escape

*I am full of dark melancholy and without hope for the future.*
                                        Joseph to Leopold

Symbolically and physically Joseph tried to escape from his
mother and her environment, which included his brothers and
sisters, courtiers and nobles. The co-regent disliked everything
his mother represented and reacted against all who were
attached to her.

When in 1770, at the age of nine, Joseph's only child, a girl
whom Isabel had borne him, died, the last spark of affection
was extinguished in the twenty-nine-year-old emperor. He was
cool to all his relatives, except Leopold, and despised his
sisters with whom he rarely corresponded after they left the
maternal house, unless, as in the case of Marie Antoinette, he
needed them for political purposes. On her death-bed the
empress found it necessary to plead with Joseph to protect her
children; but as soon as the mother died the emperor took steps
to get rid of the whole pack of them. He sent Marianne to an
abbey at Klagenfurt and Marie Elizabeth to a convent at Innsbruck. Marie Christine and her husband, Duke Albert of
Saxe-Teschen, he reluctantly appointed, according to his
mother's instructions, Governors of the Austrian Netherlands;
but Joseph despised and distrusted them both. Brother Ferdin-
and (1754–1806) was Governor-General of Milan, where,
despite his bitter protests, the emperor completely ignored him.
The youngest brother, Maximilian (1756–1801), became Archbishop of Cologne; Joseph treated him 'with contemptuous
indifference'. They all repaid Joseph with the same hatred.
Only Leopold, Grand Duke of Tuscany, was fond of his brother,
but he was a wise and cautious man, and understood Joseph
too well to come close to him.

Leopold had cause to believe that 'His Majesty's spies' were watching him: some of his letters were intercepted by Joseph's secret police. Like the rest of the family, Leopold stood a little in awe of his impetuous brother. The emperor's letters, however, were always gracious and, in personal matters, disarmingly candid. 'You admit in your letter,' Joseph once chided his brother, 'that you rarely speak with women for fear of boring them. But the court ladies who saw you have found you very charming . . . I have discovered that in order to please the ladies, one must above all know how to entertain them; all the rest comes of itself.'

As a reaction to his domineering mother, Joseph had as thorough a contempt for women as had Voltaire's royal friend in Potsdam. He considered 'petticoat rule', as he called it, the apex of all abominations. A woman's place was in the kitchen or salon, the emperor believed, forgetting the example of his mother and Catharine of Russia, two contemporary women of superior ability, one of whom acquired the dubious title 'Great', the other missed it by a fraction. No woman, except Maria Theresa, ever had the slightest ascendancy over him. The emperor 'had neither favourites nor notorious mistresses', the abbé Georgel notes in his *Mémoires*; 'he knew neither love nor gallantry. What he sought mainly was the pleasure of the senses'. 'Journellement,' wrote the French minister Durand in Vienna, 'il passait une demi-heure chex la fille do son jardinier, montrant au reste par la brévité de l'entrevue que l'engagement n'allait pas au délà du besoin'.

The emperor sought the society of women only as a means of distraction. He was never emotionally involved nor did he have the usual royal liaisons.

> I must admit [he confessed to Leopold], that the more I see of women the more they disappoint me . . . You know my views on the subject; you know my sincerity. I assure you that at the moment I am as free as a new-born baby . . . I go into society with less bitterness. I have still not been able to decide to attend balls . . . I want to know nothing of love. I do not wish to make new acquaintances, and so I go to sleep without disturbing my tranquillity.

Having, as he said, 'fortunately neither wife nor other depend-

ents', Joseph found an outlet for his energies in work and
'escape from reality' in travel. Neither satisfied his character.
'Work piles up daily,' he complained to Leopold, 'but nothing
is being done . . . I work every day until five and six o'clock in
the evening, excepting the quarter of an hour in which I dine
alone, and yet nothing seems to be finished . . . Delay makes
everything go to the devil . . . Farewell, honour and fame!'
Maria Theresa's court was much too leisurely for his restless
person: 'Things move slowly here. But I wish to God it were
only that. Even in the most important and pressing matters we
always seem to be in a situation of *Dum Romae consulitur, Sagan-
tum perit*.' He was like a leashed hound, constantly tugging at
the chain.

> I work until 1 pm, then, whatever the weather, I go out for
> fresh air. I dine at three, then I read or write reports. At five I
> visit Her Majesty and remain there until Vespers; after this I
> write some letters or play music. At eight or later I go into society,
> and usually return at eleven; I look over the newly-arrived dis-
> patches, warm my bones at the fireplace, and rarely go to bed
> before midnight. At seven in the morning I rise and everything
> starts over again, day after day.

The society Joseph visited was composed of the high noblesse,
an inner circle of about two dozen families. The wealthiest, and
hence the most distinguished, was the house of Liechtenstein,
whose annual income was the equivalent of 70,000 pounds
sterling; next in importance were the Esterhazys, with a yearly
income of 50,000 pounds. And old Count Cobenzl complained
to his friend Kaunitz that he could not get along on 75,000
florins a year. Ten pennies (Kreuzer) a day supported a soldier
in Joseph's army.

The other great families were those of Schwarzenberg,
Dietrichstein, Lobkowitz, Khevenhüller, Paar, Clary, Starhem-
berg, Harrach, Auersperg, Colloredo, Kaunitz, Windischgrätz.
Joseph's most constant and loyal women friends were the
Countess Windischgrätz and the Princess Carl Liechtenstein.
The friendships were purely platonic.

Only a few of these nobles were patrons of the arts or lovers of culture. Being supreme, with no one competing with them, the aristocrats had no need to establish lofty distance-barriers between themselves and more common people. The English traveller, Wraxall, tells that the Viennese sprigs of the nobility were insupportable, proud, bigoted, and ignorant. This was the result of Maria Theresa's fanaticism, Wraxall believed; the empress forbade most books, including Voltaire and Rousseau. The aristocrats, the Englishman observed, 'seem never to read'.

Despite the bliss of ignorance, however, Vienna was no paradise, even for the nobles. Like John Calvin, Maria Theresa aimed to make her capital and land a moral haven; unlike Calvin, she did not try to establish a theocracy, for she was born to rule by the grace of the Almighty and did not at all desire a divine competitor on earth. As early as 1753, when her husband was still alive, the empress ordered that women's skirts be lengthened so as not to arouse sinful thoughts in men by shapely calves and slender ankles. Maria Theresa may have wished to save her husband from temptation when she decreed that 'the improperly shaped bodices should by and by be made to look more decent'. The empress further announced her intention of abolishing all feminine adornments.

Maria Theresa displayed an almost pathological brutality in all cases violating her moral code. When a certain Countess Esterhazy eloped to Zürich with a Count Schülenberg, the empress, despite the protests of the civilized Kaunitz, had the count condemned *in absentia* to be decapitated by the sword and broken on the wheel. A Count Arco, who fled to Switzerland with his mistress, Maria Theresa described as 'a loathsome person'.

Under Maria Theresa Vienna became a paradise for toadies. 'Spies,' writes Wraxall, 'form a numerous, expensive, and very obnoxious branch of the state police.' The empress, in the words of Wraxall, 'actuated by the narrow bigotry of an abbess', had her spies to report to her all infraction of morals. Women accused of prostitution, especially when they were poor and therefore defenseless, the virtuous empress exiled to the unhealthiest districts of Hungary. Joseph's busy mother found time to write to her minister of police such notes as these: 'I have heard that Palm has proposed to a certain Weisin, a singer in the German theatre, to give herself to him . . . Seek out this man and try to find the truth . . . It would be frightful on the part of Palm to be such a hypocrite.'

Joseph's sardonic comment on his mother's spies was: 'When doors and windows are closed the police have nothing more to see.'

In Casanova's *Mémoires* there is a wonderful description of Theresan Vienna. The Italian adventurer, who had lived, gambled, cheated, and seduced in every capital of Europe, was a competent observer.

> Vienna [he wrote], was beautiful. There was plenty of money and plenty of luxury, but the bigotry of the empress made Cytherean pleasures extremely difficult, especially for strangers. A legion of vile spies, who were adorned with the attractive name of Commissioners of Chastity, were the pitiless tormentors of all girls. The sovereign did not have the sublime virtue of tolerance where it concerned what was called illegitimate love, and, pious to the point of bigotry, she believed herself to acquire great merit in the eyes of God by her minute persecution of the natural propensities of both sexes . . . Despite the principle of virtue which compelled her, it gave rise to all kinds of infamies which her tyrannical Commissioners of Chastity committed with impunity in her name. They carried off to prison, at all hours of the day and from all the streets of Vienna, poor girls whom they found alone, who in most cases went out only in order to earn an honest living . . . When a girl entered a house, the spy who had followed her waited outside the door and then arrested her for interrogation. If the poor victim showed any embarrassment and hesitated to answer in a manner satisfactory to the spy, the tormentor took her to prison, first, however, despoiling her of her money and jewels, which were never returned. The only means girls had of not being molested was to walk through the streets demurely with lowered heads and chaplets in their hands.

Thus Maria Theresa revenged herself for the numerous infidelities of her husband. Her contemporary, Catharine II of Russia, who had many loves and withal a robust appetite for the

3. Joseph at the age of 23

4. Prince Kaunitz, Chancellor of Austria

'natural propensities', contemptuously dubbed Maria Theresa 'Lady Prayerful'.

Life was dull and petty in Vienna. The Austrian capital had none of the brilliance of Paris, the beauty of Rome, or the charm of even so small a city as Turin. Vienna had few historical monuments and almost no artistic ones. Even today the Austrian capital, with one or two exceptions, has no medieval buildings. The old city was destroyed by the Habsburgs after the Turkish invasion and a new city took its place in the eighteenth century. With Joseph powerless and Maria Theresa ignorant and fanatical, the court attracted no intellectual or artistic luminaries. In the Theresan epoch Vienna did not have a single distinguished writer or artist, with the exception of Haydn. Mozart, Schubert, and Beethoven came later, after Maria Theresa rested in the vault of the Capuchins.

Superstition was rampant, even among the nobles. There was a widespread belief in miracles, ghosts, ghouls, devils, and saints. There were as many saint's days as there were days to be found in the calendar; time was reckoned by saints. The luxuriant growth of holy days became the weeds that choked the Austrian garden of commerce. Even Maria Theresa, at the risk of her immortal soul, had to abolish some of them; and Joseph later made a clean sweep. In the absence of a scientific tradition, alchemy was widely practiced by those who could afford the means. The future Emperor Francis II, Joseph's nephew, is said to have spent a fortune in the pursuit of the elusive element.

The sybaritic Kaunitz, who had spent three delightful years in Paris, lived the last forty years of his life in Vienna grumbling at the tedium and sighing after the various perfumed pots of the French capital. He and the rest of the aristocrats amused themselves as best they could, mainly in social gatherings, where the most charming and beautiful women could be met. The ladies, Wraxall tells, were 'elegant, graceful, and pleasing, but rarely do they possess a cultivated mind'. Brought up in convents, their chief education consisted of 'holy legends, lives of female saints and devotees, masses, and homilies'. Only mass

E

would rouse them out of bed before noon. At half-past two they
dined and an hour later they went visiting and gossiping.

Social life began at eight in the evening. The most popular
indoor sport was gambling, especially during Lent. 'I wish,'
exclaimed the exasperated British ambassador, Keith, in 1773,
'Lent were in the Pope's inside! or that a good comedy were a
part of the papist penance! Cards, cards, cards!' The best
known games were loo, whist, taroc, trissette, reversé, and tric-
trac. The women came magnificently gowned, glittering with
jewels. Even the little ladies, seven or eight years old, dressed
like their elders; 'powder, high head, a chignon, and a hoop'.
Rouge was universally used, except by Maria Theresa's
daughters; 'Girls of fifteen wear it as much as persons of thirty.'
Love affairs were carefully conducted, out of a 'respect for
appearances', that is, a fear of the empress's sharp tongue and
heavy hand. Secrecy added spice to amorous adventures, and
Vienna, even under the pious Maria Theresa, produced some
first-rate Messalinas. The Austrian woman, Wraxall observed
sardonically, 'sins, prays, confesses, and begins anew; but she
never omits her masses, not even for her lover'.

At the best houses splendid dinners were served. Fish came
from the Danube; partridges and pheasants from Bohemia;
oysters from the Adriatic; truffles from Piedmont. Each guest
was given a list of wines and he could choose from Absinthe,
*vin d'Autriche*, Razersdorf, *vin de Rhin*, Moselle, Nuitz, Champagne, Malaga, Bacaret, Alicante, Balmsec, Cerises, Tokay.
Occasionally a hired entertainer amused the guests. Prince
Khevenhüller notes such an occasion at a dinner at Kaunitz's:
'There was an Italian poetess, whose poetical name was
Corilla, but real name Morelli Fernandez, a native of Tuscany,
who chantingly versified all given themes *ex tempore*.'

There were also some amusements at the court. In the winter
hundreds of carts brought snow and scattered it on the principal streets so that royalty could go sleigh-riding.

In each [of the sleighs, about thirty] is seated a lady, dressed
in furs richly ornamented, and her head covered with a profusion
of jewels. Behind her stands the nobleman who drives, commonly

as much decorated with diamonds as the lady. The sledges themselves . . . are gilt and carved with great taste . . . and commonly
cost some thousand florins. Before each run footmen, or Hey-
duques, superbly habited, carrying long poles in their hands.
Even the horses are quite obscured under the multiplicity of
trappings, plumes, and ornaments, with which they are loaded
. . . They drive with amazing velocity, through all the principal
streets and squares of the capital.

This particular ride, described by Wraxall who was then in
Vienna, took place in January, 1778, at a moment when
Austrian troops were invading Bavaria and a war with Prussia
was imminent. No wonder, we are informed, 'Joseph . . . neither
likes the amusement, nor the expense attending it, which is
considerable'.

In its formal aspects Viennese life was more glittering before
Joseph became regent. The innumerable gala days were reduced
by him for economy's sake. 'Alas!' the witty Keith wrote in
1773:

the present imperial reign has almost totally abolished those
gaudy exhibitions, and instead of fifty days in the year in which
every grandee was permitted to give a full scope to the genius of
his tailor, and clap upon his back the produce of a thousand
acres, we have now but one solitary first of January, to air our
finery, and kick up the dust of pageantry . . . What a pity it is that
the present emperor, by an unaccountable simplicity of manners,
and hatred of show, should have prevented me from returning
often to this favourite theme.

The so-called lower classes lived in poverty, filth, and ignorance; they brawled and drank, often to excess. On Sundays
and holidays they went to church, dressed in their poor best,
and listened to pious incantations, legends and fables, designed
to keep them contented and humble.

Although Joseph went into society, he never gambled and
rarely danced. He would informally drop in to Kaunitz's or
Colloredo's, accompanied by a single chamberlain, and, without fuss, join in the conversation. 'Remember,' he always used
to say, 'that you are conversing with Joseph and not with the
emperor.' He was a delightful and animated talker. He could

tell amusing stories even when the joke was against him. In the presence of women, a contemporary traveller relates, 'the emperor would laugh heartily with the young ladies, and tell a number of excellent stories'. One story is perhaps typical of Joseph's humour.

> One of the town prisons had been pulled down; a man purchased the ground where it stood; built a house and shop there, and put my head for a sign. The magistrates of the town, thinking it disgraceful that his Imperial Majesty's head should be exposed in a place where malefactors had been confined, ordered it to be taken down. The man came to me, and complained of the expense he had been at, in having so fine a sign-post painted, and thought it hard it should be thrown away. I did not choose to contradict the magistrates; but I told the man to put a beard on the face, and a glory round the head, which would change it to Saint Joseph.

The emperor's conversation was frequently light, as he had little interest, as he himself admitted, in science or literature. 'The etcher whose business it was to form the taste of the emperor,' Riedesel, the Prussian minister at Vienna, reported to Frederick, 'has told me that he [Joseph] does not have the slightest knowledge of painting.' We shall see that the emperor treated Mozart shabbily and that despite his radicalism he forbade the publication of Voltaire's works in German, not wishing to spread the Frenchman's 'poison' among his subjects. Joseph was only interested in politics and administration, and in these matters he always encouraged contradictory opinions in conversation.

He considered games and dances puerile, unworthy of a man's time. In this too Joseph, perhaps unconsciously, imitated his great rival, Frederick of Prussia. Once when Maria Theresa invited her son to join her in Pressburg, he coolly replied, 'I shall choose, if you do not mind, a less clamorous time to visit Pressburg . . . It would be of little consequence to a man who does not dance . . . who does not wish to run for six hours through the snow chasing a ball, or to freeze, in order to see a banquet, when he can have all this at home'. Games, balls, amusements, he told Leopold, 'do not tempt me a bit'.

In the early years of Joseph's co-regency, the only public entertainment in Vienna was to be found in the French theatre, where Italian operettas and French comedies were played. Joseph, more of a German patriot than Frederick of Prussia who despised all things German (except soldiers), decided to change it because it was French and because the nobility liked it. The institution had been supported from the proceeds of legalized gambling, each faro bank paying ten ducats. Joseph forbade gambling. This blow to the French theatre made even Kaunitz angry. 'On all sides,' the Francophile chancellor growled, 'I see nothing but taboos.'

The emperor took it over, put it under the administration of the court, and officially declared it the German National Theatre.

The plays produced in this German theatre were not always the best in dramatic literature, but, then, German drama was still in its infancy. Among the plays produced in the National German Theatre (not the *Burgtheater*) between 1777 and 1782 were light comedies such as *All for Friendship, The Surprise, Who Cheated Himself?, Old Love Does Rust, The Friendship of Women, Who will Get Her?* plays entirely forgotten today.

Joseph's action in establishing the first national German theatre evoked the praise of Gotthold Ephraim Lessing. 'I honour your emperor,' Lessing told a Viennese visitor; 'He is a great man! Unquestionably he can be the first to give us Germans a national theatre, since the king in Berlin hardly tolerates the native stage and does not take it under his protection as does your monarch.'

Joseph's commonest form of escape from squabbles with his mother was to go travelling.

The emperor, always travelling incognito, visited almost every one of his provinces and acquired a more intimate knowledge of his lands than any man in his employ.

He visited Bohemia most frequently, not because he loved it but because it was Prussia's gate to Austria. Here military manoeuvres were frequently held, forts were built, and the terrain was studied. In the summer of 1766 Joseph spent six weeks carefully examining Bohemian topography, especially in the north and north-west. At Pirnau he inspected the army and rebuked the artillerists for careless shooting. He drily told the gunners that, in his humble opinion, balls which hit the target were somewhat more effective than those which just spun through the air.

The co-regent's first journey to Italy, where his family held large districts, took place when he was twenty-eight. His route was that of the medieval German emperors, probably through the Brenner Pass, through Verona and Mantua, to Rome. The 'eternal city' charmed the emperor. 'We have already seen some of the beauties of Rome,' he informed his mother, 'which, without exaggeration, are really astonishing. The church of St Peter . . . enchants and amazes one.' In Rome he was entertained, but not amused. He found 'the ladies very homely, all badly brought up, and not one amiable', and assured his mother that his 'heart will not lose its virginity'. It was Easter time and Joseph was careful to inform Maria Theresa that he went daily 'to a different church for morning service and vesper'. At the same time he complained that he was 'overwhelmed with balls . . . which bore me to death'.

From Rome Joseph went to Naples to see his sister Marie Caroline, the wife of King Ferdinand who was a philistine so ignorant that he could speak only the dialect of the Lazzaroni. Although the young queen 'enchanted' him, Joseph did not stay long in Naples. He returned north to Tuscany. At Forli he had a conversation with a Count Papini; the Italian noble did not know with whom he was speaking and expressed himself frankly. Several months later the dismayed Papini found out who the stranger was and wrote Joseph an apology.

> Nothing is more agreeable to me [the emperor replied], than the memory of the respect which you have shown me, thinking me a private person . . . The panegyrics with which we are addressed are unfortunately given more to our rank than to our merit . . . Keep me in your affection, my dear Papini, and rest assured that I should be very angry if I did not know it was the *man* for whom

you showed esteem, and that Joseph was happy at being liked
independently of the external advantages and vain honours
invented by adulation to nourish and flatter the pride of the
sovereign.

At Bologna, seat of a famous medieval university, the emperor,
as was his custom, conversed informally with various persons.
The professors of theology wanted to know his religion. Joseph's
reply was not pleasing to the orthodox: 'I am only a soldier
[what pride he always took in his soldiering!] and no theologian, but so far as I know there is only one way to heaven –
consequently, only one doctrine, I hope. You will teach this
doctrine in your schools; I mean the tenets of Jesus Christ.'

At the end of May the emperor was in Mantua, whence he
asked his mother's permission to visit Genoa. But Maria Theresa
had not forgotten that the city-republic had driven out the
Austrian troops in 1746, and vindictively she forbade her son
to honour by his presence the city that was famous and powerful when the Habsburgs were still but unknown knights.

Early in June, Joseph met General Paoli in Pavia. The
Corsican, after a vain struggle to win independence for his
island, was now an exile. It seems Maria Theresa wished to
engage his services, but Joseph advised against it. The emperor
formed a poor opinion of the later enemy of Napoleon. 'He is
not personally brave,' Joseph wrote his mother; 'he is nothing
but a rebel chief who acquired a reputation by the enthusiasm
and fanaticism with which he knew how to inspire his nation.'

Joseph's next stop was in the Savoyard capital, Turin, a
city', he noted, 'marvellously laid out in straight lines, being
absolutely the most beautiful place I have seen in Italy'.
Charles Emmanuel III, the ancestor of the dynasty which gave
Italy her first national monarch less than a century later, was
not an attractive character. The Turin court, Joseph observed,

is composed of men of spirit, but due to the negligence, age, and
jealousy of the king [Charles Emmanuel III, born in 1701], it is
governed very badly . . . The employees are old; the king wishes
to do everything himself and is incapable. There are moments
when he repeats himself, and one can clearly see that his head is

not all there. He walks unsteadily, has extremely red eyes, and consequently is unable to read or write.

The emperor left Savoy in the middle of June, going east to Milan. On June 21st he was in Como, whence he probably crossed the Septimer Pass on the way home to meet King Frederick of Prussia in Neisse, Moravia.

Joseph visited Hungary when he was twenty-three, interesting himself mainly in the rich mines. Two years later he inspected the forts of Arad, Temesvar, and Peterwardein. On this trip, a serf, with unconscious dramatic sense, presented the emperor with a petition which is perhaps the sharpest epitome of the feudal system. 'Most Merciful Emperor!' the paper read. 'Four days statute labour, the fifth day fishing, the sixth day helping the master in the chase, and the seventh belongs to God. Consider, Most Merciful Emperor, how can I pay taxes and dues?' The plea is eloquent, both from the point of view of the condition of the serfs and from the fact that Joseph's reputation as a benevolent monarch had already spread among the people. The serfs had of course no idea that their emperor, despite his indignation at their lot, was, at the moment, powerless to help them.

Joseph went to Hungary again in 1768, 1770, and 1773. Each time he was more depressed by the wretchedness of the population, most of whom were peasants. In long letters the emperor complained of the disorganized conditions in the land and of the almost complete lack of culture.

What was so painful was the knowledge that Hungary was potentially the most fertile of the Austrian provinces. This strange kingdom was a central European 'melting pot', which never melted. The Austrian metallurgist, Baron Born, on his inspection tour to the Banat in 1770 observed that the people who called themselves *Srbi*, spoke a 'corrupt Slavonian dialect' and that their manner of living was 'extremely rough'. 'They lack religion and sciences,' the baron added.

> *Kukuruz* or maize is their chief object of agriculture. However they sow likewise oats, barley, and corn . . . Biscuit of coarse ground maize, baked under ashes, which they call malai, some meat, milk, cheese, beans and other vegetables, are their common

food. . . . They confess the non-united Greek religion, *Graeci ritus non unitorum*. But in fact they have scarce more religion than their domestic animals, except repeated fastings, which almost take up half the year . . . Some of them are so ignorant as to be unable to read.

In 1772 another foreign province was added to the Habsburg dominions, the fertile Galicia, taken from Poland. The population was a mixture of Poles and Ruthenians on the land, and Jews in the small towns. For centuries the serfs had been barbarized by their brawling masters. Except, possibly, in the German-founded cities of Cracow and Lemberg, there was hardly any civilization in this muddy, roadless, thatch-hutted region. When Joseph went to inspect this new acquisition in the summer of 1773 he received a shock: used as he was to seeing deplorable conditions in his lands, Galicia was unlike anything he had yet seen. 'The peasant,' he wrote his mother, 'is an unfortunate creature who has nothing human about him except his body.' Even the Austrian administration during the first few years was incompetent and confused, unable to cope with the heritage of Polish anarchy. 'It is incredible,' Joseph indignantly wrote to Maria Theresa, 'how much has to be done here. There is an unexcelled confusion here, cabals, intrigues, anarchy.'

The emperor took the hardships of his Galician trip very good-humouredly. Back in Vienna, Joseph sardonically told Sir Robert Keith one of his experiences in Galicia, where, he said, he was 'almost devoured by bugs'. Sitting in a hut and writing a letter to his mother, a louse fell from the emperor's hair. 'I blew him off,' Joseph related,

> and finished my despatch. Just as I was about to seal it, I recollected a circumstance, which in my hurry had escaped me. Having opened the letter again, in order to insert it, to my surprise, I found the louse had got possession of his old post. I attempted to dislodge him, but he maintained his ground, and I therefore let him alone, only adding, as a postscript, at the foot of the paper, 'One of Your Majesty's new Polish subjects absolutely insists on being presented to you'.

Joseph's trip to France, in 1777, had political rather than personal motives. For years there had been rumours in France that the young emperor disliked the French and was hostile to the Franco-Austrian alliance. As early as 1767 Maria Theresa had had to assure Mercy, the Austrian Ambassador in Paris, that Joseph really had no animosity for the French, but that he was no 'flirt', as one should be with 'Madame la France'. This was only diplomatic talk, for Joseph had a profound antipathy for France, both before and after his visit. 'I passed the winter of 1777 and 1778 in Vienna,' William Coxe, the English historian of Austria, wrote, 'and frequently had the honour of meeting the emperor, in private societies, where he visited without ceremony. On these occasions he did not affect to conceal his anti-Bourbon sentiments, and seldom failed of uttering some severe sarcasms.'

There was a family reason for going to Paris. Marie Antoinette, Joseph's youngest sister, later to perish on the guillotine, was married to Louis who, in 1774, became King Louis XVI. On that occasion Joseph wrote his sister an impersonal and pedagogical letter:

> Madame, I congratulate you on your husband's accession to the throne. He will compensate France for the late government . . . The nation groaned under the burden which had been imposed upon it of late years by Louis XV. He dissolved the parliaments, gave his favourites too much power over the people, and removed the Choiseuls, Malesherbes, and La Chalotaises. He placed at the helm of affairs men . . . who plundered and distracted the kingdom. I often pitied this prince from my heart, for having made himself so much the slave of his passions, thereby degrading himself in the estimation of his respectable family, and even of his subjects.

Young Marie Antoinette, who always remained an Austrian at heart, found Versailles a hotbed of intrigue and she carelessly made so many blunders that Mercy had to complain secretly to Maria Theresa. Joseph wrote the Queen of France a harsh letter:

> So far as I know you concern yourself with a number of things which are none of your business, about which you know nothing. The intrigues and stupidities which appeal to you, as well as your vanity, make you commit one blunder after another . . . Why, my dear sister, do you interfere in removing ministers, in exiling some

to the country, in helping others win law-suits. . . ? Why do you speak of state affairs, and even use expressions, when they are incompatible with your position? Have you ever asked yourself by what right you intervene in the business of the French monarchy? What studies have you pursued, what knowledge have you acquired that you should dare imagine that your opinion or judgment is worth anything at all. . . ? You, a charming young person, who think all day only of your pleasures, your amusement, your attire; you, who read nothing, who cannot speak sense even for one quarter of an hour in a month, who do not consider, do not reflect – never reflect, I am sure – who do not weigh the consequences of your actions and words. . . ? Take my word, and listen to a friend and a man who loves you, as you know . . . Give up these stupidities; never interfere in any business . . . Try zealously to win the friendship and confidence of the king . . . Discover his tastes, and act accordingly; be as much in his company as you can . . . For the rest, read, occupy yourself, develop your mind, use your gifts.

The queen, who was afraid of Joseph but who admired him and tactlessly boasted about him like a little girl showing off the prowess of her big brother, was hurt by Joseph's scolding. 'Your letter has distressed me very much, dear brother,' she replied, 'I desire above all to have back your esteem.'

Joseph planned to go to Paris at Marie Antoinette's accession to the throne, but his mother did not relish the idea of her son being exposed to 'the frivolous and ridiculous intrigues of that nation'. What annoyed the empress most was Joseph's avowed intention of seeing Voltaire, Tissot, Haller, 'and all these wild fellows'. When Joseph, despite his mother's objections, did decide to visit France, Maria Theresa asked her friend Mercy in Paris to keep an eye on her son. She knew, she sadly admitted, that Joseph admired Voltaire, Haller, and the other 'wretches', but hoped that Mercy would make the emperor see all that was 'vile, inconsistent, and despicable in their character and conduct'. Joseph, however, changed his mind and would not go because he feared Frederick of Prussia would ascribe political intentions to his French trip; and that 'monster's' opinion, Maria Theresa complained to Mercy, influenced the emperor.

The 'monster' in Potsdam had an excellent espionage system. Half a year before Joseph finally went to France, Frederick knew of the emperor's intentions. In November, 1776, the Prussian king instructed Goltz, his ambassador in Paris, to prepare his spies and 'to watch the emperor's steps'.

It was early spring when the thirty-six-year-old emperor, travelling incognito as Count Falkenstein, went to Paris. 'My emperor,' Ambassador Keith informed a friend at London, 'is now galloping to Paris ... I'll lay a wager that not three people in France form any just idea of his character; he is so totally unlike a Frenchman, above all, a French monarch.'

The Habsburg Haroun Al-Raschid quietly entered the French capital, made his first stop at an inn, and then went to lodge at the *Petit Luxembourg*, belonging to his ambassador Mercy-Argenteau who had fifteen thousand fine bottles of wine in his cellar. Joseph partook of the rare vintages no more than he did of the hospitality of Versailles.

At court Marie Antoinette, who had boasted about her brother, eagerly awaited his coming. The Habsburg girl was proud of her brother, proud of her family, full of zest and joy of life. As the simply-dressed Count Falkenstein walked up the stairs leading to the Palace of Versailles, the young queen shocked the etiquette-frozen court by dashing forward and impetuously embracing him. How closely they resembled each other. Both had fine eyes and proud bearing; but in Marie Antoinette the Habsburg thick and drooping lower lip was more protruding than in Joseph. He was tanned and lean. 'Her skin,' a contemporary observed, 'was admirable, her shoulders and neck matched it; her bosom was rather too full, and her waist might have been more elegant; but I have never met since with arms and hands more beautiful.'

Antoinette, hoping to entertain a guest, was confronted with a pedagogue. Her older brother, disregarding the fact that she was Queen of France, lectured her on all conceivable matters. 'Even the queen's toilette,' writes Marie Antoinette's lady-in-waiting, Madame de Campan, 'was a perpetual subject of criticism for the emperor. He accused her of having introduced new fashions, and upbraided her for using rouge.' The tactful Mercy informed Maria Theresa that Joseph criticized his sister 'without offending her'.

The emperor's visit, despite his anonymity, caused a flurry in Paris. The French, for centuries used to a haughty, unapproachable, extravagant monarchy, were excited by this unassuming, simple-mannered, and gracious sovereign. The dramatic sense of the Parisians was stimulated by the conduct of this Holy Roman Emperor, heir to a thousand-year-old tradition, who dressed like an ordinary citizen, spoke French fluently, conversed with all manner of people, and was always kindly, interested, and modest. Joseph was heartily cheered wherever he was recognized. The emperor's simplicity, his curiosity, his democratic habits aroused the distrust and contempt of the stolid Louis XVI who suspected his brother-in-law (and perhaps not unjustly) of hypocrisy. Joseph's tactlessness and his Teutonic straightforwardness stirred up the sense of inferiority in the French king.

'You possess the most beautiful building in Europe,' Joseph told his brother-in-law.

'What is that?' asked Louis.

'*Les Invalides*,' the emperor replied.

'So they say,' Louis answered politely.

'What!' exclaimed Joseph, 'have you never visited the building?'

'*Ma foi*, no,' answered the king.

'Nor have I,' chimed in Marie Antoinette.

'Ah, I am not surprised in your case, sister,' the emperor smiled ironically; 'you are so busy.'

Such verbal passages did not endear Joseph to his brother-in-law. The keen-eyed emperor's judgment of the king who sixteen years later lost his head under the guillotine has been corroborated by posterity. 'This man,' Joseph informed Leopold, 'is a little weak, but not an imbecile. He has ideas and a sound judgment, but his mind and body are apathetic. He converses reasonably, but he has no wish to learn and no curiosity; in fact, the *fiat lux* has not yet come; the matter is still without form.' Joseph's impression of Marie Antoinette also shows a sense of penetration. 'She is a charming and honourable woman,' he wrote to Leopold:

> somewhat young, a little thoughtless, but essentially decent and virtuous . . . She also has spirit and a keenness which surprised me. Her first reaction is always correct; if she would only act according to it, reflect a little more, and pay less attention to the gossips, who surround her in flocks, she would be perfect. She has a strong desire for pleasure, and since her tastes are known, advantage is taken of her weaknesses . . . Her relation to the king is peculiar; she drives him by force to do things which he does not wish to do.

Joseph had hoped to derive some political advantages from his trip. The aggressions of Catharine II of Russia, and her successes against the Turks, had long made the Austrian court uneasy. Both Kaunitz and Joseph wished to check the advance of the 'Colossus of the North', and this could be done only with the aid of the French ally. Shortly before Joseph went to France, Austria sent Francis von Thugut to Paris to suggest a possible anti-Russian coalition. The French foreign minister, Vergennes, a cool-headed and intelligent statesman who had little love for the Habsburgs and who was to be Joseph's constant Nemesis, politely replied 'The last war [with Turkey] had exhausted Russia too much to make her contemplate a new attack on the Moslems. For the present, therefore, it should be sufficient to watch Russia; but should that power really decide to arm against the Porte, then it would be time enough for France and Austria to take proper measures'. Vergennes, well informed as to Joseph's ambitious political plans (Thugut was in the pay of the French foreign office), warned Louis XVI to be on guard. The French king, heartily disliking his brother-in-law, did not need much prompting to oppose blandly his imperial relative's schemes.

If the French trip was a political failure, it was a social and intellectual success. Joseph spent April and May in the capital, visiting institutions, observing, conversing, asking questions, and, to the delight of the French, making *bon mots*. When, Thomas Jefferson relates, the emperor was asked by a curious

French lady what he thought of the American Revolution, he replied, 'It is my trade to be a king'. Joseph spent two hours in conversation with Madame du Barry, the mistress of Louis XV. The two went out for a walk in the garden and Joseph tried to take the Countess's arm, but she hesitated to accept so great an honour. 'Madame,' the emperor gallantly said, 'beauty is always queen.' When the librarian of a Paris library expressed his regrets that the light was poor and therefore he could not show the emperor the works on theology, Joseph replied drily, 'Oh, my dear sir, where there is theology there is never much light.' Count Falkenstein went to pay his respects to the great Jean-Jacques Rousseau, whom he found occupied copying music. Joseph asked him why he did that, 'Well,' Rousseau replied, 'I have tried to teach the French how to think, and did not succeed, so I decided to instruct them how to sing.'

Every day the emperor saw new sights and met different people – artists, diplomats, writers, burghers. He interested himself in everything, looked, asked questions, smiled, and made complimentary remarks. *Il observe tout*, said a French lady, *ne critique rien*.

This odd monarch charmed and puzzled everyone. 'He was a man,' a French noble said of him, 'more surprising than admirable, more singular than rare, more amiable than attractive, more brilliant than solid, and more extraordinary than great . . . in a word he possessed a thousand fine qualities which are of no use to kings.'

All Paris talked about him. He spent a great deal of time in the house of Minister Necker, whom he considered a man of spirit, character, and genius. One evening at the Neckers' there was a distinguished gathering, composed of the Academicians Marmontel and Leroy, and the famous historian Gibbon. Joseph had been there for two hours conversing about politics. At nine-thirty the Marquise du Deffand entered; the men rose and bowed. Joseph went up to Necker and said, 'Introduce me'. The marquise made a deep bow and sat down. Joseph wanted to talk to her but was tongue-tied. Embarrassed, he looked at her *sac à noeuds* and said, '*Vous faites des noeuds?*' She smiled: '*Je ne puis faire autre chose.*' Again he did not know what to say and murmured, '*Cela n'empêche pas de penser?*' The witty woman relieved him with a quick compliment: '*Non, et surtout aujourd'hui que vous donnez tant à penser.*'

The fat little historian of fifteen centuries of emperors looked on with ironic eyes at the Holy Roman Emperor who was talking with a clever woman about knots.

The Marquise du Deffand, however, found the emperor to possess a 'charming simplicity'. To illustrate his character she related a characteristic anecdote about him. Joseph was travelling incognito and found an overturned carriage on the road; he offered the passenger a place in his own, and the man accepted. To amuse his host, whom he did not know, the stranger asked him to guess what he had for dinner.

'Fricassée of chicken,' said Joseph.

'No.'

'Leg of mutton,' Joseph guessed again.

'No.'

'An omelette?'

'No,' said the man, and patting him on the thigh told him what he had for dinner.

'We do not know each other,' Joseph said, 'and now it is my turn to make you guess. Who am I?'

'Perhaps a soldier.'

'Perhaps,' replied Joseph, 'but I also may be something else.'

'You are too young to be an officer,' the stranger said: 'are you a colonel?'

'No.'

'Major?'

'No.'

'Commander?'

'No.'

'Are you a governor?'

'No.'

'Who,' the exasperated man asked, 'are you? Are you then the emperor?' Joseph maliciously patted the man's thigh: 'You guessed it.' Crestfallen and humiliated, the stranger wanted to

leave the carriage. 'No, no,' said the emperor; 'I knew who
I was when I took you in and did not know who you were.
Nothing has changed; let us continue our trip.'

Ambassador Mercy accompanied his sovereign on many
institutional visits – and sent minute reports to Maria Theresa
in Vienna. Joseph generously left donations at the hospitals,
showed great interest in a veterinary school, and was curious
about an institution for deaf-mutes. Like Peter the Great,
Joseph visited shops, laboratories, and factories. Trudaine,
member of the Academy of Sciences, and director of bridges and
highways, had his corps of engineers show the emperor 'models,
machines, and plans'. The engineers, Mercy reported, 'were
surprised at the questions which the emperor put to them, and
at his penetration'. To find out the state of French finances,
Joseph had Mercy introduce him to the financier, Jean-Joseph
de Laborde, who gave the emperor an exact account of 'the
king's revenues, expenses, the organization of the royal treasury, and of the general mismanagement'. Joseph was much
surprised at the frankness with which Frenchmen generally
volunteered confidential information.

After attending a session of the Paris *Parlement* and listening
to the pleadings of the lawyers, Joseph was taken to the *Académie
des Inscriptions et Belles-Lettres*. The *savants*, flattered by the
imperial presence, asked the distinguished visitor to preside at
the meeting, which he refused to do. Next day, May 17th, the
emperor went to the *Académie Française* to attend the lectures.
Fifteen scholars and scientists were present. Marshal Duras
introduced them all to the emperor. The meeting was then
called to order, and d'Alembert read an essay on manners,
with some complimentary references to the emperor. D'Alembert also related a number of anecdotes about Fénelon. La
Harpe recited verses from the poem *Pharsalia*, Marmontel read
some history. After an hour and a half, Joseph rose, and made
a flattering address to the Academy, singling out d'Alembert
for special distinction.

Considering the intellectual and social ferment in France at
this period, which twelve years later exploded in a violent

F

storm, Joseph's contact with the intellectuals and with the most advanced spirits of the time was of some significance. The French thinkers – the *philosophes* – who had been criticizing existing institutions for two generations, who had been dreaming of an age of reason, and hoping for a rational, enlightened government, could not but be struck by the difference between their own stolid and indifferent monarch and this foreign emperor who interested himself in art, science, and intelligent administration, and who did not erect lofty barriers between himself and common mortals. To the credit of Louis XVI, it must be said that he had sense enough to appreciate the danger of Joseph's presence in France.

Before leaving Paris for the provinces, Joseph summarized his impressions of the French capital. 'There are highly interesting things to be seen here,' he wrote to Leopold:

> buildings whose splendour and appearance are magnificent . . . Everything is for show; but when one tries to penetrate beneath the surface, one meets with disappointment . . . There is a pretence of greatness . . . For this everything else is sacrificed; and in this Babylon, one knows neither the laws of nature nor of society – it is all but a varnish of politeness . . .
>
> The court at Versailles is different; here rules an aristocratic despotism . . . The king is but an absolute lord in order to succeed from one slavery into another. He can change his ministers, but he can never become master of his business . . . Petty intrigues are treated with the greatest care and attention, but important affairs, those which concern the state, are completely neglected. The whole judiciary and all the nobility . . . constantly clamour against the rulers, asking for a change; but if an attempt were made to touch this loathsome form of monstrous despotism which each official exercises, then all would combine to prevent it, because everyone hopes to derive some advantages for himself. The king is badly brought up, his appearance is against him, but he is honourable, possesses some knowledge, yet he is weak in the presence of those who know how to intimidate him . . . The queen is a very beautiful and charming woman, but she thinks only of her pleasures, has no love for the king, and is drunk with the extravagance of this country; in short, she does not fulfil either the duties of a wife or of a queen . . . for as a wife she neglects the king . . . has little interest in his society . . . She does not do her duty, and this

may have dangerous consequences in the future . . . Her environment prevents her from thinking of anything else but pleasures.
Everything around her sustains her in this frenzy and how can I
alone combat it?

My life at court is very simple; I play the courtier . . . In Paris
I go out mornings and afternoons to see all kinds of things, and
in the evenings I visit some distinguished personality; at ten in
the evening I get home.

At the end of May Joseph left Paris to visit the provinces. His
trip took the form of a circle round the coasts of France, from
Normandy to Marseilles. He skirted the coast southward to
Bayonne, and made the shocking observation that the land was
'depopulated and abused; during thirty-six hours of travel I
have not found three villages'. After a flying trip to St Sebastian
in Spain, Joseph rode to Toulouse. The province of Languedoc,
the French California, he found, 'has a culture which really
delights me'. In the south, Joseph visited most of the important
cities and ports, including Montpellier, Nîmes, Aix, Marseilles,
and Toulon ('The most beautiful port I have yet seen'). 'The
French navy,' Joseph confided to his brother, 'does not inspire
me with any confidence. The ships are poor and in bad form;
I judge this from the manoeuvers which I have seen, where the
vessels were constantly being damaged.'

Early in July Joseph travelled northward, along the Rhone.
At Lyon the emperor had a long conversation with Prost de
Royer, lieutenant of police and friend of Voltaire. Royer insisted upon treating Joseph as Count Falkenstein. 'Very well,'
the emperor said, 'we will meet this evening and put our elbows
on the table.'

In the evening Count Falkenstein and the police lieutenant
met to converse as befitted two enlightened citizens.

'We will be sorry at your departure,' Royer said; 'but our
nation is convinced that you do not admire it and that you like
it even less.'

There was a moment of silence, and Joseph asked, 'But what
could be the motive of this prejudice?'

'Monsieur le Comte,' the Frenchman replied, 'one remem-
bers the terrible instant, which you have not forgotten, when

Maria Theresa took you in her arms and presented you to the Hungarians, asking their aid against France.'

'But it was Louis XV and his cabinet who had made that war,' Joseph exclaimed, 'and they are all dead today.'

'In Paris,' Royer persisted, 'you have spoken of the French. You have exclaimed, "Charming nation!" Nothing more. This is but slender praise.'

'I have told the truth,' the emperor said seriously. 'When one considers the court and the capital, one sees only a charming nation, and nothing more. But in the cabinet, among the scholars, among our friends [here Joseph mentioned men like Turgot] . . . there are highly interesting people in every respect.'

Royer said, 'One believes you to be enamoured of conquests, a person who seeks glory only in war.'

'I desire only the glory of government,' the emperor answered.

The Frenchman wanted to know why Joseph did not imitate in Austria his brother Leopold's enlightened Tuscan administration.

'I am unable to do it,' Joseph replied with more truth than perhaps Royer realized; 'I am nothing but the first Councillor of Her Majesty.'

Leaving Royer, Joseph, tired of his trip, wrote to Leopold:

You are a better man than I am [Is this a reference to Royer's comment?], but I am more of a charlatan, and in this country one has to be. I, personally, am a charlatan because of calculation and modesty. I exceed in appearing simple, natural, reflective, even to excess. All this has aroused enthusiasm which really embarrasses me. During my trip I did not attend any theatre, any amusement, in order not to show myself too much. Everywhere I have conversed with well-instructed persons, at all hours . . . I have entered into their minds; I have satisfied them . . . Everybody wanted to hear me talk, and I passed for an oracle, for the rare is very precious . . . I quit this land very content, but without regret, for I have had enough of my role.

On his way home Joseph passed close to Ferney, the home of Voltaire. The great Frenchman had expected the emperor's visit with pathetic eagerness. In June, Voltaire had received a letter from Potsdam, in which Frederick expressed the hope that

Joseph 'would wish to see and hear the man of the century, the
Virgil and Cicero of our day. If this should take place,' Frederick added ironically and a trifle jealously, 'you will proclaim
him above Jesus.' The old philosopher at Ferney prepared a
splendid dinner, appropriate verses, and his own collected
works for the illustrious traveller. To Voltaire's chagrin, Joseph
drove by the home of the most famous man in the eighteenth
century, without stopping and without a word of explanation.
When near Ferney, the emperor was asked whether he would
go in to see Voltaire, he is reported to have replied drily, 'No,
I know him too well already'.

Voltaire never quite got over the slight, and contemporaries
were harsh in condemning Joseph for this deliberate insult to
an old man. Frederick of Prussia understood the reason for
Joseph's strange behaviour. 'I have learned from a reliable
source in Vienna,' the Prussian king wrote, 'that the empress
has forbidden her son to see the old patriarch of toleration.'
This is the truth. Under ordinary circumstances, the emperor
might have ignored his mother's request, but she was ill at the
moment, and he was quarrelling with her over the Moravian
Protestants, so he did not wish to make matters worse. To
Voltaire's credit, it must be recorded that he did not repay the
insult with his customary biting comments. One may search
Voltaire's voluminous works and correspondence, and never
find a word of condemnation of Joseph. The sage of Ferney
may have compensated himself with reading the poem which
Frederick had sent him in anticipation of the emperor's visit:

> Oui, vous verrez cet empereur,
> Qui voyage afin de s'instruire,
> Porter son hommage à l'auteur
> De *Henri Quatre* et de *Zaïre*,
> Votre génie est un aimant
> Qui, tel que le soleil attire
> A soi les corps du firmament,
> Par sa force victorieuse
> Amene les esprits à soi:
> Et Thérèse (Maria Theresa) la scrupuleuse
> Ne peut renverser cette loi.

Joseph a bien passé par Rome
Sans qu'il fût jamais introduit
Chez le prêtre que Jurieu nomme
Très-civilement l'Anté-Christ.
Mais à Geneve qu'on renomme,
Joseph, plus fortement séduit,
Révérera le plus grand homme
Que tous les siècles aient produit.[1]

---

[1] This may be freely translated as: Yes, you will see the emperor, who travels to instruct himself, do homage to the author of *Henri Quatre* and *Zatre*. Your genius is a magnet, which draws to itself the intellects, as the sun attracts the heavenly bodies. And Maria Theresa, the scrupulous, cannot reverse this law. Joseph has passed by Rome, without entering the home of the priest whom Jurieu very civilly calls Anti-Christ. But at Geneva, Joseph, more definitely attracted, will pay homage to the greatest man the centuries have produced. *Oeuvres de Voltaire,* vol. 50, 243-4.

# CHAPTER 5

# Aggression

I

*The emperor seems to have a great appetite . . . I hope you will give him such a good indigestion that he will lose all desire for further glory.*
Prince Henry to his brother King Frederick of Prussia

'That man is a genius and a marvellous talker,' is what Joseph said when he rose from the table after a conversation with the formidable enemy of his house, Frederick the Great. The place was Neisse, Moravia; the time, August, 1769. The twenty-eight-year-old emperor and the fifty-seven-year-old king were discussing the fate of Poland.

Poland, lying between the Habsburg and Romanov empires, stretching like a huge, lazy, anarchic giant across the flatlands, forests, and marshes of central Europe from the Baltic Sea almost to the Black Sea, served as a buffer state between Europe and Russia in the east, and between Christendom and Islam in the south. For centuries the Polish land had been a battleground for Prussians and Wends, Germans and Lithuanians, Russians and Poles, Hungarians and Bohemians, Tartars, Swedes, Mongols, and Cossacks. This unfortunate geographic position had left an indelible impress upon Polish institutions and character; the Poles became something not quite European and not quite Asiatic. Polish instability, disorder, and venality became proverbial; *Polnische Wirthschaft* is still a German byword to describe sloppiness and anarchy.

The Polish aristocracy – *Szlachta* – formed about 8 per cent of the population, about 900,000 persons; the rest of the people were mainly serfs. The majority of the nobles, forbidden to engage in any livelihood except that of knights, were but a privileged proletariat; they were the lackeys, flunkeys, and henchmen of the sixteen or seventeen great families who owned and ruled the country. These families maintained splendid courts, kept standing armies, and carried on their own foreign policies. They usually sold themselves to some foreign power. General Mokronosky, for example, who was a famous Polish 'patriot', received 20,000 livres annually from the French Government. These magnates kept Poland in a constant state of anarchy, continually brawling, intriguing, and fighting. No force existed to restrain and check them. They throve on anarchy.

With ill-defined boundaries, lacking natural frontiers, corrupted by strife and disorder, weakened by a preposterous governmental system, Poland was ready for the executioner. It required only the historical moment, a favourable combination of circumstances, and a will to do the inevitable job. The will was supplied by three of the most ruthless rulers of the eighteenth century.

What Joseph and Frederick were discussing at the memorable interview in Neisse was how to stop Catharine of Russia from dominating Poland. The czarina, who was, incidentally, Frederick's ally, had put her lover, Stanislaus August Poniatowski, on the Polish throne. She poured money and troops into that country and soon acquired a stranglehold there. The result was a civil war, into which Turkey, incited by Vergennes, the French minister at Constantinople, was drawn.

The Habsburg empire, wedged between a powerful Russia and an enlarged Prussia, with a crumbling Turkey too weak to offset the balance, found its position uncomfortable.

Joseph, Maria Theresa, and Kaunitz realized the seriousness of the situation. What was to be done? Peace, at any price, said Maria Theresa. Let us get in on the game, urged the ambitious Joseph. The wily chancellor shook his head. He agreed with both sovereigns in their aims, but disagreed as to method. In his opinion it was necessary to come to an understanding with the King of Prussia, the man on whom depended the peace of central Europe, Austria's enemy for twenty-eight years. Frederick himself, unwilling to be embroiled in a war, had given

Austria an opening. 'We are Germans,' he told the Austrian Ambassador in Berlin;

> What matters it to us that in Canada or on the American isles the English and the French are squabbling; that Paoli causes trouble to the French in Corsica; that the Russians and the Turks are tearing each other's hair? So long as we two, the House of Austria and myself, have a good understanding, Germany has nothing to fear from war.

Vienna decided to send Joseph to talk things over with Frederick. 'I consider it not unjust,' Kaunitz pointed out, 'that Poland, in order to save herself from Russian slavery and imminent destruction, should voluntarily provide the King of Prussia with the necessary compensation.' The chancellor's idea was that Austria should permit Frederick to take whatever he wished in Poland, on condition that he return Silesia to Maria Theresa.

Provided with minute instructions by Kaunitz, Joseph set out to meet the famous Prussian hero who had defeated his mother's armies in so many battles. The young emperor was eager to see Frederick, whom he admired above all other mortals.

'The German emperor,' reported the Turkish governor of Belgrade to His Majesty the Sultan at Constantinople,

> has withdrawn from government affairs because of liver and spleen trouble, and has left Vienna in order to find distraction from his illness on trips to Venice, Prussia, and Hungary; the empress, his mother . . . encouraged him to go travelling to cure his palpitation of the heart.

Such was the espionage system of the Sublime Porte.

The two rulers of Germany met for the first time on August 25, 1769. The young emperor, hook-nosed, blue-eyed, and thirsty for fame, gazed with unconcealed admiration at the little Prussian king, hero of innumerable battles, lean, sharp-tongued, and disillusioned. Frederick was unusually cordial; Joseph was honoured and delighted but not duped.

'Dearest Mother,' Joseph wrote four days after the first meeting,

> The King has overwhelmed us with politeness and friendliness . . . I believe he wants peace, not out of the goodness of his heart, but because he realizes that it is advantageous . . . I have questioned him on all sorts of things; it would be impossible to write it all, because we converse about sixteen hours daily . . . He is very discreet on the subject of religion . . . His health is very good . . . He does not resemble any of the portraits that you see of him . . . The servile attitude which his brother and nephew have towards him is incredible. During meals, which last a dreadfully long time, they dare not open their mouths . . . As regards the army . . . his officers are better disciplined than ours, more active, and execute the king's commands more effectively than ours.
>
> We went to dinner (August 25th, noon), which lasted almost three hours . . . After that I went home . . . Soon the king came to visit me, and we talked for about three hours . . . I asked him to tell me about the battles of the last war, which he did very modestly . . . After supper (August 26th) . . . we smoked and talked . . . about Voltaire . . . He asked me whether I thought it advisable that he should report our interview to Russia. I told him he ought to decide that for himself . . . We talked about Russia. He told me it was necessary to stop that power . . . The king always assumed an exaggerated politeness, was full of assurances of friendship, but one may be sure that his old distrust is still in his soul and . . . in his character.

'That young prince,' the Prussian king summarized Joseph's character, 'affected a frankness which suited him well . . . Desirous of learning, he had no patience to instruct himself. His exalted position made him superficial . . . Certain traits of character broke through in spite of himself, revealing the boundless ambition which was devouring him.'

In Vienna Maria Theresa was disturbed. She feared her Catholic son would be corrupted by the free-thinking Prussian king who was worse than a Lutheran, for he was a friend of Voltaire. The mother poured her heart out to her chancellor. Kaunitz, tongue in cheek, consoled the empress, assuring her there was no danger that Joseph would be affected by such a knave as Frederick II of Prussia.

The meeting at Neisse settled nothing. Russian military

victories over the Turks threatened to disturb the balance of power in the east. Action was called for, and Kaunitz decided to meet Frederick personally.

Joseph and Kaunitz met Frederick at Neustadt in Moravia, on September 23, 1770. The Austrian chancellor had never met his arch-enemy, the Prussian king, and he went forth to the diplomatic battle to slay the Potsdam Goliath with a portfolio packed full of advice. Kaunitz carefully drew up what he called a 'Political Catechism' to teach the innocent Frederick some elementary politics. Button-holing the witty and cynical King of Prussia in a casement, the humourless chancellor bade the king 'to listen tranquilly and without interruption' to what he had to say. Despite his keen sense of humour, the absolute master of Prussia was startled; no one, since his father's un-lamented death, had ever dared lecture him. But Kaunitz was imperturbable. Frederick, with a sigh and wry smile, resigned himself to listening to a long dissertation on international politics. Frederick was so grateful when Kaunitz finally ended that he jumped up hastily and smothered him in an embrace. The chancellor was flattered. 'My conversation,' he modestly informed Maria Theresa, 'has made upon that prince a most vivid impression.' The smiling Frederick confided to his ambassador in Vienna that Kaunitz 'has taken me for nothing but a soldier who has no conception of politics, and I cannot deny that he has amused me quite a bit'.

Frederick was a perfect host. He entertained his Austrian guests with military parades, theatricals, and good dinners. He knew precisely when to flatter. With Joseph he got along beautifully, for the old soldier was rather fond of the spirited emperor.

The ubiquitous Prince de Ligne, who later wrote volumi-nous memoirs, recorded some of the conversations at the royal table. Frederick and Joseph discussed what each craved most. De Ligne, asked for his opinion, replied: 'I would like to be a pretty woman till I was thirty; a commanding general with success and ability till sixty, and a cardinal till eighty.' Both monarchs laughed. 'Everyone cannot have the same thing,' Frederick said to Joseph,

It all depends on the situation, circumstances, and the power of states. What suits me would not suit Your Majesty. For instance, I sometimes risk a political lie . . . I conceive a piece of news, for example, which I know will be seen to be false at the end of twenty-four hours. No matter; before the truth is known, my news has done its work.

Joseph remembered and smiled.

'I have just returned from a long trip,' Frederick informed Voltaire after leaving Neustadt; 'I was at Moravia and visited the emperor who thinks of playing a great role in Europe. Brought up in a bigoted court, he discarded superstition; reared in splendour, he adopted simple manners; fed with incense, he was modest; eager for glory, he sacrifices his ambitions to filial duty.' The king also told his friend that Joseph surprised him by reciting 'a number of verses from Tasso and the whole Fido'.

The interview at Neustadt again led to no positive results, except a clarification of issues. The Austrians wished that Catharine would withdraw her troops from Poland and make peace. Frederick agreed in principle, but refused to bind himself to any action.

Early in 1771, Frederick and Catharine signed a secret convention to partition Poland. The court of Vienna, upon hearing the news, began to mobilize the army, and concluded a treaty with Turkey. Kaunitz and Joseph were both opposed to war. The rattling of the sword was merely a bluff to frighten Russia and Prussia, as Maria Theresa inadvertently informed the Prussian ambassador. Austria could not afford to allow Prussia and Russia to strengthen themselves at the expense of Poland and Turkey. But Vienna, outmanoeuvred, had only two choices left: either to engage in war; or to join in a dismemberment of Turkey or Poland. Kaunitz embittered by Maria Theresa's babbling, left the decision to her and to Joseph.

Joseph pointed out that there were three possibilities. Russia and Turkey might end the war without indemnities for either side, but this, he reasoned, was out of the question. Austria, Russia, and Prussia might come to an agreement about Poland.

Finally, Russia and Austria might unite to prevent a partition of Poland. Joseph maliciously favoured the last plan, for it meant snatching the prey from Prussia. Maria Theresa and Kaunitz agreed. They were actuated by different motives. The empress sincerely hoped to preserve the peace and to save Poland. The ambitious Joseph, who cared little for Poland, hoped that things would develop in such a way as to bring Austria some territorial gains, without the risk of war. Kaunitz, shrewder than his sovereigns, pursued his tortuous policy, intending, if possible, to save Poland, and at the same time to leave a loophole open to share in the partition, should it take place.

Unfortunately for Poland, Austria's decision to co-operate with Russia came too late. The Russians were by this time distrustful of Kaunitz. As the Russian minister, Panin, expressed it to his ambassador in Vienna, Kaunitz had better realize 'that we have settled everything already, and that it would therefore better repay the court of Vienna also to make acquisitions'. Kaunitz realized it very well. Early in 1772 he knew he would have to join in some partition; but he wished to save Poland at the expense of his ally Turkey. Joseph sharply objected. He had changed his mind, and wished to fight. Austria, he urged, should follow Prussia's example and occupy the Polish cities of Cracow, Lemberg, and Sandomir, with the declaration that she would 'relinquish them and . . . withdraw her troops as soon as . . . Russia and Prussia did the same'. This, the emperor concluded, would be a guarantee for Austria not to be left empty-handed in case 'the Turks could not be persuaded to pursue the war'. Joseph's position resolved itself to this: win or lose, Poland would pay the price.

Kaunitz, in a long explanation, demolished Joseph's arguments. Reluctantly the emperor admitted that the chancellor was right. Kaunitz was now neutral as to which country, Poland or Turkey, would be partitioned, provided Austria would get an equal share with Russia and Prussia. The great obstacle, however, was Maria Theresa. She considered any kind of dismemberment a crime and a sin, and as regards Turkey, a double crime, as it also meant a breach of treaty. To Kaunitz's sober argument that if the two neighbouring states increased their territory, Austria, to preserve the balance of power, must do likewise, the empress replied that if two powers acted unjustly it did not necessarily follow that a third must do the same. 'Even if the whole thing were necessary,' she wrote, 'I am by no means convinced that it is just.' She positively refused to dismember Turkey. 'We have allied ourselves with the Porte,' she pointed out indignantly; 'we have taken money from her . . . There can be no question of our enriching ourselves at her expense.' At any rate, she added more practically, such provinces as Moldavia and Wallachia (the chief states of modern Rumania), which would fall to Austria, were unhealthy and desolate; they would be of little value to 'our monarchy'. She admitted the only thing left was to partition Poland, it being 'the lesser evil'. Joseph received his mother's moral outburst – the 'Jeremiad', as she herself called it – coldly. His mother's fits and scruples were not formidable when they were, as in this case, opposed by the masterly Kaunitz and himself.

After lengthy negotiations between the three courts, during which Austria made exorbitant claims, the treaty partitioning Poland was signed on August 5, 1772. 'In the name of the Very Holy Trinity', Russia, Prussia, and Austria made claims to certain 'rights' in Poland. Austria was given Galicia, with the important salt mines of Bochnia and Wieliczka, which gave her a salt monopoly in central Europe, but this did not prevent Maria Theresa from deploring the sad fate of poor Poland. Galicia was to be the only acquisition of territory under Joseph, the thwarted monarch who dreamt of great conquests.

By the first partition Poland lost 4,000 square miles of land. Poland did not recover from the blow. The process could not stop: the first partition logically and inevitably led to a second and a third until Poland was nothing but a name. The dismemberment of Poland brought Russia to central Europe and made her a dangerous rival and enemy of Austria.

## II

*A genealogist proves to a prince that he is a descendant in
straight line from a court whose relatives once made a family
pact, three or four hundred years ago, with a house the very
memory of which no longer exists. This house had remote claims
on a province whose last master died of apoplexy. The prince
and his council then conclude without any difficulty that the
province belongs to him by divine right. The province, which is
a few hundred leagues away, protests that it does not know
him, that it has no desire to be governed by him . . . This does
not even reach the ears of the prince, whose right is incontestable. Forthwith the claimant finds a great number of men who
have nothing to do and nothing to lose; he dresses them from
a large blue roll of cloth . . . stitches their caps with white
yarn, makes them turn right and left, and marches them to
glory. The other princes who heard about this frolic soon
participate, each according to his ability, and cover a small ex-
panse of land with murderous mercenaries the like of whom
could not be found even among the followers of Genghis-Khan,
Tamerlane, and Bajazet.* – Voltaire*

Such, precisely, was the method by which Frederick of Prussia
claimed, and acquired, Silesia from Maria Theresa. It was in
exactly the same way that Joseph tried to seize Bavaria. Joseph
was no Frederick, but the adventure is of considerable interest.

Bavaria was a large south German state contiguous to
Austria. Like the other German provinces, it was independent,
although nominally part of the Holy Roman Empire; that is,
under the titular jurisdiction of Emperor Joseph. The emperor,
however, had no more rights or power in Bavaria than he had
in Brandenburg, Saxony, or anywhere else, for the empire as a
political unit had ceased to exist for over half a millennium.

Austria had long coveted Bavaria, either in part or whole,
and Kaunitz spent a good deal of time scheming the possibilities
of annexation. Central Europe, one must remember, was still
feudal, and medieval law governed interstate relations. Almost
any noble house of long lineage could claim kinship to, and the
inheritance of, almost any other noble family, for aristocratic
intermarriage was the universal rule. It was all, as Voltaire
acidly put it, a question of genealogy. At the death of the

Bavarian Elector, who was childless, Maria Theresa could thus claim the fiefs of the Upper Palatinate on the ground that the Bavarians had once bequeathed them to the Bohemian crown, which she now wore. As Archduchess of Austria, Maria Theresa could demand Lower Bavaria by virtue of the investiture granted Austria by Emperor Sigismund. She had rights to the *allods* (freelands) because she was a descendant of Anne, who was great-granddaughter of Albert and the wife of Emperor Ferdinand I (died 1564), and also a descendant of Mary Anne, who was the daughter of William, who was the fifth Elector of Bavaria. Furthermore, at the end of the seventeenth century, the daughter of Leopold I, Maria Theresa's grandfather, had married the Elector of Bavaria. And Joseph, in his capacity as emperor, could rely upon the medieval law which provided that in case a prince died without heirs, his fiefs should revert to the empire. All that was necessary was to prove these claims – for which a staff of clerks and a historian were employed by Vienna to dig in the archives – and an army to back these demands.

The childless Maximilian Joseph of Bavaria died on the last day of the year 1777. Within twenty-four hours a messenger dashed into Vienna and whispered the news in Kaunitz's ear. The court was amusing itself at the moment. Kaunitz called out Joseph and whispered in his ear; Joseph ran back to the hall and whispered in his mother's ear. Maria Theresa changed colour and dropped her playing cards. The court broke up. The empress hastened into her apartments for a conference with Joseph and Kaunitz. The chancellor spread out a map of Bavaria and pointed out the districts to be claimed; Joseph eagerly supported Kaunitz. The sixty-year-old empress, however, was agitated and frightened. 'In God's name,' she exclaimed, 'take only what we have a right to demand! I foresee that it will end in war. My wish is to end my days in peace.' She had lived through fifteen years of war, and she had had enough. She recalled that her formidable enemy was still alive and active in Potsdam.

'Even if our claims to Bavaria were better established,' she told her belligerent son, 'we should hesitate to start a general conflagration. We should do this for the sake of the immense expenses which would oppress our people anew with debts . . . I do not oppose settling the matter by means of conciliation and negotiation, but never by force of arms.' The empress was not supported by Kaunitz, who, for once allowing himself to commit a great blunder, aided Joseph in his aggression.

In June the Austrian troops invaded Lower Bavaria. They met with no resistance. Both the emperor and the chancellor were sure they would meet with no opposition from anyone in Europe. France was occupied with the American colonies in their revolt against England; Russia was engaged in another round of her perpetual war with Turkey, and Frederick of Prussia was anxiously watching both arenas. 'The conditions in Europe seem favourable,' Joseph enthusiastically wrote to Leopold. 'Everyone is occupied . . . consequently I flatter myself that this coup will succeed without war, and our acquisition even though incomplete, will always be worth while for having cost nothing.'

Thirty-seven years of experience should have taught Vienna that Frederick was not the man to permit plunder on his frontier without himself participating in it.

The one thing that Frederick could never permit was a strengthening of Austrian power. At the death of the Bavarian elector, the King of Prussia wrote to his foreign minister, Hertzberg: Austria's 'conduct will be my compass'. Frederick warned Riedesel, his envoy in Vienna, 'to keep a watchful eye', and ordered Hertzberg to prepare the legal documents and records relating to Bavaria, and to draw up the 'laws of the empire which forbid alienation and dismemberment of its great fiefs'.

Kaunitz sent a note to Prussia, explaining Austria's 'incontestable rights' to Bavaria. That sounds just like Austria, Frederick growled; 'that cannot go on'. To Goltz, Prussian ambassador in Paris, Frederick wrote that Joseph's right to Bavaria was that of 'a highway robber who puts a pistol to a traveller's throat and demands his purse'. On such conduct, Frederick's opinion was that of an expert. It had been his own procedure in Silesia.

The Bavarian struggle was in the first stages only a battle of

G

wits. Each side employed all the pressure, chicanery, and diplomatic verbiage of the period. As a propagandist, the King of Prussia had few peers. 'The best way to interest the French ministers,' he wrote to Goltz in Paris, 'is . . . to point out to them the underhanded ambitions of the emperor; that, animated as he is by such passion, he could equally revive the ancient claims to Alsace, Silesia, Belgrade . . . It is time to stop this torrent in its course.' When Austria tried to bribe Frederick with the duchies of Julich and Berg, which did not belong to Vienna and to which Prussia had claims anyhow, the king sneeringly replied that Austria's offer was a 'lure to shut my mouth in order to have a free field for her depredations'. He had no intention, he said, of being 'the dupe of her fraudulent policies'.

The Prussian king ordered the troops mobilized and the men recalled from their leave. He did not mean war, although he was determined, so he said, to 'bridle the ambition and despotism of the House of Austria'. When Kaunitz refused to answer the insistent Prussian notes, Frederick, furious at Austria's 'abominable conduct' thundered that she would be 'punished as she deserved' and hired spies to report to him the movement of the Austrian armies. Early in March Frederick learned that sixteen regiments of Austrian cavalry, thirty-four battalions of infantry, and 20,000 Croats – a total of 80,000 men – were on the move, menacingly enough, towards Bohemia and Moravia, which pointed at Prussia.

And what was Joseph doing? 'He burns with impatience and activity,' Riedesel reported to Frederick on March 11th.

> He has prepared his campaign equipment . . . He already sleeps on his camp cot and speaks of nothing but the next war. He has said that he runs no risk, since if he is defeated it will be by the hero of the century. Her Majesty, the empress, on the other hand, is disconsolate. Considering the fury of the emperor, and the ascendancy he has gained over his august mother, I do not believe that it will be possible to check the imperial court by means of negotiation.

This truthful report made Frederick swear. Why, he wanted

to know, does not Maria Theresa, who boasts about her love for peace, curb her unbridled son?

This was exactly what the empress was trying to do. In letter after letter she appealed to her son. She pointed out that Austria's army was 'surely inferior' to the Prussian. 'Prussia,' she wrote, 'has fortresses, and we have none; we have a vast stretch of territory to cover . . . which we will have to expose to all the invasions and revolts.' She did not see a single friend in Europe who would aid her. 'The sword once drawn,' the empress concluded pleadingly,

> negotiation will become impossible. The well-being of thousands upon thousands of men, the existence of the monarchy and the preservation of our house are at stake . . . I am not saying this out of . . . personal cowardice. I still possess the same forces I had thirty years ago, but I cannot lend a hand to the ruin of my house and my states.

After this letter was dictated to a secretary, Maria Theresa added this postscript as a final warning: 'If the war breaks out, do not count on me at all. I shall retire to the Tyrol, and there finish my days in isolation, bewailing the unhappy destiny of my house and my people.'

The mother's appeal had no effect on Joseph who was drunk with the dazzling prospect of enlarging his territories and of 'crossing swords' with the most redoubtable general of the eighteenth century. To Joseph, Frederick was the overshadowing spirit, both to be emulated and humbled: 'I shall affirm by the sword that which Frederick has gained by the pen.'

They will not catch me napping, Frederick said, and busied himself with his diplomatic campaign. Catharine of Russia, when appealed to by the Prussian king, replied piously she hoped the affair would be 'terminated amicably'. Frederick was more successful with Austria's ally, France. Here ruled men who hated Joseph. Louis XVI spoke of his brother-in-law's 'ambitious and despotic temper'. The French foreign minister, Vergennes – 'a man of cool head, penetrating judgment, and refined address' – had received his training as ambassador in Constantinople, and was an enemy of the Austrian alliance.

Besides he was being engaged in giving the rebellious English colonies in America as much aid as his pretended neutrality permitted. Vergennes pointed out to Louis that it was vital for France to maintain Prussia's power in Germany as an equilibrium to Austria.

Prussia now threatened to fight, unless Austria withdrew from Bavaria. Could Vienna yield without a struggle? Retirement from Bavaria meant a humiliation which no great power could undergo without suffering a blow to its pride and prestige. A pall of gloom hung over the court of Vienna. Maria Theresa's eyes, a contemporary reports, were 'perpetually red with weeping'. Kaunitz, especially after the French rebuff, became 'gloomy, thoughtful, and less communicative'. Only Joseph appeared 'unaffectedly gay, constantly in action, on horseback before the sun is risen, and ready to receive with alacrity the various troops on their arrival'.

On all sides it was hoped there would be no war. Frederick did not really want war. He was sixty-seven years old, war-worn, for he had spent the better part of fifteen years on battlefields; but he had no intention of letting the young Habsburg cub brow beat him. Joseph, however, had so great an admiration for the 'enemy' that he was willing to plunge Europe into a war to prove that he was Frederick's match. He assured the Prussian king of his 'high esteem' and 'sincere friendship'. Frederick, muttering a plague on both 'your' esteem and friendship, gave answer as 'an old soldier'. He bluntly told the emperor what was involved: whether or not 'an emperor had the right to dispose at will of the fiefs of the empire'. Frederick emphatically denied the right. 'As for me,' he added, 'as a member of the empire . . . I find myself directly engaged in maintaining the immunities, the liberties, and the rights of the Germanic body . . . I have no personal interest in the matter . . . I love and honour Your Majesty . . . It will certainly be hard for me to fight a prince so endowed with excellent qualities, and one whom I personally esteem.'

Frederick was willing to negotiate, but was canny about it. He threw out a suggestion about a portion of Saxony or Lusatia, without specifying his demands, expecting Austria to make the first offer. Not at all, thought Joseph; we will not be 'the first to propose' anything. 'The answer to France will decide everything,' the emperor told Leopold.

It was a peculiar battle. Frederick boxed Joseph with one hand, kept an eye cocked on St Petersburg; and Joseph parrying the thrusts, looked over his shoulder towards Paris. What will Catharine say? How will Louis act? Baron Sacken, the Saxon ambassador in St Petersburg, wrote that the czarina considered it proper that Berlin should 'ardently' oppose Vienna, and that she would like to see 'the constitution of the Holy Roman Empire protected and preserved'. Louis XVI, or rather, Vergennes, likewise sided with Frederick, who, he said, was 'pleading our own cause'. France now took a further step. She had not only refused to aid her ally, but she now began to oppose her. Vergennes wrote to Berteuil that France could not calmly stand by and see the Habsburgs take possession of a 'great military stream which would open an outlet to Alsace and Lorraine'. Knowing that Louis sympathized with the 'very natural' feelings of Marie Antoinette, who suffered on account of her brother, Vergennes persuaded the French king to remain firm nevertheless. 'No equivalent,' he wrote Louis, 'could compensate Your Majesty for the damage that would be caused by the least increase in the power of that house [Austria].' Louis took the cue, and all the insinuations, tricks, and pleadings of Kaunitz, Mercy, and Marie Antoinette could not budge him. Like a wise husband, the French king did not argue with his tearful and angry wife. He simply avoided the subject.

With Louis obstinately hostile, Catharine unfriendly, and Frederick intransigent, Joseph became more and more furious and bitter. Was Bavaria to slip from his grasp? Was he to be humiliated before the whole world? It was summer now, and there was still no decision. He was no further on in July, 1778, than he had been in January. Only the situation had become aggravated. His warlike passion had considerably cooled. How could he wage a war when Maria Theresa was passionately opposed, and Kaunitz had withdrawn into Sphinxhood? Could he fight Frederick singlehanded, especially when Prussia had the sympathies, and possibly the aid, of France and Russia? He could not even withdraw with dignity. So, sick in body and in spirit, the frustrated emperor defied his rival verbally. He wrote to Frederick:

> My Brother. Since the death of the Elector of Bavaria you wish to act the part of a protector in the contest for the succession. You assume the character of a guarantor of the Westphalian peace, in order to mortify Austria. . . .
>
> I hope you will kindly allow me, as head of the empire, some knowledge of our imperial constitution; conformably to which every state of the empire may enter into treaties with the Magnates, by an amicable agreement, with respect to claimed lands, and may, after the agreement, take possession of such lands. Least of all do I believe that Your Majesty will expect Austria should submit to the tribunal of the Elector of Brandenburg, in a case where he has no other authority than such as belongs to him as a member of the empire in a general assembly.
>
> You opposed neither the negotiations concerning the succession of Bavaria, nor the taking possession of it . . . You began to doubt when the time for doubting was gone by; and you were irresolute in an affair, the uncertainties of which had long before been removed by agreements. Perhaps you fancied yourself as living at the epoch of the death of Charles VI and of your acquisition of Silesia.
>
> It appears to me, that it is too much in your recollection that you have been a successful general, that you have had an experienced army of 200,000 men, and a colonel who has written a commentary on the work of Caesar's *de bello Gallico*. Providence has given this advantage to several other powers besides Prussia; if it gives Your Majesty pleasure to lead 200,000 men to the field of battle, I shall be there with the same number; if you wish to make the trial whether you are still a successful general, I am ready to satisfy your passion for fighting. . . .
>
> I hope to find you on the banks of the Elbe, and when we shall have fought, and given Europe a spectacle of obstinacy, we will return our swords into our scabbards. *Je savois bien que vous êtes fâché contre moi.*

The order now was: *À gloire, dragoons!*

## III

On a cool April morning the emperor rose at four, dressed hastily, and went out on the ramparts, impatiently waiting for the day to break. His brother Maximilian joined him and when the sun rose the two men went to their mother's apartment, and then all together to chapel. They spent an hour in prayer on their knees. Maria Theresa rose, embraced her sons, and parted from them with deep sobs. Her sons were going to the front.

Joseph joined his troops – about 190,000 men – near Prague. Farther to the north, at Frankenstein, the King of Prussia was at the head of his armies. 'When it is a question of fighting,' Joseph muttered, 'he [Frederick] rises up earlier than other people, but he shall never find me napping.'

King Frederick commanded 80,000 veterans and had 433 guns; his brother, Prince Henry, had an equal number of men and cannon. The Austrian marshal, Loudon, had under him 70,000 men and 252 guns; the emperor himself commanded the bulk of the army, 128,000 soldiers, with 423 cannon. The Austrians took up a 'fine position' behind the Elbe – and negotiated.

While the Teutonic armies were facing each other in Bohemia, Voltaire – 'the meteor of the reading world' – was dying. At Strawberry Hill in England, Horace Walpole was wondering whether Voltaire's 'royal friend of Prussia' would cede the 'throne of war' to 'young Caesar'. From Paris, Baron Grimm informed his friend Catharine at St Petersburg that only she was 'capable of digesting the thickest diplomatic soup'. And in Vienna old Kaunitz spent his time in minute analyses, 'never saying what he thinks', as Maria Theresa complained in exasperation.

Would the Austrians and Prussians fight? Everybody, including Joseph, wondered. The emperor was torn between ambition, fear, and filial love. Maria Theresa's letters to him undermined his self-confidence. 'I bow my head,' the mother wrote him to the field, 'and say, *Fiat voluntas tua.*' She trembled for the safety of her son: 'I fear only for this precious and dear Joseph.' There were thousands of other sons, even more exposed, for whom she did not fear. Her son suffered at this time from rheumatism of the legs, which was aggravated by the raw weather. 'The cold and wet weather,' Maria Theresa wailed, 'drives me to despair.' A boil, constantly increasing in size, spread on the crown of Joseph's completely bald head; he was worried it might suppurate and affect his brain. Such were the feelings and moods of the monarchical commander-in-chief on the even of a dynastic struggle.

Early in July the negotiations were broken off. Would the clash now occur? In Passy in France, Benjamin Franklin, Arthur Lee, and John Adams thought it would. 'A war in Germany,' they wrote on July 20, 1778 to the President of Congress in Philadelphia, 'between the Emperor and the King of Prussia seems to be inevitable'.

The whole Austrian army occupied a triangle, the left wing under the Livonian-born Scotsman, Loudon, the centre under the mediocre generalship of the Russia-born Irishman, Lacy, and the right commanded by the emperor in person. The Austrians were in a good strategic position, covering the whole apex of north Bohemia. They were trained to manoeuvre for position; its object being the destruction of the opponent's supplies and the occupation of strategic points. The later Napoleonic device of manoeuvring the enemy so as to force him into decisive action was at this time not yet employed, except occasionally by Frederick. The Austrians were traditionally averse to bold action; and the King of Prussia was now too old and cautious to attack with his former impetus.

The Prussians were in Austrian territory, but they did not fight much. The opposing armies marched and counter-marched, exchanged a few random shots, manoeuvred back and forth – and waited. According to their custom, the Prussians ravaged the land, dug up the fields, requisitioned provisions, cut down trees, and destroyed what they could not take. It was the Bohemian peasant and not the government, who paid for Joseph's desire for glory.

Meanwhile Maria Theresa, frantic with fear for the safety of her son, secretly sent the astute Thugut to Frederick with a letter signed by 'a mother of a son in the war'. The Prussian

king eagerly accepted the proffered hand; but Joseph, when he
heard of it, was infuriated. He told his mother he 'neither could
nor would have anything to do' with 'this incredible negotiation', which, he said, was the greatest humiliation of his life.
'Nothing more dishonourable, more injurious, and more
destructive could have happened,' the emperor bitterly confided to his brother. His pride was, of course, more important
than the lives and property of hundreds of thousands of people.
Maria Theresa pleaded with him not to hate her, that her
'intentions were pure'. Against pure intentions even an emperor
cannot prevail. 'We must try once more,' he desperately informed his mother, 'what success our arms may have against
an enemy of our house.'

But Frederick would not be budged, especially as he had
hopes that Maria Theresa would succeed in checking her son.
There is also some reason to believe that Loudon had secretly
'promised Maria Theresa not to give battle', at least so Ligne
affirms. We know that the old Scotch warrior was disgusted
with the whole affair. 'This dog of a political war,' he growled.

Was this war? It was against all rules. Frederick did not play
a fair game; the canny Prussian would not engage the enemy.
A few shots here and there, several shots here and there, several
minor skirmishes, some casualties mainly due to sickness – was
this all the redoubtable Prussian hero was capable of?

Joseph cursed, the officers sneered, the soldiers shivering in
the cold grumbled and dug potatoes to feed themselves. The
rain came down in torrents and the men, with rough humour,
said this was nothing but a Potato War.

The Prussians stolidly bided their time; twenty-five thousand
of them deserted or died of exposure, but men were cheap in
Prussia and Frederick could always find new material. There
was no point in wasting precious *thalers* on ammunition. It did
not cost much to feed Prussian soldiers; they despoiled and
ravaged the land. Why, Frederick thought grimly, not let the
impatient Habsburg wear himself out? 'We drift here in the
same cruel uncertainty,' the despairing Joseph wrote, 'far
from the enemy, separated from him by thick forests and

ravines . . . It is beginning to be unbearable. Prince Henry's army, which occupied a large terrain, took horses, men, cattle, everything that could be found, and the Saxon peasants in the rear of the army pillaged the rest.' This was a fine situation for an ambitious, glory-loving, proud commander-in-chief. With almost 200,000 men he could not even defend his own land from marauders who were only a few miles away. And the humiliation of it – Saxon peasants pillaging the land under the very nose of the emperor, within range of his five hundred guns! 'If ever we have a stroke of good luck,' the emperor shouted in impotent rage, 'Saxony will have hell to pay!'

The rain was heavy, the mud deep, the cold execrable. The soldiers could not keep warm. And in Vienna, the empress informed her son, there was 'a furious lack of money', no commissariat, no quartermaster, the 'monthly accounts . . . in confusion', millions lost, and 'the credit abroad declining every day'.

*Ce chienne de guerre politique!* The morale of the Austrian army sank into the mud. Profound and utter disgust reigned everywhere. The soldiers personally liked Joseph who was brave, comradely, sympathetic, and bore hardships with the rest. He slept on the ground, fraternized with his men, and sometimes shared their food; but the emperor's comradeship could not make up for his ignominious campaign. In Vienna, too, Joseph's prestige declined; he was sharply criticized in public. Wraxall, who was in the capital, relates that 'an officer of distinction' said:

> Never since the accession of the . . . Empress . . . have the Austrians exhibited so inglorious a spectacle to Europe . . . If ever offensive operations were necessary in order to inspire the troops with ardour, they were so in the present campaign . . . But what has the Emperor done? He has impressed an indelible conviction on all his officers and soldiers, that whatever may be the justice of his cause, he feels his inability to maintain it in the field . . . Joseph beheld the finest provinces of Bohemia plundered, without daring to make an effort for their defence . . . How can it be otherwise? The Empress . . . only wishes for peace. The Emperor breathes war, but knows not how to conduct it, though he

aspires to superintend all operations in person. Prince Kaunitz fluctuates between both; desirous of repose, yet anxious to gratify a Prince whose passion is ambition, and who may soon become his sole master.

Ominous news came from the west and east. In France, Vergennes, prophesying that Joseph would have 'a sad end' unless he controlled his 'greedy tendencies', secretly encouraged Russia to oppose him. The czarina, her vanity excited by the role she was invited to play as arbiter of central Europe, sent an army to the east Galician border and offered to act as armed mediator. Catharine's move frightened even Kaunitz and terrorized Maria Theresa. The chancellor urged Joseph to hurry to Vienna, for 'every moment is precious'. The empress added an hysterical postscript, pleading with her son to come immediately, because 'the monarchy is at the point of collapse'. The monarchy was always collapsing in Maria Theresa's time.

Joseph replied that he would come as soon as possible; he could not leave at once, for 'the King of Prussia is again on the move', and that it would be treason to 'my duties, service and country' to desert the field at the moment. He doubted, he wrote, that the Russians 'would push things to an extreme'. It would take thirty-six hours of 'jolting on these dreadful roads' to go from Prague to Vienna. Meanwhile he gave his mother permission to negotiate for peace: 'I implicitly subscribe to everything.'

When the frustrated hero finally arrived at Vienna he looked 'burnt out and thin', but to conceal his discouragement and failure he appeared gay. He found everybody, including Kaunitz, 'gloomy and joyless'. Maria Theresa was dejected, 'pensive and frequently in tears'. The emperor also found widespread popular discontent. The poorer classes, a contemporary noted, 'murmur at the increase of taxes, and look forward with natural apprehension to their probable augmentation'. Everyone dreaded the continuation of the ludicrous but expensive war. And so Joseph was compelled to capitulate and to tolerate (for he never publicly approved) the assembling of a peace congress to terminate a war which was no war.

The peace congress met at Teschen in March, 1779. According to sacred custom, each participant made lofty claims. The Austrians, perhaps goaded by Joseph's intransigent hostility, showed themselves intractable until news arrived that Russia and Turkey had made peace again, which meant that the Russian army was free to turn against anyone whom Catharine disliked. On May 13, 1779, birthday of Maria Theresa, the peace was signed between Austria and Prussia and between the other German states involved. Russia became the guarantor of the Peace of Teschen. Emperor Joseph put his signature to the document on May 16th, and, with a certain *Galgenhumor*, appended all his titles to the name.

Who was the victor? Austria was given a small section of Bavaria, the so-called *Innviertel*, a little triangle on the Inn River, thirty-four square miles in extent. It cost Frederick 25 million crowns to thwart Joseph, to preserve the 'indivisibility' of Bavaria, and to play the role of protector of the small German states. In the long run it was worth the price, for in the nineteenth century Bismarck and the time-serving historians, publicists, and other Prussian apologists harped upon the traditional Hohenzollern role of protectors of the German states.

At the moment only Catharine came out victorious; to the end of her days she was to be the arbiter of Germany. Maria Theresa was happy at the outcome. 'I am overjoyed,' she wrote. 'Everyone knows that I have no partiality for Frederick, but I have to do him full justice, and recognize that he has acted nobly. He has promised me to make peace on reasonable conditions, and he has kept his word. For me it is an inexpressible happiness to have prevented a great effusion of blood.' *Felix qui potuit rerum cognoscere causas!*

Maria Theresa may have been happy, but the whole affair was a tragedy to her son. Not only did Joseph lose prestige, so essential to a monarch, but his first great military-diplomatic setback had a dangerous effect on his personality. Thwarted in his first adventure (which was a conscious and subconscious attempt at imitating his rival Frederick's career), Joseph's narcissism drove him in later years to various rash 'imperialistic' ventures. It was as if he desperately strove to assert that sense of superiority which had been so deeply outraged in the Bavarian struggle.

His immediate escape was into irony. After the Peace of Teschen he wrote in a Byronic letter:

> A considerable number of ambassadors immediately assembled, and for three months applied themselves with great wisdom in arranging a peace, by which Austria received only a small part of Bavaria, when the whole country was in her possession.
>
> They did not fail to convince the Empress, my mother, of its advantage . . . Immediately a number of compliments were exchanged, and 99,000 *Te Deums* were sung and celebrated in Vienna on the occasion . . . In order not to grieve the empress, I approved the peace. . . .
>
> I am like a Venetian general, who in time of war commands the land-army and receives his commission from the republic. When the campaign is over he obtains a pension.
>
> Live contented like a wise man; enjoy all the charms of your private station, and by no means envy the happiness of kings.

# IV

For years it had been Kaunitz's aim to dismember Turkey, an object which Joseph favoured. To partition the Ottoman empire, Russian and French aid was needed. But after the Bavarian war the Austro-French alliance was badly shaken. Only Russia was left as a potential friend. Catharine, however, was the staunch ally of Frederick.

Joseph and Kaunitz decided to break the Russo-Prussian alliance and draw closer to Catharine. Conditions were favourable, for with western Europe entangled in the war of the American colonies, Russia could once more proceed with the conquest of the Crimea from the Turks. Here Austria could be of help. Furthermore, an Austro-Russian accord would isolate the hated Prussian king. Thus reasoned Joseph, who was still smarting from the humiliation inflicted upon him by Frederick.

The King of Prussia kept up his friendship with Catharine by excessive flattery and undignified fawning. The ardent czarina was beginning to tire of her old diplomatic love, ridiculing Frederick for his senility. The straw that finally broke the alliance was a letter which the King of Prussia wrote to the czarina, in February, 1779, proposing that Russia, Prussia, and Turkey ally to keep Joseph at bay. The suggestion was surprising coming from so adroit a politician as Frederick. For, obviously, Catharine had nothing to fear from Austria, and, on the other hand, a great deal to gain from hostility to Turkey. The czarina's angry comment was that Frederick's proposal meant that Russia's 'Turkish policy should become dependent upon the court of Berlin, and would be favourable only to the Turks, as Russia did not at all need Moslem aid'.

Joseph decided to take advantage of the favourable situation. Early in the spring of 1780 Catharine was to go on a tour in western Russia, and the emperor made up his mind to pay her a visit. But Maria Theresa's scruples had to be overcome first. The pious empress had a deep hatred and contempt for the adulterous and free-thinking czarina. She was shocked at the thought that her son should come in contact with so wicked a sinner as Catharine. 'You can imagine how such a project appealed to me,' Maria Theresa confided to a friend; 'for the character of the Empress of Russia fills me with aversion and horror.'

The empress, however, was a practical woman despite all her tears, and, at Kaunitz's appeal, she withdrew her objections. Through Prince Gallitzin, the Russian ambassador in Vienna, Joseph informed the czarina he would like to make her acquaintance. Catharine declared herself delighted. The city of Mohilev, not far from the Austrian border, was chosen as a meeting place for June 7, 1780. The emperor then asked Kaunitz to draw up instructions for his guidance. Joseph thanked the chancellor for his 'good advice and sage counsel', and promised to obey the instructions.

The emperor was in high spirits. The trip was not only political, but personal. It gave him an opportunity to pay off his score to Frederick for the humiliation suffered during the Bavarian war. 'I cannot deny,' the emperor wrote to his friend

Lacy, 'that I am curious to make the acquaintance of Catharine. If only through this I could so gall the beloved Frederick that he would burst.'

Joseph warned Cobenzl, his ambassador in Russia, that he would travel incognito as Count Falkenstein and that he wished no demonstrations made in his honour. Nor did he want any gifts from the czarina. If Catharine insisted upon being generous, the emperor added significantly, 'then the only jewels which would cause me pleasure would be Schweidnitz, Glatz, Neisse, and Kosel' (these were the strongest fortresses in Silesia which Prussia had taken from Austria).

Count Falkenstein crossed the Moravian-Hungarian mountains on horseback and then descended into Galicia, where he found the cattle poor, the land uncultivated, 'the country sparsely settled, many forests, and marshes'. A month later he arrived at Mohilev. Here Potemkin, Catharine's lover, brought him an excessively flattering letter of welcome from the czarina.

Catharine was fifty-one, plump, white-skinned, vivacious. She had had many lovers, enjoyed life, loved good food, delighted in conversation. She received many fawning letters from the most distinguished men in Europe. Voltaire, Diderot, Rousseau flattered her with fulsome compliments. Grimm's letters were almost obscene in their flattery. 'The nourishment of my soul,' he called her, 'the consolation of my heart, the pride of my mind, the joy of Russia and the hope of Europe.' She relished those words, was charmed by the flowery French phrases. The *literati* spread Catherine's fame throughout Europe.

She was reputed to be an 'enlightened' ruler. She spoke readily of 'Reason' and 'Justice' and 'Humanity'. Millions of Russians were sunk in abject slavery; the czarina distributed large diamonds to her lovers. The family of her lover Orlov was given an estate of 45,000 peasants and 17 million rubles in jewels and palaces. Lieutenant Vassiltschikov loved his imperial mistress for twenty-two months and was given 350,000 rubles and an annual pension of 20,000. Catharine loaded her lover Potemkin, with whom she lived for two years, with 9 million rubles worth of gifts and made him a prince. Savodovsky, who lasted eighteen months, was paid with 10,000 peasants and presents amounting to 260,000 rubles. Zoritz, Catherine's only lover who was not a Russian, lasted only one year, but his prowess was rewarded with presents worth 1½ million rubles. There were many others.

When Catharine died after thirty-five years of autocratic power, Russia was as she found it, poor, rotten with corruption, enslaved.

> The great population
> In your lands
> Longs for freedom
> From your hands.
> Then spake she full of noble zeal
> *Messieurs, vous me comblez*,
> Whereupon she extended serfdom
> To the Ukraine also.
> *Alexei Tolstoy on Catharine*

She was now driving toward Mohilev to meet the Holy Roman Emperor. Over thirty years ago as Sophie of Zerbst she had been an insignificant little German princess, a daughter of a fanatically Lutheran Prussian general. It was Frederick of Prussia who had engineered the match between Sophie and the half-witted Grand Duke Peter of Russia. Sophie's father had obstinately refused to permit his daughter to turn Greek Orthodox; his daughter's soul was worth to him more than a Russian throne. The cynical King of Prussia had smilingly argued with the pious parent. To every argument the father had only one answer: '*Meine Tochter nicht griechisch werden.*' Frederick then bribed a Lutheran parson to persuade the general that the Greek and Lutheran rituals were the same. Sophie's father kept muttering in a daze: '*Luthersch-griechisch, griechisch-luthersch, das gehet an*' (Lutheran-Greek, Greek-Lutheran, that is all right).

Sophie went to Russia, abjured her faith, became Catharine, and married the brutal Peter, whom she ultimately dispatched in Muscovite style. 'I count it among the finest days of my life,' Frederick wrote her after her betrothal,

5. Marie Antoinette, Joseph's sister

6. Catherine II, Czarina of Russia

when I have seen the elevation of Your Imperial Highness to that dignity. I should believe myself very happy to have contributed to it, considering that it will be a service which I have rendered to the Empress of Russia, my dear ally, and to all the vast empire, that of procuring a princess of your merit as a sleeping companion for the grand duke.

That was thirty-six years ago and in the intervening time she had beaten the Turks in the name of Christianity, suppressed a peasant revolt, half-destroyed Poland, and introduced vaccination to Russia. The grand duke her husband, was long dead and she, Catharine, had other companions.

Catharine made her pompous entry into Mohilev, 'a vile city', Joseph noted, 'built of wood, and the streets full of mud'. The autocrat of all the Russias drove in magnificent style, her gilded carriage surrounded by gay nobles, dashing hussars, glittering cuirassiers, gold-braided generals. The unostentatious emperor watched the procession with an ironic smile, and then splashed through the mud after the cavalcade. In a big wooden house Potemkin introduced His Majesty to Her Majesty. Joseph, in simple military uniform, stooped to kiss her hand, but the czarina put her white and plump arms around him and pressed him to her ample bosom. The czarina overflowed with amiability.

Catharine set up her court in the mosquito-ridden town of Mohilev, and tried to entertain herself and her distinguished guest. Joseph was interested neither in the parades nor in the improvised opera, he confided to his mother, for he had to keep in mind his chief object, which was political. He observed that Catharine was an attractive woman who knew how to play to royal game.

Joseph's simplicity and charm won Catharine's admiration. The emperor made a special effort to fascinate Catharine. The czarina was, she never forgot, an upstart; the Holy Roman Emperor was the proud son of the oldest and haughtiest ruling house in Europe. Others had flattered her too, but they were only bourgeois scribblers. And Frederick of Prussia? The Hohenzollerns were not a much better family than her own.

But the Habsburgs! From the moment Catharine met Joseph she lost all interest in Frederick. 'She talked of him,' says a contemporary historian, 'as superannuated, rapacious, wholly devoted to his own interests, and actuated by a perfidious and crooked policy.'

Joseph spoke of Frederick's malice against him. 'That is his old wives' prattle,' the czarina retorted; 'living alone, the king accepts gossip from all kinds of petty folk, and his false reports will yet bring him to a point where he won't be believed even when he tells the truth.' Giving Joseph a shrewd side glance, Catharine asked if it were not appropriate for the Holy Roman Emperor to have Italy, and especially Rome, for his heritage. Joseph caught the point and smiled as if the suggestion were a jest. But seeing the czarina was serious, he answered astutely that Rome would be somewhat difficult to acquire, whereas the Russian Rome – Constantinople – was much easier to conquer. At this neat thrust, Catharine was startled and murmured that she had no such intentions.

The czarina urged the emperor to accompany her to St Petersburg where they could exchange ideas more freely. Joseph could not refuse. On the way the two sovereigns conversed more frankly, Catharine reproaching Joseph with his support of the Turks, and the emperor complaining of her friendship for Prussia. Catharine again came back to her insinuation that Joseph should make Rome his capital. It was clever and unscrupulous talk.

The emperor went on a flying visit to Moscow, while the czarina travelled to St Petersburg. Joseph found Moscow attractive. 'It is a superb city,' he wrote his mother; 'the surroundings are fertile and cheerful, and the company, especially the women, is good and very charming.' He saw the all-powerful Potemkin three times, and was careful to give him a rich present. Catharine's favourite promised his attachment and loyalty to Austria. 'He is,' Joseph observed, 'a very indolent person, extremely cool . . . and insouciant.'

From Moscow Joseph went to St Petersburg, where he spent three weeks. He was not a social success in the capital. The

Russian nobility resented his aloofness and reserve. He never visited them and never concealed his contempt for them. He considered them barbarians, which they perhaps were, and mercilessly satirized their conduct and ridiculed their appearance. Even Catharine, the grand actress, could not conceal her annoyance at the emperor's tactlessness. True, St Petersburg society was not equal to that of Paris or even Vienna, but why show openly one's scorn? Catharine deplored, as she said, 'his chatter, levity, and thoughtlessness'. And the Russians, used to showy royal claptrap, wondered what kind of a monarch this foreigner was anyhow: he had none of the trappings, neither horses, nor equipages, nor chamberlains, nor flunkeys, nor crown, nor jewels. And he did not even get drunk like their own dear unlamented 'Little Father' Peter!

Joseph took care to send to Vienna two sets of letters; one by private courier, and another through the regular post. The post letters, everybody knew, were opened by the government's spies and the contents reported to the czarina. The best indirect way of letting Catharine know something was to send a letter through the post. Joseph wanted the czarina to understand that he admired her capital. He wrote a regular post letter to Maria Theresa:

> I will again reiterate what I already had the honour of repeating to you in every letter, that my sojourn here is very agreeable, that the public establishments and the tasteful and magnificent monuments which the Empress of Russia has built, much surpass anything abroad . . . I am neither an enthusiast nor an exaggerator, but I will say that any traveller who, curious and desirous of seeing beautiful and great things which elevate the soul, does not come here, is very much mistaken.

In a secret dispatch, sent by courier, Joseph explained to his mother that he held 'long and frequent conversations' with Catharine. The czarina was willing to treat with Austria, but did not consider the time opportune for breaking with Prussia. She was angry at the French, wanting to know why they 'absolutely insist upon having the Moslems in Constantinople'. On every occasion, Joseph concluded his letter, Catharine warmly insisted that Rome was Austria's real capital, and that only there could be the emperor have 'a great field for glory and immortality'.

The seed for an alliance was sown. When Joseph left, Catharine wrote him a farewell letter in the grandiloquent royal style of the period: 'The land which Count Falkenstein leaves is filled with the deepest veneration for his distinguished virtues.' There was a touch of the comic in all this mummery, for Catharine was eager to be decorated with the Order of the Golden Fleece; Joseph was in consternation lest she ask him for it outright. He knew that Maria Theresa would be indignant at any suggestion that the sacred order should go to a woman with the morals of Catharine; fortunately the czarina did not ask for the tinsel directly.

On his return Joseph had to cross through Poland where he got stuck in the mud. There were no roads. It rained constantly. In the downpour the emperor had to traverse thirty miles of forest, ditches, sand, underbrush, and swamps. 'When one reflects on the size, fertility, and excellent rivers of Poland,' the dripping emperor commented, 'and realizes that such conditions as these can exist, one begins to tremble at the consequences and effects of a wretched and feeble government'.

In Vienna a honeyed letter awaited the emperor. 'I no longer address Count Falkenstein,' Catharine wrote, 'but the chief of the Holy Roman Empire, who has returned to his residence.'

'At the moment when I read your letter,' was Joseph's unctuous reply,

> I thought to myself: Thou hast not wasted thy years – Catharine is satisfied with thee, and I refuted the prognostication which Voltaire had made of me when I passed his residence without going in to see him. He said that the other sovereigns and great men had already secured all the virtues and brilliant qualities, so that they left me only one . . . namely, modesty; but that I have taken possession of this and paraded it. But when your letter arrived I was no longer modest and could not restrain myself from showing it to my mother and a few good and sincere friends

'Happy is the moment,' Catharine answered thrillingly, 'when

I had the satisfaction of making the acquaintance of Count Falkenstein.'

The fawning correspondence between the two imperial doves continued for the next ten years, until the very day Joseph died. It was to lead to the greatest disaster in the emperor's career, and probably cost him his life.

CHAPTER 6

# *Sic Transit*

No sooner did Joseph return from Russia than he planned a new trip, this time to England, a country which he admired. The ailing Maria Theresa was bitter. She hated Protestant England, especially as in June, 1780, a riot had broken out against the Catholics in London. 'The heterodox,' she said in disgust, 'attack the true religion, but to us they preach toleration.' In deference to his suffering mother, Joseph gave up his planned trip across the Channel, but announced his intention of visiting Holland, another Protestant country. 'I wish,' Maria Theresa confided to Marie Antoinette, 'that these journeys would once and for all come to an end . . . It is becoming worse every year, and increases my sorrow and anxiety at a time when in my age I need aid and consolation.'

Early in November Maria Theresa's complaints increased. She bewailed her ill health and lack of support. Her face was pock-marked, and she was so corpulent that her legs could hardly carry her. A special machine had to be constructed to take her up and down the *Gloriette* at Schönbrunn. Asthma and a weak heart made breathing difficult. She was easily fatigued and perspired at the slightest exertion. 'I feel inside,' she said, 'that I am turning to stone.' To cool the heat that fat generated, she always kept the windows open and drank quantities of iced lemonade. Soon she was attacked by a choking cough and fever, but insisted upon attending mass regularly.

Joseph did not believe his mother's condition serious, but he thought it his duty to summon Leopold and the sisters to her bedside. The emperor spent the nights in the vestibule leading to his mother's bedroom. From time to time he would enter and make her comfortable in her armchair, for she could not breathe in a lying position.

On the night of November 27 to 28, 1780, she grew worse.

Dr Störck urged her to receive extreme unction. At four in the morning the children were summoned to her bedroom. They all knelt, while the empress, propped up in her armchair and praying in a clear voice, received the last sacrament. Then she addressed her offspring, thanking them for their love for her, and urgently commending them to Joseph. There was suppressed sobbing in the room. Weeping loudly, Joseph fell on his knees, his body trembling. Maria Theresa blessed her eldest son, while he kissed her hands. She then blessed the other children, kissed their foreheads, and gently ordered them out of the room.

During the day the empress and her son held long conversations. In the evening of the 28th – her last – she sat with her children at the table, leaning heavily on her elbows. 'I feel cold in my bones,' she said. At night and on the following day she was in fever and could not quench her burning thirst. She conversed with Joseph in French, although she customarily spoke German to her children. The sky was murky and when evening came there was a cold nasty drizzle as only Vienna knows in November. 'This is bad weather for so long a journey,' the empress murmured. At nine in the evening of November 29th she rose from her chair and sank on the edge of the bed. Joseph hastened to make her comfortable, saying, 'Your Majesty lies in a bad position.' 'Yes,' she replied, 'but good enough to die.' With these words, she died.

The ante-chamber was packed with courtiers and women. Joseph opened the door, pale and haggard. Without speaking, he handed his friend Lacy a little note with the words: *Tout est dit.*

Philipp Cobenzl, the friend of Joseph and Kaunitz, hastened out to bring the news to Kaunitz. He found the chancellor entertaining guests. Cobenzl, knowing that it was forbidden to mention death in Kaunitz's presence, simply placed himself behind a couch on which a lady was sitting, and looked straight at the chancellor. Kaunitz caught his glance; Cobenzl nodded. Kaunitz understood. Suddenly there was a deep silence in the room. Two tears fell from the eyes of the seventy-one-year-old man who had never been known to have any emotions. This was his particular tribute to the woman he had faithfully served for almost forty years.

The same night Joseph wrote a touching letter to Kaunitz. 'My dear Prince. The terrible misfortune is already known to you. I have ceased to be a son . . . Remain you my friend; be my aid, my guide in the burden which falls upon me.' The chancellor replied he would not change in his attachment and service to the emperor, 'whom I love no less than I do myself'.

Early next morning Joseph was already deeply at work in his mother's cabinet, sorting her papers. Her testament, he complained, was 'an unhappy confusion of ideas and diction'. After lengthy examination and analysis, the will was found to provide a bequest of 1,500,000 florins to be distributed among the troops as a month's wages, and a stipulation that each one of Maria Theresa's sons should receive 45,000 gulden annually, while the unmarried daughters were to get only 24,000.

The funeral took place on December 3rd. The Theresan regime had been one long agony for the common people, which, however, did not prevent cringing German historians and time-serving poets from calling it glorious, and her 'the noblest mother of the fatherland' and 'the greatest German woman'. The poet Klopstock penned a dithyramb in which he spoke of her as 'a whisper of the voice of the Gods, a word of flames'. In all the forty years of her reign she never did a generous thing and never thought a noble thought. Limited in her outlook, she considered the masses of her subjects as existing merely to work, sweat, and bleed for the monarchy, church, and nobility. Narrow in her sympathies, Maria Theresa left her land in a morass of corruption and inefficiency, and but for her son the Habsburgs would not have for long escaped the fate of the Bourbons. The starving masses repaid the mother of the fatherland with a deep hatred – a hatred which had been aggravated in the last period by a burdensome drink tax. Dumb, sullen, and threatening, the Viennese lined the streets as the funeral procession was wending its way to church. They cursed the dead woman and threw stones and mud at the coffin. The grenadiers had to shield the hearse from greater violence.

There was an ironic climax to Maria Theresa's career. She, who had ardently loved and protected the church all her life, was refused by Pope Pius VI the funeral service usually accorded in the papal Church to Catholic monarchs. The pope said that such services were not customarily held for women. When the papal legate in Vienna, who knew the dangerous consequences of such an insult, protested to the Holy Father, Pius retorted: 'It matters little to me whether the emperor takes amiss this act of mine or despises it.' In his next official dispatch to Rome, Joseph added a postscript in his own hand, 'It matters not at all to me whether the Bishop of Rome be well- or ill-bred.' The pope lived to regret his slight.

At the moment Maria Theresa was buried Joseph realized his isolation. 'I am alone in the world,' he wrote to Leopold: 'Providence has wrested from me wives, children, father, and mother. I pray you sincerely to retain your friendship for me.'

And Marie Antoinette, to whom the domineering mother had always been a friend and adviser, tearfully wrote to Joseph from Paris: 'Oh my brother, oh my friend! Now I have nobody but you in a country which has always been and will always remain dear to me.'

In Potsdam the old and morose Frederick exclaimed: 'Maria Theresa is no more. A new order of things begins.' And he was suddenly afraid of his dead enemy's revengeful son in Vienna.

# PART THREE

# The Autocrat

## (1780–1790)

*Your son will rule, striving*
*Ringing, yearning, weeping for glory;*
*Ah, but will he excel thee!*

Klopstock

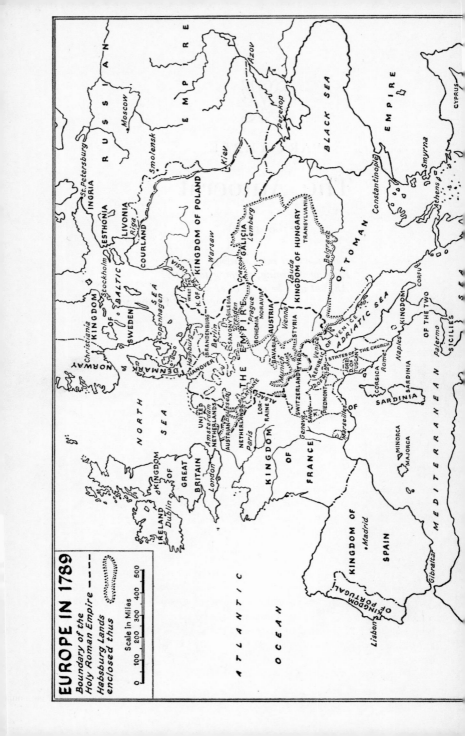

EUROPE IN 1789

Boundary of the
Holy Roman Empire — — — —

Habsburg Lands
enclosed thus

Scale in Miles

0   100  200  300  400  500

# CHAPTER 7

# State

## I

*The government of more than twenty million souls weighs*
*upon me as a heavy burden, which can be felt only by monarchs.*

Joseph to his sister Marianne

At last Joseph was free. He was

> By the grace of God, Emperor of the Romans, always august,
> King of Germany and of Jerusalem, King of Hungary, of Bohemia,
> of Dalmatia, Croatia and Slavonia, Archduke of Austria, Duke of
> Burgundy and of Lorraine, Grand Duke of Tuscany, Grand
> Prince of Transylvania, Duke of Milan, of Bar, etc., Count of
> Habsburg, of Flanders, of Tyrol, etc., etc.

He was the master of central Europe. His word was law from
the Carpathians to the Apennines, from the Dniester to the
Rhine. There was no lawful power, under God, to whom he
owed any account.

'*Mon ami*,' he communicated to Choiseul in France soon after
his mother's death:

> the empress, my mother, has left me a great state . . . I always
> entertained the greatest respect for her virtues and character . . .
> With respect to the officers of state, this princess has given proof
> of considerable knowledge of government . . . With the governors
> of the provinces I am not quite satisfied. I shall pay some attention
> to their mode of conducting affairs . . . The influence the clergy
> have hitherto exercised in the government of my mother will be
> another object of my reform . . . The state of finances of the
> Austrian dominions also requires an alteration . . . I must make
> retrenchments . . . These matters are yet new to me; I must
> better ascertain my real position; to the duties of my new station
> I must add a perfect knowledge of their objects, otherwise I should
> be a monarch like the Grand Seignior, who is well acquainted
> with the pleasures, but not with the duties of his station.

Live happier than myself: I have hitherto hardly known what happiness is, and before I have finished the career I have marked out for myself I shall be an old man.

This was a new Joseph speaking. Here is an assurance of power, of aim, of destiny. 'I must' this, and 'I shall' that. He casts doubts on his mother's government; she had a 'considerable knowledge', yes, but the undertone is: 'not quite good enough'.

The emperor entered his duties without any ceremony, without any coronation. He demanded no homage. He would not be crowned in Hungary, as was the custom, because he considered such an act ecclesiastical and medieval. In any case he did not wish to receive the crown from any outside power. He would brook no restraints. The governors received the oath of allegiance from the Estates, and the officials were simply confirmed in their positions.

The first step was to reorganize the administration. He must have an efficient machine to do his will. The Council of State was hardly ever assembled, and Joseph almost never presided over it. The individual councillors would submit reports of their departments to the emperor, with whom rested the final decision.

Many of the older men, and in particular Kaunitz, Hatzfeld, Swieten, and Kressel, were retained. The chancellor still remained the unquestioned head in all matters pertaining to foreign policy. With one or two exceptions, Joseph yielded to Kaunitz's experience and insight in foreign affairs. But the chancellor had no voice, and probably little interest, in internal administration. He rarely opposed the emperor's domestic acts. Even when he disapproved, as in the case of Joseph's harsh treatment of Belgium, he hardly voiced his protest. So long as the old man was given a free hand to play the *Grosse Politik* he was content. Joseph trusted him implicitly, made him read and correct his diplomatic and state papers, and had him act as regent when he himself went travelling.

The ablest members of the foreign office were Count Ludwig Cobenzl, who was ambassador in St Petersburg from 1779 to 1795; his nephew Philipp Cobenzl, who was vice-chancellor;

Gottfried van Swieten, former ambassador in Berlin; and Cardinal Count Francis Hrczan-Harras, Austrian plenipotentiary at Rome. The Austrian diplomatic organization was farflung and was maintained at huge expense. In 1786, the embassies and the diplomatic agents and spies cost the country 2,025,000 florins. The couriers alone cost 343,343 florins that year, while in 1785, during the trouble with Holland, the expense of the couriers was 800,000 florins.

Among the administrative experts were the court chancellor, Count Blümegen, who was succeeded by Count Kolowrat (from 1782 to 1808); Count Haddik, in military affairs; Count Seilern, in justice; Count Zinzendorf, in accounts; Gottfried von Swieten, in education; and Count Rudolf Chotek, in finances.

The most enlightened and interesting members of the new government were privy councillors, Franz Kressel von Qualtenburg (1720–1801) and Tobias von Gebler (1726–1786). Kressel, a liberal and a man of culture, was the active spirit behind the church reforms. Gebler had literary aspirations and was in constant communication with the foremost writers of the age. He was interested in coinage and mining.

The intellectuals of the epoch, the men who gave the Josephan era its theoretical foundation, were Professors Anton von Martini and Joseph von Sonnenfels. Martini taught law at the University of Vienna, and Sonnenfels lectured on political science and economics. Both men were Joseph's teachers and had a lasting influence on his despotic inclinations. Martini and Sonnenfels (the latter a converted Jew) developed the theory – *jura majestatica circa sacra* – that the ruler's sovereignty over the church was part of the authority which belonged to him since the formation of the original contract (Rousseau's Social Contract). This theory was taken up and further developed by other Austrian jurists, mainly Gmeiner, Pehem, Riegger, and Rechberger, who went farther than the French thinkers by insisting that the church came under the jurisdiction of the secular ruler. If church law, they argued, was opposed to state law, it was contrary to natural law and hence to Christ's will; consequently the monarch had a right to oppose the church whenever he found the latter in conflict with the state.

Joseph's aim was to create a centralized and unified bureaucracy wholly devoted to the state and its ideas. The officials had to fill out a questionnaire every six months, giving their outside incomes, years of service, abilities, effort, conduct, knowledge – fifteen questions in all. To assure them economic security, the emperor decreed in March, 1781, that they be eligible for pensions at the end of ten years of service. After twenty-five years a man would receive one-third of his salary; up to forty, one-half; and over forty, the whole. Widows were to get one-third of their husband's salary, plus a stipend for the children.

The officials were peremptorily informed that henceforth they were nothing but servants of the state. Nor were they allowed, if they were German, to feel any superiority to their non-Teutonic colleagues. 'All jealousies and prejudices between province and province, nation and nation, must cease,' the emperor decreed in his Pastoral Letter (*Hirtenbrief*), 'in the body politic the whole suffers when even one member is sick. The distinctions between nations and religions must disappear, and all citizens must consider each other as brothers.' The officials were to give their bodies and souls to the state; they were to have no outside interests or occupations. 'In the business of the state,' Joseph ruled, 'personal inclinations should not have the slightest influence. Everybody must give his best and carry out his duties regardless of rank or ceremony.' Everything and everybody for the service of the state, was his motto. 'The State,' he said in a phrase that was to become famous, meant 'the greatest good for the greatest number.' He realized that his conditions were hard; hence he warned those who could not sacrifice themselves 'to leave an office of which they were neither worthy nor capable'.

The emperor strove to establish an officialdom that was honest, educated, and efficient. He warned Kolowrat, Chancellor of Bohemia, that appointments to the Aulic Council should go only to those 'who possess a knowledge of the country', and who had ability and experience.

7. Frederick the Great, King of Prussia

No official was safe from the emperor's interference or wrath. One could never tell when he would drop in for inspection. On a cold November morning Joseph once unexpectedly walked into the office of the Austro-Bohemian chancery and grimly sat down with paper and pencil to take notes. 'You will excuse me,' he said to the flustered chancellor, 'if I listen-in today.' One winter morning, on his way to a meeting, the emperor met a councillor going up the stairs. 'Ah,' said the monarch to the embarrassed official, 'we are both late today.' At a prolonged administrative session, a councillor surreptitiously glanced at his watch; it was three o'clock. The emperor also looked at his watch. 'Indeed,' he remarked to the official, 'it is somewhat late, but, you know, time passes quickly when one is in good company.' On a sudden inspection at the Vienna Municipal Hospitals Joseph found the man in charge in his shirtsleeves reading a newspaper. Without being permitted to put on his coat, the mortified official had to take his emperor through all the corridors and rooms of the building. But the joke the emperor relished most, and gleefully repeated, was the one about the government official and the priest. The bureaucrat asked a priest why the clergy had become too proud to employ the humble mount of the Saviour. 'We are forced to have recourse to horses,' the clergyman answered coldly, 'because the emperor has taken so many jackasses into his employ that there are few left for us to use.'

Joseph could be blunt to the point of brutality, especially to the nobles. When he deprived Prince Furstenberg of the governorship of Bohemia, he told Princess Furstenberg harshly: 'I must tell you, Madame, that in future, things can no longer go on in Austria as formerly . . . Give your consort the assurance of my regard, and at the same time remind him, that, in future, in matters relating to the state, I expect his own immediate reports; I am not accustomed, in affairs of my empire, to correspond with – ladies.'

Joseph did not even spare Kaunitz's chancery. Once when a note of his to the foreign office took four months before it was attended to, he burst into fury. 'Nothing is done,' he stormed,

'but only bare facts and obstacles . . . When, after experience,
I make certain propositions, I expect them to be accepted, and
not considered merely as a lamentation of mine on which you
should utilize your wits for the sole purpose of making a lawyer-
ish plea for the preservation of precedents.' His letters to Leopold are full of complaints against the bureaucracy. 'I find
difficulties and bitter work,' he wrote. 'There is an absolute
lack of men who can conceive and will; almost no one is animated by zeal for the good of the fatherland; there is no one
to carry out my ideas.' Leopold, who was wise, cool, and without much faith, told his brother calmly that his great design of
simplifying, clarifying, and unifying the administration was
admirable; 'but the work which you have undertaken is most
formidable, difficult, and discouraging, for you will find infinite
obstacles among the employees, accustomed to the old regime,
who do not like any innovations'.

Complain as he might of his officials, and urge them, as he
did, to go to the university 'to improve their ignorance' yet the
despotic son of Maria Theresa brooked neither interference nor
independent thinking on the part of his bureaucracy. The
Chotek incident showed this. The experienced Count Chotek
did not agree with the emperor's revolutionary tax patent of
1789. He protested that the economic ideas in the tax reform
were unsound and dangerous. Joseph ignored his subordinate's
plea, and Chotek, after eighteen years of service, found himself
compelled to resign. 'I realize,' he sadly wrote to his emperor,
'that with eight children and a moderate income my resignation will be hard on my family; but there are circumstances in
life when a man of honour has to sacrifice everything to preserve
his self-respect, which he could not do if he remained in a
position where he would be forced to act against his principles.'
This is strangely reminiscent of Joseph's own struggles with his
mother. But did the emperor sympathize?

Whatever your decision [was the imperial answer], I will not
change my actions, not even out of respect for you . . . Accustomed
as I am to ingrates, this does not surprise me. But that a man of
spirit like you, out of sheer obstinacy and quixotism, should take

such a step when, even if the tax patent were really harmful, the blame would not fall on you – that, I admit, has astonished me.

With or without aid and co-operation, the absolutist monarch instituted a regular 'paper regime'. Edict followed edict with lightning rapidity. At the end of the ten-year reign there were six thousand decrees, and over eleven hundred and forty-seven folio pages. Every conceivable and inconceivable matter was regulated, rearranged, and prescribed. The emperor was trying to create a rational, mechanized state, soulless and will-less, but one that should function like a well-greased machine. The thoroughness with which he went to work on this monster, which he called the State is appalling. Nothing was left to chance, imagination, or initiative. He meant well, of course. His people were to be made happy in spite of themselves. He was to be to them a father, a harsh and brooding, but just and solicitous father.

In 1784 Joseph issued minute instructions for the guidance of his district commissioners who were to travel through the land for periodic inspections. They were to observe:

Whether the censual and vital statistics registers were kept.
Whether the houses were numbered.
What was the condition of the buildings.
Whether the population was industrious or lazy; well-to-do or poor; and why.
Whether the conscription books were kept in order.
Whether the barracks were habitable.
How many men could be quartered among citizens and peasants.
Whether the army behaved properly towards the civil population.
Whether the population had sufficient protection.
Whether the toleration edicts were observed.
Whether there was any superstition.
Whether the clergy were respected, and what their discipline was.
Whether divine services were properly carried out and whether the churches were in good condition.
Whether the preachers delivered indiscreet sermons.
Whether anyone cared for the orphans, foundlings, and homeless children.
Whether anything was being done for the blind, deaf, and crippled children to make them ultimately self-supporting.
What was the condition of the schools.
Whether there were roving clowns and jugglers on the land.

Whether the restrictions against drunkenness were carried out.

Whether there was a need for more workhouses and prisons.

Whether the laws were carried out.

Whether the judges were obedient to the superior courts.

Whether the roads were cleared.

Whether there were sufficient precautions in the sale of poisons.

Whether the sale of contraceptive methods was prohibited.

Whether the church penances and the dishonouring punishment of unfortunate girls were abolished, and whether there were institutions for the saving of such girls, and foundlings.

The officials had to investigate, observe, and report upon hundreds of such questions, which the emperor drew up himself. He would leave nothing to the doubtful intelligence of his subalterns.

Nor was this all. With his mania for systematization, the eternally suspicious despot created a far-flung espionage system and reorganized the official police. Previously the police had been under the administration of the provincial governments. In 1786 the emperor unified all the police in his lands, except Hungary. Provincial police chiefs were to report to Count Pergen, the Minister of the Interior, in Vienna, and Pergen was to communicate directly to Joseph to whom he had access at all hours. Pergen received ten thousand gulden every three months for his secret service. To each provincial capital Joseph sent a specially trained police commissioner who was to work together with the governor, without, however, being responsible to the latter. The secret police, which became the basis for the notorious state-police under Metternich, a generation later, was not created to watch revolutionaries, but to keep tab on the officials, the army, and the clergy.

Here, too, Joseph left nothing to the imagination or initiative of his subordinates. He composed an elaborate 'Secret Instruction' for the use of his minions. The public, the instruction read, should have no knowledge of the 'secret service'. Only the governors and the police chiefs should know of the existence of the spies. The official police was to be a cloak for the secret one. The agents were to 'detect dangerous plots and expose them before they ripened'. The government, the emperor reasoned, 'must from time to time have reliable information as to the true feelings of the subjects, so as to be able to take the proper measures . . . and to be able to uncover and destroy the hidden enemies who are dangerous to the public safety'.

The secret police were to keep an eye 'on the doings of the officials and to discover how the public is satisfied with them, whether they receive bribes, whether they have relatives abroad with whom they correspond, whether they have contact with suspicious strangers to whom they give official secrets'. Such findings should be reported to Pergen. The agents were to find out 'what the public says of the monarch, and his government, what its mood is from time to time, and whether there are any malcontents'. The army was to be watched to see whether 'there are any individuals who are in communication with foreign powers'. Furthermore, 'the clergy, whose tendencies, in general, are hierarchical, are to be strictly watched to see whether or not they promulgate principles which are contrary to their subjection to the ruler and to the interest of the state'. The agents should observe whether 'the laws of the land are neglected . . . whether money is being taken out of the country, and whether anything else is done to the prejudice of the state'. An eye should be 'kept on suspicious foreign persons, false recruiters, spies and forgers'. The frontier police were to go over all private correspondence 'for interesting news . . . and also to track down unfaithful officials'. This, however, was to be done carefully so 'that the police should not compromise itself'. Observations were to be made 'on those who under-handedly try to spread sectarianism and errors among the credulous mob'. Particularly 'suspicious persons' on their way to Vienna should be reported immediately.

The second half of the instructions dealt with 'ways and means'. The police should keep a list of all suspects. Everybody, particularly strangers, should be registered. Servants should be carefully employed to spy on their masters. This, the emperor pointed out, would serve a double purpose: 'It would keep this class in order,' and it would be easy for the police to watch them. The post should be placed in the hands 'of persons on whose uprightness and dependability the police can rely'. The police should employ anybody who could be of any use, no matter what their position: 'Messengers, drivers, nay under certain circumstances, even Jews who sometimes do good service. Nobody should be considered too low.' No consideration was to be shown to suspects, 'because the duties to the state permit no mercy and no regard'. 'It is self-evident,' Joseph concluded, 'that this instruction should be kept as a veritable state secret and locked by the chief with his own key, and absolutely shown to no one, no matter who he may be.'

Following the emperor's encouragement of inter-bureau spying, a certain subaltern denounced his chief, who, after being suspended from office for half a year, was found to be innocent. The victim asked the emperor that his denouncer be punished.

'I cannot do that,' Joseph replied; 'for this would frighten those who might reveal truths to me, and I must utilize all means to discover rogues.'

'But by this,' the official protested, 'Your Majesty will bring things to a point where no one will be safe from accusations.'

'The honest man,' the emperor answered, 'will surely justify himself and be cleared, as was your own case.'

'True,' the man said; 'but it is no trifle to be for six months under suspicion as a scoundrel.'

'You will not die of it,' was the imperial answer, 'and no one will die of it. He who has nothing to reproach himself with, can rest assured that his innocence will be proven in the end. I myself could easily bear to have my enemies laugh at me only to see them fooled in the end.'

Despite his police regime and his distrust, Joseph was always accessible to his subjects. He encouraged direct complaints and his antechambers were crowded with petitioners who never had long to wait. 'I was accustomed,' the emperor said, 'to pass too many hours in my father's antechamber not to know from experience how unpleasant such a detention must be to others.' The monarch was not only unaffected, but cordial, sympathetic to the poor, and ready to grant prompt aid or redress wrong.

Your Majesty [a trembling peasant addressed the emperor], the rascal, I beg your pardon, has gone off with my last piece, money and beast; we are reduced, my wife and children, to beggary. I always said: Our emperor would not allow this; but he answered: Our emperor has nothing to do with it. We gave him all we could, and now he wants more money or forced labour. You must wait, I said to him, I am going to see the emperor, and I'll tell him . . .

That is enough, my good man. Can you read and do arithmetic?

Yes, Sire; I can show you.

If I believe you; wait a moment. Give this rescript to that honest collector; you take his position.

Must I deprive him of his bread?

Do not let it bother you. That man gets only what he deserves.

[The emperor was not so generous, however, to aristocrats, officials, and snobs.]

What do you wish, madame? [he brusquely asked the widow of an official]. You have heard of the suppression of the pension. How can I live on five hundred florins? I demand justice from Your Majesty.

It is precisely because of justice that you will not get that pension.

I thought that the services of my late husband, and the standards to which I am accustomed, would militate in my favour.

The services of your husband [the emperor replied dryly], were recompensed by a salary. As to your standards, or those which you believe you are entitled to, I must consider also my other subjects. I am not merely the sovereign of Vienna, and you are not the only person I have to serve. Am I to assist you at the expense of the unfortunate poor? Justice demands that I should not accord to you what could support five or six thrifty families.

But what will become of my daughter? She is without resources. She can go to work.

My daughter – work! But Your Majesty. . . !

Work [snapped the emperor], yes, work! I, too, work!

## II

*Every subject expects safety and protection from the ruler;*
*it is therefore the duty of the ruler to specify clearly the rights*
*of the subjects which are to be arranged with a view to the*
*general and individual welfare.*

Paragraph I of the Josephan civil code

Austria, like most European states, was blessed with a diversity of laws. Generally, the Roman law was prevalent; but there were also the medieval Saxon and Swabian codes (*Sachsen und Schwaben-spiegel*), the imperial law (*Kaiserrecht*), and the local and municipal laws (*Land und Stadtrecht*). There was neither unity nor method nor system in all this accumulation. Emperor Leopold I had made an attempt at codification; he drew up a *Codex Austriacus*, listing all the ordinances since the time of Ferdinand I (1556–64) in alphabetical order. In 1752 Maria Theresa had supplemented the Codex with an inclusion of those laws – from 1524 to 1720 – which had come after the earlier code, and added the laws of 1721 to 1740. She had appointed a commission to collect all the laws of the monarchy, but the work was not completed at the time of her death.

Joseph dissolved his mother's commission and appointed one of his own. The new Compilation Commission acted in a different spirit. It made a distinction between civil and criminal laws, and introduced order into the vast mass of irrelevant and trivial decrees. The aim was a rational code based upon general principles.

The judicial body worked for six years before it completed the civil code. Being lawyers, the members of the commission were too conservative for the emperor. Only with the aid of liberal councillors like Kaunitz and Kressel was Joseph able to overcome the obstinacy of the precedent-ridden jurists. It hurt the lawyers to see the emperor ride roughly over their beloved precedents, customs, ancient judicial decisions, and other legal superstitions. They opposed Joseph in his advocacy of greater personal liberty, in his attempt to destroy the privileged estates, in his disregard for customary law; they fought the emperor – in vain – when he ordered the abolition of all the privileged feudal and ecclesiastical courts and jurisdictions.

The gentlemen of the law being too slow, Joseph decided not to wait for the completion of the code and to issue civil decrees. In January, 1783, he promulgated a new marriage law, based upon the doctrine that 'marriage is in itself a civil contract, and consequently the government has the right to decide on the

validity or invalidity of the marriage contract'. The angered
clergy considered the law a violation of the sacramental character of holy matrimony. Joseph explained that the decree
applied only to the contractual aspect of marriage and did not
violate the sacrament. But the clergy were not satisfied: the
decree challenged one of their vital privileges. The Hungarian
Ecclesiastical Council protested that the law was contrary to
the Council of Trent. Joseph did not see what decisions of
ecclesiastical councils had to do with the laws of a modern
state. Concerning divorce, the emperor ruled that the bishops
– and as a last recourse, the secular authorities – had the right
of dispensation. Protestants and Jews had, under certain circumstances, the right of divorce.

Another imperial decree revolutionized the law of inheritance.
Henceforth individuals could leave their estate to whom-
ever they wished. It was a blow at the nobles with their ancient
privileges of primogeniture and entail; some large estates,
however, were exempt from the new law. At the same time,
Joseph abolished the old usury laws, permitting interest at
5 per cent.

By 1787 the second and third part of the civil, property, and
criminal codes – *Bürgerliche Gerichte, Concours Ordnung, Jurisdiction und Gerichtstand* – were completed. A year later criminal
procedure was regulated.

In his penal code Joseph showed his eighteenth-century enlightenment. The death penalty was abolished and brutal
punishments, which existed everywhere in Europe, were done
away with. The emperor, one must keep in mind, lived in an
age of judicial torture, flogging to death, the rack, and the
wheel. As late as the nineteenth century sailors were flogged to
near-death in the British navy. Frederick William of Prussia,
the father of Frederick the Great, was in the habit of cudgelling
witnesses, women and children, until they were crippled.

Joseph's penal code abolished the crimes of witchcraft,
apostasy, and marriage between Christians and non-Christians.
A distinction was made between civil and political crimes.
Under the latter head came *lèse majesté*, treason, revolt, riot,

public violence, abuse of office, forging of state papers, counter-feiting, assistance in desertion, murder, assassination, bigamy, rape, robbery, seduction, kidnapping, stealing, robbery, and arson; all other crimes were considered civil; wood-stealing, poaching, gambling, etc. Duelling was forbidden, the surviving duellist, even if he were an army officer, was to be treated as a common murderer. 'I will suffer no duel in my army,' Joseph wrote to a general:

> I despise the principles of those who attempt to justify the practice, and who run each other through the body in cold blood . . . Officers who bravely expose themselves to every danger in facing the enemy . . . I esteem . . . highly. But should there be men among them who are ready to sacrifice everything to their venge-ance and hatred, I despise them; I consider such a man as no better than a Roman gladiator . . . Such a barbarous custom, which suits the age of the Tamerlanes and Bajazets . . . I will have suppressed and punished, even if it should deprive me of one half of my officers.

In cases of extreme crime the offender was not to be executed but condemned to the galleys. The criminal code, for the first time, recognized the principle of motive in crime. Political offenders were to be treated with consideration; there were to be no unfair tricks or torture, and judicial decisions in political cases were to be made within eight days after examination. The code considered even an accused person as a human being with definite rights, honour, and personality.

Joseph was too much a child of his age to do away with all barbarous judicial practices. Among the remaining barbarities were the stocks, flogging, and branding. Flogging, however, was to be strictly regulated. When Sonnenfels submitted the draft of the penal code to him, Joseph made a marginal com-ment on the paragraph dealing with punishment: 'In this article you must add where the lashes are to be given; on the buttocks, but never on the loins or shanks, and always stretched out on a bench.'

The significant thing was that the new code recognized no distinction between classes. A criminal was to be treated as such, whether he be a duke or a serf. One of Joseph's favourite chastisements was to make upper-class offenders sweep the streets. It was an unheard-of scandal. Caroline Pichler, a friend of Maria Theresa, raged against this indignity in her *Mémoires*. 'This severe justice,' she wrote, 'levelling everybody before the law, seemed to me unfair; to condemn a count, a councillor, or a distinguished citizen to street-sweeping, just as if they were ordinary workers or domestics!'

A number of criminal cases of the period caused a sensation. The most notorious was that of Zahlheim, the last man to be broken on the wheel. Zahlheim, a clerk in the Vienna magistracy, stabbed to death a rich old relative in 1786. The man confessed the murder and was sentenced to be executed. The emperor, although he was shocked at the torture inflicted on the criminal (his flesh was torn with glowing pincers), upheld the verdict. A pamphlet appeared which attacked Joseph for brutality. But this was the last case of capital punishment. Contemporary with the Zahlheim case was that of the peasant-worker Paul Reininger of Styria. In the course of seven years Reininger had brutally murdered six young girls. The courts condemned the man to be executed; but the emperor interposed. 'This villain,' Joseph decreed, 'should be branded, be given one hundred lashes every day for three days in succession, be chained for life in jail, be fed only bread and water, and be brought forth every three months for new punishment.' This was of course infinitely worse than execution, but the emperor had a philosophical horror of capital punishment.

Another case that aroused a fierce attack on Joseph was his punishment of an aristocratic officer, Székely. The lieutenant had taken 97,000 gulden from the military treasury and used the money in an alchemical search for the elusive philosopher's stone. The courts condemned Székely to eight years confinement in a fortress. Joseph commuted the sentence to four years, but had the officer ignominiously stuck in the pillory two hours a day for three days. The aristocracy, hitherto practically exempt from punishment, raged madly. It was bad enough to be penalized, but to be treated like plebeians was unendurable. The nobles thought the sun was being extinguished in their heaven when the emperor had the temerity to order an aristocratic young forger, Count Podstacky, to sweep the streets of Vienna, chained to common felons, in prisoner's garb, and with shorn head.

What Joseph did for Austria in the 1780s Napoleon was to do for France a quarter of a century later. There was a difference, however. The Corsican not only had a united nation behind him, but also, what is vastly more important, a people with a revolutionary tradition, eager for reforms and efficient institutions. In Austria Joseph had neither a nation nor a revolutionary tradition; the Germans, Slavs, Magyars, Italians, and Belgians were all, unfortunately for the emperor's reforms, priest-ridden, steeped in the incense of ecclesiasticism, and dozing in drugged provincialism and superstition. The mistake Joseph made was that he expected his subjects, shackled by centuries of slavery, to love him for the benefits he jammed down their throats.

# CHAPTER 8

# Interlude

*This is the only province of my states which I do not know.*
Joseph on Belgium

Six months after Joseph came to power, months of ceaseless activity, he was seized with the old wanderlust. The *Mémoires* of Count de Neny, describing Belgium, fell into the emperor's hands, and he suddenly decided to visit the Low Countries. He ordered the bureau of the Netherlands to send him the original protocols dealing with those provinces, read them hastily to acquaint himself with conditions there, and began to prepare for the journey. To Ambassador Mercy at Paris he revealed his intention of spending two months in Belgium and 'four or five weeks with the queen' at Versailles; he asked Mercy to tell him frankly whether his trip to France would be considered desirable there or not. When Kaunitz was consulted, he replied he had no objection; he would keep the emperor informed of everything. Perhaps the old chancellor was not sorry to rid himself for a while of the driving master.

In May, 1781, Joseph, travelling incognito as Count Falkenstein, left Vienna in the company of one doctor, three nobles, and two secretaries. On the day of his departure he appointed Kaunitz regent and issued a decree admitting Jews to schools and trades. He took the shortest route – from Regensburg, through Frankfürt, Mannheim, and Trier – and arrived at Luxemburg in nine days.

At Luxemburg a noble insisted upon giving the emperor a formal reception. 'My dear count,' Joseph said, 'I did not come to Flanders to devote myself to pleasures, but to occupy myself with very serious things.'

On the way to Namurs Joseph received a letter from Mercy informing him that Marie Antoinette was eager to see him: 'It would be terrible if I were deprived of the sight of my brother,' the queen had said. As for Louis XVI, Mercy wrote diplomatically, he would see his brother-in-law 'with that pleasure of which his moderate and tranquil character is capable'.

At Namur the emperor held long conversations with the mayor, consulted the magistrates, received the bishops and clergy, and chatted with the officers of the garrison; the emperor was friendly and produced 'an excellent impression'. To the President of the Council Joseph broached his plans for reforming Belgium. 'There is a Flemish proverb,' the Fleming replied significantly, 'which is sometimes good to remember: What one is not sure of being able to do on Monday, he should postpone until Sunday.' The emperor would have been wise to heed this advice.

After visiting Mons, Courtrai, Menin, Ypres, and Dunkirk, Joseph arrived at Ostend. Here he inspected the army and then went to see the salt refineries, sawmills, and rope factories; he gave the workers advice on how to make ropes. In the evening he went to the theatre, where he was warmly received. After a conversation with the British consuls Joseph entertained the idea of visiting the island across the channel. 'It is not a little tempting to a man like myself who has seen almost all of Europe,' he wrote to Belgiojoso, his ambassador at London, 'to be six or eight hours away from England and not be able to go there; but why did the English ministry, since 1755, please to pile up stupidities on stupidities?'

The imperial traveller's next step was Bruges, where he offended the religious sentiments of the ardently Catholic population. There was a church service and Joseph accompanied the procession to the cathedral, carrying a taper. On the way the bishop blessed the faithful who fell on their knees. Somebody solicitously offered the emperor a cushion to kneel on. Joseph stood up proudly, refused to bend his royal knees, and only inclined his head slightly. 'A population essentially religious,' a contemporary observes, 'did not look with pleasure at this affectation of philosophism.'

The itinerary from Bruges led through Ghent and Oudenarde. At Oudenarde Joseph visited the battlefield where, seventy-three years before, Eugene of Savoy and Marlborough had inflicted a crushing defeat on the French. The pious military pilgrimage accomplished, Joseph crossed the Scheldt River on a bark, and, in the afternoon of June 19th, he arrived at Antwerp amidst the banging of cannon and the pealing of bells. Since time immemorial sovereigns visiting Antwerp had stayed at the Prinsenhof palace; Joseph characteristically ignored tradition and put up at the Hôtel du Grand Laboureur. After dinner he went to the military academy and spent several hours investigating the instruction given to the cadets. Next day he received the civil and religious dignitaries, asking for information about commercial, philanthropic, and military conditions. He repeated the same procedure at Malines and Louvain a day or two later. At Louvain he delivered an address to the university, visited the library and the botanical garden, and promised money to buy instruments for the physics laboratory.

At Brussels, as elsewhere, Joseph was received with enthusiasm. Since the time of Charles V and Philip II no monarch had visited Belgium. Maria Theresa's conservative government had pleased the ruling elements in the Low Countries; she had disturbed neither their privileges nor their religion. The Austrian governors, especially Duke Charles of Lorraine (Joseph's uncle) and Count John Charles Cobenzl, had been popular. Now the emperor would continue his mother's policies of leisurely do-nothingness.

Joseph had no such intentions. He was irritated to see the decline of the once rich land. While the northern element of the Low Countries, the Dutch, had broken with Rome and grown rich in commerce, the southern part, Belgium, lay stagnant in a pool of tradition and medieval conservatism. Joseph restlessly explored conditions in the Belgium capital. 'My occupations,' he wrote to Leopold, 'are immense. Mornings I frequent the various tribunals; from eleven until three I give audience to everybody, then I dine alone and work. At six daily the ministers and councillors come to see me, and we discuss finances, commerce, justice, administration.'

He was popular. Rumours of his goodness, simplicity, and democratic habits spread among the population. This was not a taciturn and extortionate Charles V, nor a bloodthirsty, sadistic Philip II. 'It pains me that I cannot make everybody happy,' he told some Flemish magistrates. The words were winged. Common folk repeated amazing stories in awed tones. At the barracks, people said, he ate the soldiers' bread to see how it tasted; he examined the mattresses to see whether they were comfortable. In one town, folk related, he sent away the honorary guard with the words: 'My guards are my subjects; my security rests on their love.' One legend had it that he sharply berated an officer who cursed a common soldier: 'Sir, you forget yourself, this soldier is as good a man as you are. He is your brother as much as he is mine; I will not stand for it to see mistreated those of my subjects who devote themselves to the service of the fatherland.' More credible is his rebuke to a nun who tried to kiss his hand. 'No, no,' the emperor told her, withdrawing his hand, 'my hand is not a relic.' The people thronged the streets to catch a glimpse of their lord. He was *le bon Joseph*.

There were large crowds in the streets, eager to see the emperor. Joseph, incognito and on foot, elbowed his way through the people, smiling and happy; he enjoyed such comedies. A girl pressed by him, jolting him. 'Where are they all rushing to?' Count Falkenstein, in simple military uniform, asked the girl. 'Have you not heard,' the girl answered, 'that the emperor is coming along this street? Please let me pass.' 'Do not hurry,' he told her; 'I assure you he will not come that way; all these people will not see him today.' The girl looked dejected: 'I am unhappy not to be able to see that prince of whom so much good is told; I was given special leave to go out today, and it is all in vain.' Joseph, smiling, delighted, took out a gold coin, pointed at his image on it, and said: 'Possibly you have seen him without recognizing him; here, look, and have it.' He hurriedly left the speechless girl.

After a stay of fifteen days in Brussels, Joseph left for a hasty visit to Holland. On July 6th he arrived at Rotterdam and stopped at a private hotel. In the morning he went to Mass, then visited the admiralty magazines, and inspected the docks and wharves. Later in the day he paid a visit to the tomb of William the Silent and the statue of Grotius. Strange pilgrimage for an emperor of the House of Habsburg! In the evening, incognito, he promenaded in the gay streets of Rotterdam, mixing with the crowd, and envious of the city's prosperous appearance. Three days later Count Falkenstein was at The Hague, thence he went to Leyden, Haarlem, and Amsterdam. Everywhere he saw and admired ships, canals, hospitals, museums. Why could not his own province be like that? In Amsterdam, with majestic impartiality, he visited Catholic, Protestant, Jewish, and Quaker churches. On the 15th he was at Utrecht, whence he wrote to Kaunitz 'I have been very content with my circuit through Holland; I have found there not only beauty of location, incredible and incomparable industrial wealth, but also kindness and attention on the part of the inhabitants which was entirely unexpected to me'.

From Utrecht Joseph went, through Aachen, to Spa; at the gates of that city his horse died, so he had to enter on foot. He stayed at the lively resort for two days, had dinner with the French writer, Raynal, and met his enemy, Prince Henry of Prussia, Frederick's able brother. Two days later he drove through Liége without stopping, passing the night at Louvain. Next morning he quietly entered Brussels.

The Belgians were annoyed. What was the idea of their emperor slipping in and out of their capital like a fugitive from justice? The good people wished to do their sovereign honour; they wanted to wave their flags, show their horses, beat their drums, and display their uniforms. Was it not a monarch's business to put up a grand show? The fat burghers felt themselves insulted. He talked to them as man to man, true; but who wanted this kind of royal democracy? His business was to be haughty, inaccessible, imperial.

Joseph ignored all suggestions for parades, displays, pomps, and ceremonies. Why did they want to waste their money and his time on such puerilities? He had made Ostend a free port

K

and was planning to revive Belgian commerce, make this province a fit rival for Holland. He was scheming to found an East India Company, and spent his last days in Brussels discussing the feasibility of such an undertaking.

At the end of July Joseph was in Paris. How he hurried! Unceremoniously he put up at Mercy's, hastened to embrace Marie Antoinette, and to greet stodgy Louis. He stayed in France only six days, and after he left, Marie Antoinette 'locked herself up in her room and cried much', Mercy reports. She never saw him again.

Ten days later Joseph was back in Vienna. He could not remain still. No sooner had he arrived than he dashed off to Bohemia for the army exercises. Back from Bohemia, he went off – this was still in August – to Hungary for a short visit. How long could such a frenzied life last? Leopold was troubled, and scolded his brother. 'Permit me to tell you,' the grand duke wrote Joseph, 'that the fatiguing life you lead in these camps, and in the four days you stayed in Vienna, instead of resting, you have been overwhelmed with affairs and worked day and night.'

# CHAPTER 9

# Church

I

*Fanaticism shall in future be known in my states only by the contempt I have for it; nobody shall any longer be exposed to hardships on account of his creed; no man shall be compelled in future to profess the religion of the state, if it be contrary to his persuasion and if he have other ideas of the right way of insuring blessedness. In future my empire shall not be the scene of abominable intolerance . . . Tolerance is an effect of that beneficent increase of knowledge which now enlightens Europe, and which is owing to philosophy and the efforts of great men; it is a convincing proof of the improvement of the human mind, which has boldly reopened a road through the dominions of superstition, which was trodden centuries ago by Zoroaster and Confucius, and which, fortunately for mankind, has now become the highway of monarchs.*

Joseph to van Swieten

In 1763, when Joseph was still crown prince, there appeared in Germany a book which shook the foundations of the Church. The reverberations of this Latin work with the long Latin title (*De Statu Ecclesiae et legitima Potestate Rom. Pontificis L. ad Reuniendes Dissidentes*) were heard even in the Burg at Vienna. The pope, realizing the book contained dynamite, had promptly put it under the ban. This was enough to arouse Joseph's curiosity, especially since sixteen of the foremost German bishoprics, including that of Vienna, allowed the dangerous work to circulate freely.

The author was short, stout, and learned. His name was Johan Nicolaus von Hontheim, but he wrote under the pseudonym Justinius Febronius, and was, properly enough, a suffragan bishop. He laboured on the book for eighteen years, and when it was published it had so tremendous a success that another edition was put out a year later and translated into German, French, Italian, Spanish, and Portuguese. With the ripe wisdom of an eighteenth-century ecclesiastic, Febronius, following the example of Voltaire, took care to dedicate his work to the 'Prime Bishop, Clement XIII, Christ's Vicar on Earth', as well as to Christian kings, princes, and bishops.

Febronius's modest aim was to bring reason into Catholic dogma and to heal the breach between Catholics and Protestants. The erudite bishop, imbued with the ideas of the British constitutionalists and the sentiments of French *philosophes*, especially Montesquieu, rejected the dogmatism of the Church, argued in favour of the laws of nature, and urged that the Church return to its pristine liberties which were based on the custom of the first Christian centuries and the words of Jesus.

The Catholic bishop did not oppose Catholicism; he did not even object to the pope's primacy over Christian churches. On the contrary, he quoted with approval Christ's words to Peter: 'Thou art Peter, and on this rock I shall build my Church,' perhaps the most significant sentence in the world, for on it is based the whole imposing Catholic structure. Febronius even added to this Cyprian's well-known dictum: *Qui Petri cathedram deserit, in ecclesia non est*. His chief quarrel was with papal absolutism.

The Febronian artillery was directed against the papal monarchy. Jesus, he argued, had never intended the Roman bishop to have divine powers. The pope was nothing but *primus inter pares*, simply the Bishop of Rome and, consequently, only the first bishop in Christendom. Jesus did not give the keys to the Bishop of Rome but to the whole Christian community. 'The pope,' Febronius wrote:

> can be called king; he is a prince of princes, and lord of lords; he is as God on earth. He stands above right, above law, above the canons . . . He can make arbitrary exceptions to God's commandments . . . he can, without excuse, deprive one church and enrich another, and no one can say him nay . . . He is bound by no contract and no concordat. The pope and Christ make a consistory of one; the pope can turn injustice into justice; he can

transform the essence of things and create things that are not there. He can square a circle.

Febronius continued his argument with an accusation of papal usurpation. The pope was not a monarch, he insisted; he was never intended to be one. The sovereignty of the church resided, not in the pope, as the Romanists claim, but in the episcopate, representing all Christian believers. 'In order to intimidate the rebellious', the bishop went on sarcastically, 'the Church threatened people with the crime of sacrilege, by saying: To question the power of the pope is sacrilegious, for the pope is the cause of causes; therefore you must not question his sovereignty because the first cause has no higher cause.' Febronius bluntly denied that Christ gave the Church such an interpretation. 'I say, He made the Church free and sovereign.'

The Church, Febronius proposed, should be reorganized and the bishops given back their pristine power and independence. Rome should have no political influence over the episcopate. The freedom of the Church could be gained only when legislative and judicial powers were taken from the pope (shades of Montesquieu!). An eighteenth-century libertarian who admired Locke and who recognized only the authority of the Bible, tradition, and human reason, Febronius urged that the people be enlightened on the subject, that a general council with full freedom be convened, that national synods be assembled, that secular rulers should resist all papal decrees, and that Catholic princes take concerted action to overthrow papal absolutism and establish national churches in their dominions.

The author was, of course, unsuccessful. The Protestants, although enjoying the attack on the papacy, cold shouldered him. 'Not since Luther,' the Protestant Leipzig *Acta Eruditorum* pointed out, 'had anyone come forth from the bosom of the Roman church and so bravely attacked its disgusting corruption and presumptuous papal power as did Febronius.' But to the Protestants it was merely another 'monk's squabble' which was no concern of theirs. Febronius himself, on his death-bed at the age of seventy-seven, was forced to recant his heresy.

'He renounced with complete sincerity', says the inspired
*Catholic Encyclopedia* (VII, 464), 'his erroneous doctrines'.

Nevertheless the book had a tremendous influence in Germany, a country traditionally hostile to foreign religious domination and whose struggle with the papacy went back to the
eleventh century. In 1769 three of the foremost German
ecclesiastics – the Archbishops of Mainz, Cologne, and Febronius's own Trier – sent delegates to a conference at Coblenz,
under Febronius's direction, and drew up thirty grievances
against the papacy (*Gravamina trium Archiepiscoporum Electorum,
Moguntinensis, Trevirensis et Coloniensis contra Curiam Apostolicam
Anno 1769 ad Caesarem delata*). Nothing came of the conference,
mainly because Joseph, who as emperor was the titular secular
lord of the Catholic world, refused to participate on account of
Maria Theresa's hostility.

## II

In Emperor Joseph, Febronius found a disciple who was in a
position to carry out many of his proposals. Joseph was a
nationalist, a centralist, a rationalist, and Febronius's words
struck a responsive chord in him.

Joseph lost no time in reforming the Church and depriving
it of its privileges. His first blow was the famous Edict of Toleration, an act which is perhaps his best claim to remembrance as
a champion of human rights and which undermined all the
entrenched interests and institutions in his dominions. To the
clergy and nobility it was a veritable calamity.

'His Majesty,' the Edict read, 'being persuaded of the injurious effects of all coercion which does violence to the human
conscience, and believing that the greatest benefits to religion
and to the state emanate from that genuine spirit of tolerance
which is agreeable to the principles of Christian charity' – proceeded to grant to all his subjects, Jews as well as Protestants,
freedom of worship. The Council of State opposed so revolutionary a measure; only Kaunitz and Gebler supported it as an
act of justice and humanity. But the emperor – 'to adorn my

diadem with the love of my people and to act according to just, impartial, and liberal principles' – paid little attention to the opinions of the reactionary councillors.

The Law of Toleration aroused the wrath of the clergy. As for the Catholic population, they had not yet reached the point of being able to appreciate the meaning of either freedom of person or liberty of conscience. Joseph made the erroneous assumption that the average man cared anything about liberty or justice.

The emperor had little love for Protestants and even less for Jews; nevertheless his law allowed Lutherans, Calvinists, Greek Orthodox, and even Jews to have their prayer houses, meeting places, and schools. The non-Catholics were permitted to own houses and lands, to enter the professions, and to hold political and military offices. In five years the Protestants more than doubled in number: from 74,000 to 157,000. No wonder the Catholic clergy fulminated and the Lutherans praised. A Protestant minister in Nuremberg compared Joseph to Martin Luther, a compliment which the emperor may or may not have appreciated.

Joseph's aim was a well-organized, centralized state with obedient subjects. Men, his mother had taught him, needed authority to keep them in leash. The Church, any church, was, he well understood, an effective 'spiritual police', to quote a candid Napoleonic phrase. Catholicism need not be the only religion; it simply happened to be dominant in his lands. But any other ecclesiastical organization would serve the same purpose. Therefore it could do no harm – might, in fact, do good – to give recognition to Lutheranism, a church traditionally servile to authority.

Toleration, however, had its dangers. If men were not forced by the sword, the wheel, and the rack to worship as their rulers prescribed, what was to prevent them from throwing off the yoke of ecclesiasticism altogether? Where, then, would discipline be, and respect for authority? Would they not begin to espouse wild creeds, join undisciplined sects, preach subversive dogmas? There were, indeed, such symptoms of disintegration, and Joseph feared them. In 1783 the emperor learned that several hundred Bohemians had publicly declared themselves Deists. Deists? A new word that smacked of rebellion. Joseph promptly decreed that as soon as any person, man or woman, came out as a Deist or anything else, 'he should, without further investigation, be given twenty-four lashes with a leather whip on his buttocks, and then be sent home'. This was to be repeated as often as the sectarian affirmed his faith, 'not', Joseph explained, 'because he is a Deist, but because he claims to be something without knowing what he is.' Experience, the emperor said, had shown him that sectarians acted 'partly out of stupidity, or ignorance, and partly out of frivolity and *Wanderungslust*.' So stupidity was made a crime.

Together with toleration came the abolition of the censorship. In Austria censorship had been rigorously enforced since the time of the Reformation. An edict of Emperor Charles V (1548) provided for the punishment of buyers of forbidden books, pamphlets, and even pictures. In 1600 more than 10,000 books were burned at Graz, 500 at Völkermarkt, and eight wagonloads at Laibach. In Bohemia the Jesuits burned more than 60,000 books. As late as 1713 persons who possessed Bibles were banished from their homes. Under Charles VI, Joseph's grandfather, those who denounced Protestant books received a fee of ten gulden.

Joseph's mother had continued the repressive regime. She forbade even non-religious works which were slightly original and faintly critical. 'Is it any wonder,' Professor Martini exclaimed, 'that darkness reigned so long, when the light was systematically shut out? In 1750 it was worth one's position and safety even to have intimated an acquaintance with Montesquieu's *Spirit of the Laws*.' When the cultured Gerhard van Swieten was appointed to the Censorship Commission there was some relief. Febronius's book was freely circulated, though Moses Mendelssohn's *Phaedra* was forbidden.

Under Maria Theresa the newspapers were severely censored; the editors had to submit their articles to the authorities, and sometimes even to the empress for approval. Denouncers were assured as much as one hundred ducats. The newspapers,

therefore, were a wretched lot, never daring to print anything
but a few innocuous facts. The *Posttäglicher Mercurius*, which
started in 1703, appeared when the post arrived: every three
or four days; this paper merged with the *Wienerisches Diarium*,
and became the only Viennese news-sheet up to 1780, when the
*Wiener Zeitung* was founded.

Under the Theresan regime both Rousseau and Machiavelli
were *persona non grata*. The Frenchman's *Emile* was put to the
flames. Even the cultivated van Swieten considered it a 'disgrace for anybody to touch a book like Machiavelli's'. The
crowning irony of the censorship was the prohibition of the
famous papal *Index librorum prohibitorum* – which listed all the
books which no Catholic may read at the risk of his soul – lest
curious readers find there precisely the titles of books they
would like to peruse. Forbidden books were smuggled into the
country, but they could not be had in the libraries. To read a
book in the Court Library special permission from the papal
nuncio was required. Secret service agents were in the habit of
raiding book stores, burning the prohibited publications and
punishing the dealers. Three days before Maria Theresa died,
she ordered that confiscated books should not be destroyed but
given to the university library.

With his mother out of the way Joseph was free to modify the
censorship. Complete liberty of opinion and expression existed
nowhere on the continent. It is to the emperor's credit that, in
this respect, he attempted to make Austria more advanced than
any other European state. Before leaving for Belgium he appointed a Central Book Censorship Commission to draw up a
new code; the law was promulgated after Joseph returned from
his trip.

The new regulation abolished all provincial censorships; the
Commission in Vienna was to be the sole literary arbiter. The
law did not grant complete freedom of the press; certain books
were still prohibited, among them works containing 'immoral
utterances and unclean obscenities', and those which systematically attacked Christianity. But a great many publications
were permitted. Scientific works were to be entirely free.

Learned publications were allowed, provided some authoritative person – scholar, professor, or prelate – vouched for their authenticity. Anyone was free to print and distribute foreign books, which, the emperor blandly explained, 'are to be considered merely as a branch of commerce'. As for criticisms and lampoons, Joseph decreed that 'so long as they are not libels, are not to be forbidden, no matter whom they attack, from the sovereign to the lowest subject, providing the author publishes his name so that he can be held responsible for the truth.'

The books listed in the papal *Index* were made free. The *Index* consisted of thirty-eight folio volumes, and contained the most brilliant names in German (and foreign) literature: Goethe, Haller, Jacobi, Mendelssohn, Michaelis, and almost everybody who was anybody. The formerly prohibited books were now put in libraries where scholars had free access to them. To the horror of Catholics, Protestant books were freely circulated. Interestingly enough, the censorship law provided for no punishment in case of violation, in contrast to Frederick the Great who sent the publisher Rüdiger to jail for printing a book against Christianity.

A distinction was made between three kinds of manuscripts to be printed: political; journals and literature ('less important things'); and newspapers. Novels dealing with political or religious matters fell under the 'political' clause. It was a little complicated, for Voltaire's works were forbidden in German but tolerated in the original French, probably because Joseph was sure most people could not read that language.

The emperor was merciless with publications containing bigoted or superstitious matter. 'The book, *The Friendship in the Convent*,' he declared:

> by all means deserved to be banned, and likewise the *Nine Day Prayer to the Mother of God* should not be allowed publication in Prague, because it contains fabulous miracles, apparitions, revelations, and such things, which would lead the common man to superstition, arouse disgust in the scholar, and finally give non-Catholics an opportunity to ascribe such weaknesses to the Catholic religion itself.

Scholars the emperor permitted as much freedom as possible; in fact, he was often their chief protector against bigots. Zumer, a professor of physics at the University of Innsbruck, once dared to demonstrate in the classroom that the world was much older than the biblical 6,000 years. Fourteen pious students indignantly protested to the authorities. The students' complaint reached the emperor; Joseph's reply was swift. 'The fourteen students,' he decreed, 'should be sent away from school, because heads as poor as theirs cannot profit from education.'

The censorship was extended to cover all ecclesiastical publications and even announcements. Everything relating to the Church was to come under the jurisdiction of the secular authorities. The prelates bitterly protested. Archbishop Migazzi of Vienna complained especially against the publication of Born's *Monachology* which compared monks to insects and other forms of animal life taken from Linnaeus' classification. Joseph was irritated by Migazzi's tactless defence of the monks. His answer was a decree that the common people should be permitted to possess and read the Bible, and that no clergyman should dare any more to make house searches for prohibited books. The Archbishop of Cologne was so incensed that he sent a sharp protest to the emperor. The angry archbishop told Joseph that not the secular authorities but 'the spiritual pastors' had the right to decide what should or should not be read. 'No bishop,' the prelate concluded, 'can obey in this matter without betraying his office.' This lecture by a churchman made the Habsburg blood boil. But he controlled himself and sent the archbishop a mocking and cynical reply. 'I would be of the same opinion,' he wrote:

had I not studied people sufficiently to realize that only few read, that even less understand what they read, and that only a slight number make use of their reading. I am even acquainted with some who do not know what they write. With such creatures prohibition of books is more to be feared than bad publications; for the former makes possible the reading of the latter. Without the unfortunate prohibition which had led our first father to temptation, we would still be promenading naked in the earthly paradise and would never have had the chance to discuss these important problems raised by Your Electoral Highness.

The partial lifting of the censorship resulted in a Niagara of publications, foreign and domestic. It was like a raging stream whose dam had broken. Feelings, desires, images, notions, repressed for centuries, burst forth. Here was magnificent fury, earthy, obscene, lusty, and naive. This outlet of repressed hostilities was a veritable catharsis, and may have saved the Habsburgs from the fate of the Bourbons.

Vienna became a paradise for pen-pushers, lampooners, and pamphleteers. There were over four hundred professional scribblers. They sat in the smoky cafés, puffing at pipes, sousing beer, exchanging ribald tales, and collecting gossip to put in pamphlets. The whole world was their kingdom: church and state, society and God, king and prince, highborn ladies and other women of questionable virtue. The ladies surreptitiously read these 'Viennese Writings' and, whether they blushed through their rouge or not, took care to be properly indignant.

Vienna was flooded with obscene books and tracts. What lusty male or curious dame could resist titles like: *Nun's Letters*; *Mama Wants Me to Enter a Monastery*; *Concerning Viennese Housemaids*; *Concerning Chambermaids*; *Concerning Bourgeois Maids*; *Concerning Court Maidens*; *Concerning Viennese Girls*; *Magister Jocosus Hilarius' Wonderful History of an Old Virgin Who Remained Unviolated for 30 Years, Told in Clean Rhymes*; *Flora, a Journal by and for Ladies*; *Bawdy Houses are Necessary in Vienna, No Matter What Herr Councillor Sonnenfels May Preach from the Pulpit Against Them?* 'From France,' Caroline Pichler comments indignantly, 'also came to us, at this time . . . a mass of books which fostered the spirit of mockery, infidelity, opposition . . . Under the cloak of philosophy, love of truth, impartial research – the yardstick, the plummet, the anatomical knife were applied to all that was beautiful, noble, and sacred.'

It must be admitted, in all justice, that many pamphlets were serious and aimed at enlightenment. Thus when the pope made his visit to Vienna, numerous publications stirred the people with such elementary questions as *What Is The Pope?*

*What Is a Parson? What Is a Bishop? What Is The Church? What Is The Devil?*

Much was translated into Hungarian. Magyar nobles and prelates did not like the masses either to read or to question, any more than did their Austrian colleagues. Baron Patachrich, Archbishop of Calocza, came to Vienna to find out from the emperor the whys and wherefores of this outrageous freedom of the press. The conversation between emperor and prelate has been preserved:

*Joseph:* Now all kinds of things are being written here, and people begin to think and write more freely and intelligently.

*Archbishop* [with arms raised in protest]: *Ach, du lieber Gott!* Alas, more than too much is being written. I pray Your Majesty in the name of God to put a stop to this levity, through which even Your Majesty's sacred person is being violated.

*Joseph:* Eh, do you read the tracts which are being published?

*Archbishop:* I read them all, and have to do so on account of my office, so that I could see whether these people say anything new and whether such writers as Curalt, Plarrer, Eybel, and others, say anything against the church which might be dangerous.

*Joseph:* Ah, this Curalt; this ex-monk is the sort of man who attacks or defends whatever one wishes. Plarrer is a fool, a fanatic. But we have to let these people talk; they do not spare me either. They have even put out a book in which they compare me to Luther. Have you read it?

*Archbishop:* *Ach, ja wohl*; surely I have read it, and am amazed at the author for transgressing against Your Majesty in so horrible a manner. The very title – *Kaiser Joseph und Luther* – is *lèse majesté*. The author tells what Luther did during the Reformation, calls him the blessed Luther, and ends up with these words: 'Thus much did the blessed Luther achieve, and it was left for Emperor Joseph to complete that which the blessed Luther started'.

*Joseph:* I sent that book to the censorship and was told that it contained nothing indecent.

*Archbishop:* That is just the trouble, Your Majesty. The censorship. . . .

*Joseph:* Yes, but I also sent it to the theological faculty, and especially to Rautenstrauch [Abbot of Braunau] who is supposed to be pretty skilful in theological matters.

*Archbishop* [shrugging his shoulders]: Yes, but that is the trouble;

I do not wish to cast any aspersion on the prelate Rautenstrauch, but. . . .

*Joseph:* Well, if *such* people do not understand these things, then I can do nothing more about it.

The censorship was mild at first. Despite criticism and abuse, Joseph, in 1787, went a step farther and granted the city of Vienna complete liberty of printing and publishing. But the regulations were constantly violated and the libels, particularly anonymous ones, were beginning to irritate the emperor.

## III

*Since I have ascended the throne . . . I have made philosophy the legislator of my empire . . . As I myself detest superstition and the Sadducean doctrines, I will free my people of them; with this view, I will dismiss the monks, I will suppress their monasteries . . . In Rome they will declare this an infringement of the rights of God: I know they will cry aloud, 'The greatness of Israel is fallen' . . . To these things we owe the degradation of the human mind . . . The principles of monachism . . . have been directly opposed to the light of reason . . . Instead of the monks, I will have the priest to preach, not the romances of the canonized, but the holy gospel and morality . . . I shall take care that the edifice, which I have erected for posterity, be durable.*

Joseph to Cardinal Hrczan

'The influence which the clergy possessed during the reign of my mother,' Joseph communicated to Choiseul when he ascended the throne, 'will be another object of my reforms. I do not like to see people, to whom the care of the future life is committed, give themselves so much trouble to make our life here below an object for their wisdom.' Joseph believed in the principle that the things which are Caesar's should be rendered unto Caesar and the things which are God's should also be rendered unto Caesar.

The emperor had reasons for dissolving the monasteries. They represented idle wealth, property which Joseph considered both a usurpation and a waste. He could not see why monks who, like the lilies of the field neither spun nor wove, should live in luxury. If he could lay his hands on those monastic meadows, those fertile fields, and vineyards, and woods, and buildings, he would pour new life-blood into the economic veins of his lands and make his cities flourish and his villages groan in superabundance.

An empire which I govern [Joseph told the Archbishop of Salzburg], must be swayed according to my own principles; prejudice, fanaticism, partiality, and slavery of the mind must cease, and each of my subjects be reinstated in the enjoyment of his native liberties. Monasticism has considerably increased in Austria. The number of ecclesiastical establishments and of monasteries has risen to an extravagant height. The government until now, according to the rules of these people, had little or no right over their persons, and they are the most dangerous and useless subjects in every state, as they endeavour to exclude themselves from the observance of all civil laws, and on all occasions have recourse to the Pontifex Maximus in Rome . . . When I shall have torn away the veil from Monasticism, when I shall have removed from the chains of my universities Andromache's web of the Ascetic doctrine, and when I shall have converted the monk of mere show into a useful citizen, then perhaps some of the party zealots will reason differently about my reforms.

I have a difficult task before me: I have to reduce the host of monks, I have to transform fakirs into men: those, before whose tonsured head the common people fall down on their knees in veneration.

Joseph was not alone in his violent hatred of the monks. Numerous ribald and obscene pamphlets against monks and nuns, which people read with glee, bear witness to the dislike which even the pious population had for the friars. Born's *Monachology* was perhaps the most lustily satirical burlesque on the cowled brethren ever penned.

In the autumn of 1781 a scandal occurred in the Carthusian monastery at Mauerbach, and the vice-governor of the province proposed the abolition of the cloister. The question came up in Vienna, where opinion as to the legality of such an act was divided. Joseph brushed aside all opposition. Here was his great opportunity. The Councillors said the emperor had no legal right to dissolve the monasteries, which were sacred private property. The emperor, however, had more than right; he had force. On November 29, 1781, he issued the death sentence of most monasteries:

> Not only this specific case, but the long-existing evidence that those orders which are entirely useless cannot be pleasing to God, causes me to order the chancery to register in my hereditary dominions all those institutions both for males and females which neither run schools, nor maintain the sick, nor engage in studies; their incomes and property, as in the case of the Jesuits, shall be taken over, and the individuals be temporarily given pensions and be free – since they are not so numerous – either to leave the land or to appear before the authorities to arrange to enter the secular clergy. This is to apply to all the Carthusian, Camaldulensian, Eremite orders, as well as to all the female Carmelites, Clarissians, Capuchins, etc., who do not educate the young, maintain schools, or take care of the sick, and who, males as well as females, only lead a *vitam contemplativam*.

The money from these orders was to be utilized 'for the best of religion and benevolence'.

There were in the Austrian lands 2,163 monasteries with almost 65,000 inmates. The value of the property was estimated at about 300 million gulden. The commissions appointed by the government travelled through the country, registered the real and movable property, checked the treasures and archives. They were instructed to proceed with consideration, monks should not be deprived of personal possessions they had in their cells, and old men and cripples should be allowed to remain in the monasteries.

In the Germanic provinces (Styria, Carinthia, Carniola, Austria), 309 institutions for males and 104 institutions for nuns were suppressed. Altogether over 700 monasteries were abolished and the number of monks and nuns were reduced from 65,000 to 27,000. There remained, however, 1,065 monasteries and 360 nunneries.

The papacy raised a vehement protest, for this reform struck the Church at a most sensitive spot; it undermined its economic foundation. The Hungarian chancery contested the emperor's right to dissolve the monasteries. Joseph ignored the opposition. The suppression of the monasteries resulted in a minor economic revolution. It was the most durable and perhaps the soundest of all Josephan reforms. The wealth frozen in this ecclesiastical mortmain was thawed out and put into circulation. It is necessary to remember that the Church held three-eighths of the land in Austria. The government itself was astonished at the vast wealth the monasteries, even the mendicant orders, possessed. Joseph and Kaunitz took the attitude that ecclesiastical property was a patrimonium reserved for the public welfare, and hence had no compunction in confiscating it for the same use. In 1782 the confiscated property amounted to 10 million gulden: from 1782–7, almost 15 million gulden; in 1788, about 17 million and in 1789, over 18 million – about 60 million in all. The sum would have been higher had there been greater care in the sale and leasing of the property.

The government did not take the money for itself. A Religious Fund was established, the income from which, amounting to over 2 million annually, was to go for the support of schools, charitable institutions, pensions, and parish priests. The ex-monks either received pensions or were made state teachers. Even the mendicants were given aid. Benefices which had no care of the souls were abolished. The maximum episcopal salary was set at 12,000 gulden. The unsuppressed monasteries were to reduce their personnel to two-thirds. The mendicant orders were forbidden to take on novices and were not allowed to beg. Monasteries were deprived of their time-honoured right to inherit property. The administration of the convents was taken from the hands of the abbots and provosts and given to laymen or secular clergy. The Brotherhoods, of which there were 642 in Austria (121 in Vienna alone), were abolished, and their property used for charitable institutions. All ecclesiastical possessions, suppressed or not, were registered by the government, and a law was passed forbidding their alienation, sale, or exchange. In brief, the government not only confiscated part of the Church's property, but also controlled what was left.

Some of the money from the Religious Fund was used to

L

excellent purpose. With it Joseph established in Vienna a General Hospital, a Lying-in Hospital, a Foundling Asylum, a Medico-Chirurgical Academy, and an Institution for the Deaf and Dumb. This was the beginning of Vienna as a world medical centre.

The old monastic buildings were turned into schools, shops, and factories. Joseph sent out Professor de Lucca to search the monasteries for treasures, manuscripts, and ancient codices. A register of the books and manuscripts found in the monasteries is still preserved in the National Library at Vienna. Many of the old books were given to the universities, particularly the University of Vienna. As in the time of Henry VIII in England during the dissolution of the monasteries, a great many books and codices were either destroyed, lost, or sold.

The dissolution of the monasteries did not cause a ripple of protest or indignation among the people, but it brought Joseph into sharp conflict with the papacy. But the time of Canossa had passed, and Joseph was not Henry IV. Indeed, he handled the pontiff with a roughness that would have been the envy of his predecessors, the medievalemperors of the Hohenstaufen house. 'Holy Father,' Joseph replied to a vehement papal protest:

> I have suppressed the useless monasteries, as well as the still more useless Brotherhoods; the funds from them I have destined for the endowment of the new parishes, and for better instruction in schools . . . the funds of the state and those of the Church have not the smallest connection with each other . . . I perceive you have not the logic in Rome which is prevalent in my states . . . If Your Holiness had taken pains to obtain from the proper sources information as to what has been undertaken in my states, much trouble would have been avoided . . . I hope you will excuse my brevity; I have neither time nor talent for writing a *thema*, particularly one so extensive as those which are usually met with in a Roman Museum. I pray to God that he may preserve you long to His Church, and that he may cause one of his angels to pass before you to prepare your way here below. Your most obedient son in Christ, Joseph.

# IV

The Church was a state within a state. It possessed privileges, orders, wealth, and an independent administration. It was ruled by its own law and obeyed foreign superiors. To Joseph the pope was, from a political point of view, nothing more than the Bishop of Rome and, at best, an Italian prince who had to be treated as any other foreign potentate.

To the nationalist emperor it was galling to see many Austrian bishoprics ruled by foreigners. This was especially true of the episcopal sees of Styria, Tyrol, Carniola, Bohemia, Silesia, and Galicia. Many prince-bishops, like those of Passau and Salzburg, held dioceses whose boundaries spread over into foreign land. Joseph set out to destroy this Catholic internationalism.

It was necessary first to cut the link between the Austrian clergy and the papacy. Joseph ordered that the papal Bulls *In coena domini* (condemning heretics: 1362) and *Unigenitus Dei filius* (attacking the Jansenists: 1713) be ignored and blotted out. Another decree provided that no papal regulation or instruction be published or obeyed in Austria without the government's permission (the *Placitum regium*). Bishops, at their installation, were compelled to swear an oath of obedience and loyalty to the secular authorities.

The bishoprics were reorganized on a national basis. Some diocesan boundaries were reshaped and others were created. In Bohemia the archbishopric of Prague and the bishoprics of Königgratz and Leitmeritz were retained; a new one, Budweis, was founded. In Moravia there were Olmütz and Brünn. Galicia had Lemberg, Przemysl, and four Greek Orthodox bishoprics; to these were added the Catholic see of Tarnow. In Austria proper the bishopric of Linz was established and the see of Neustadt was moved to St Pölten. Graz, Lavant, Gurk, Laibach, Görz were left intact in the duchy of Styria, while the bishopric of Trieste was transferred to Bourg. In Hungary and Transylvania no change was made.

Whenever possible the emperor installed native bishops. Rome constantly protested. Some incumbent bishops likewise opposed the new episcopal regulations. Cardinal Migazzi, the Archbishop of Vienna, thought this intrusion into the ecclesiastical system unwarranted. 'In matters of faith and morals,' Migazzi wrote, 'the pope is the supreme judge. Every Catholic has to obey his decisions . . . Once the majority of Catholics recognize the papal judgment as true, it acquires the stamp of infallibility and he who opposes it is an apostate.' Joseph did not mind being called an apostate. He went on undisturbed even when the Council of State raised doubts as to the legality of his actions.

In connection with the reform of the bishoprics came an increase in the parishes. Many sections, especially the newer settlements, had no adequate parochial facilities. Joseph built new churches and established new parishes. In Lower Austria alone 260 parishes were founded; in Styria 156 parishes and 145 chapters; in Tyrol 74 parishes and in Moravia 180.

This was not purely an act of piety on the part of the emperor. To each new parish a school was attached; the priests were to act as teachers. Despite the employment of ex-Jesuits and ex-monks, there was a lack of consecrated clergy. The emperor played with the thought of recruiting monks from the remaining monasteries, as he would soldiers, but gave up the idea.

The difficulty was that many young men left the seminaries because, as one bishop explained it, of pecuniary conditions and the lowering of clerical prestige. The Study Commission suggested that the requirements of celibacy be done away with in order to attract vigorous young men; but the emperor objected. Instead, he encouraged students to enter the ministry by granting stipends, reducing or abolishing tuition fees, and lowering the academic standards; this was done to attract children of poor parents.

Joseph replaced the old diocesan seminaries – which he considered seats of superstition – with five general theological schools at Vienna, Pest, Freiburg, Louvain, and Pavia, together with subsidiary affiliated institutions at Graz, Olmütz, Innsbruck, Prague, and Luxemburg. Wishing the young priests to be brought up in the spirit of liberalism, the emperor reorganized the curriculum by adding secular knowledge and natural science to their studies, and appointed his own men as directors of the seminaries. The new clergy were to become, to all intents and purposes, state officials. But this took time. As late as 1793, 2,505 parishes had only 1,099 priests.

So far there was little disturbance among the population. But when the emperor began to reform church usages and customs people rebelled. Some of these minor reforms were rather petty. Like Calvin, Joseph ordered that 'unnecessary' church decorations: relics, votive-tablets, statuary, and lamps, be thrown out. The emperor forbade lights on sacred graves; prohibited clothes on the statues of Mary; stopped the distribution of amulets, the touching of pictures, rose wreaths, kissing of relics, and 'other such things'. Divine services, their length and number, were rigorously regulated; likewise the usage of the altar, church music, litanies. Pilgrimages and processions, unless approved by the authorities, were forbidden.

Some reforms were quite ridiculous. In 1784 the emperor ordered that coffins be made only with flat covers (called nose-squeezers) and of soft wood; and, seven months later, a new decree forbade the use of coffins for burial altogether – corpses were simply to be buried in a sheet or in a linen sack. This particular regulation almost brought about a revolution, and less than half a year later the emperor had to revoke it. Joseph's letter in this connection is amusing. 'Since a great many subjects,' he wrote to Kolowrat,

> did not want to understand the reasons for the regulations concerning the burial sacks, which, considering the rapid putrefaction, were instigated out of regard for the health of the population; and since, moreover, they display so great an interest in their bodies even after their death, without realizing that they are then nothing but stinking cadavers, His Majesty no longer cares how they bury themselves in the future.

The reform of the Church required a mass of other regulations. The emperor forbade all talk and other disputation on the subject of religion in coffee houses, saloons, and beer cellars. In 1784 German litanies began to be sung in the churches. Kaunitz wondered whether the vernacular songs had quite the charm and potency of the Latin; indeed, he considered the native songs too watery and simple, and wished to have the poet, Denis, compile an appropriate song collection. Priests were deprived of the privileges of getting free drinks in the inns.

Monks were ordered to stop wasting their time in choir singing, and to devote themselves to more intellectual pursuits; monkish literature was crushed to pulp in the mills. University professors were freed from taking the customary oath on the Immaculate Conception of the Virgin. The population was ordered not to kneel in the street when the host was carried by; people were simply to take off their hats. 'Theatrical style' of church music was forbidden. Ribaldry and buffoonery in the processions were put down. All pilgrimages and processions were reduced to one: on Corpus Christi Day.

The exterior aspect of religion had too long been an ingrained part of the common people. They could not forgive the emperor for depriving them of the only show and good time they had. They could not realize that His Majesty wished to do away with abuses in order to establish a rational, moral, pure church. The good people were not sure that their emperor was religious. Scribblers had, thoughtlessly, compared him to Luther. In reality, His Majesty was a fairly good Christian, although, being what he was, he never quite bothered to clarify his attitude towards God and the cosmos; theology and metaphysics were not his sphere. According to a regulation of his, persons who mocked religion were to be considered, and treated, as insane. A Tyrolese nobleman who had once used a censer to beat a priest with was condemned by the emperor to three years in an insane asylum.

The reform of the Church was a logical step in the consolidation and centralization of the Austrian lands. It brought Joseph into conflict with the papacy, recalling the days of the medieval emperors.

## V

*You eat the bread of the church and protest against all my innovations; I eat the bread of the state and defend and renew its rights.*

Joseph to the Archbishop of Trier

The clerical opposition to the emperor's reforms was not united. A united front was, indeed, impossible, as the law forbade all such action and the bishops feared for their promotions. Nor did the episcopate have the unqualified support of the lower clergy. As during the French Revolution, so in Austria likewise there was a class struggle within the clerical order; many poor parish priests had little love for their prince-bishops who lived in luxury.

Protests came only from Rome and from individual bishops. 'Each authority has its limits,' Garampa, the papal nuncio in Vienna argued: 'the ecclesiastical laws had, until now, served all the rulers of the Austrian monarchy ... Among the numerous princes of the German empire there has never been one who dared to exercise his authority to the point of arbitrarily controlling church property ... to dissolve the laws which the church had solemnly approved.' Swift and sharp came Kaunitz's answer. He told Garampa that the reforms were intended to do away with the abuses in the Church, that in this matter the Holy See had no business to interfere, and that His Majesty would act in future as he saw fit. Coldly the chancellor informed the nuncio that just as the emperor had no intention of withdrawing from the Roman Church in matters of dogma, so would the pope please not meddle in His Majesty's secular affairs. Garampa offered a humble apology. Kaunitz drily told him never to bring up the subject again.

A stubborn opponent was the Archbishop of Trier, who, not being under the immediate jurisdiction of the emperor, could afford to be bold. The archbishop protested against the dissolution of the monasteries, the abolition of ecclesiastical immunities, the robbing of benefices, the suspension of the two papal bulls, and the attenuation of the censorship. Joseph replied with irony.

How much I am obliged to your Electoral Highness for the interest you take in all I do, and even in the welfare of my soul, of which I think I may be sure, without allowing myself to be lightly disturbed on the subject. Unfortunately, I have nothing with me here but the instructions of the Great Frederick to his generals and the memoirs of Marshal Saxe. My Quesnel, my Busenbaum, and even the orthodox Febronius are at home in my library. How can I then expect to answer fully the important questions which your Electoral Highness has been pleased to address to me in five points? I should not have time to attempt it, if a shower of rain did not enable me at this moment to moralize with you, instead of exercising my troops.

As regards the *Placitum regium*, it appears to me that if the visible head of the Church, as he is called, sends forth an order from the Vatican to the faithful in my dominions, I, as sensible and real head, ought to be informed of it and have some influence in the matter.

As for the abolition of the immunities of certain religious orders, it is well known to Your Highness that a complete sovereign authority is not obliged to submit or to defer to any other. I should never forgive myself if I led the papal court into error, or confirmed it in error, by asking for something which does not belong to it. That would be to overlook my own rights.

As for the spoliation of benefice in case of violation of the laws, Your Highness has yourself the goodness to remark that I have indirectly that right by the seizure of the temporalities. But as the indirect course is that of the false or the weak, I prefer the direct one, being neither one nor the other.

In relation to the two Bulls, *In coena domini* and *Unigenitus*, your Electoral Highness, it seems, disapproves the former; but the expression of my ordinance 'to tear them out of the rituals', appears to distress you. Allow me to suggest that in your own diocese a paper should be pasted over them with these four words: *Obedientia melior quam victima* [It is better to obey than to be a victim]; words, which if I am not mistaken, Samuel addressed to Saul in relation to certain Amalekites. The Bull *Unigenitus* is posterior to any oecumenic council, and is therefore far removed from the infallibility of a decision of the whole Church. It has been accepted by some, and rejected by others, so that it would seem that an order, such as I have given, to say no more about it, is not superfluous. Fortunately my good Austrians know nothing of either Molinos or Arminius; and would ask if they were Roman consuls. I myself once knew a greyhound called Molinos, who would kill a hare single-handed. So little do we know of the controversies of grace. Nothing more will be said of them here, and it would have been as well to say nothing for the last thirty years.

'Yes,' the prelate, protected by a safe distance of some four hundred miles, thundered in reply, 'with the liberty of the office with which I am entrusted, I am telling Your Majesty this: No matter how great now may be the hardness which makes you pursue your course, a day will come when you will be inconsolable. May that not be the day of eternity!' Joseph dismissed the archbishop's sermon with a Voltairean sentence: 'You letters are quite tragic and mine comical, and although Thalia and Melpomene did not always live in sisterly harmony on Parnassus, so permit me nevertheless to await the day when our sisters, offspring of Helicon, will unite more closely.'

The most determined opponent was the Viennese archbishop, Migazzi, a Hungarian magnate. Migazzi was not so much interested in theology. Maria Theresa had given him the bishopric of Watzen, the income of which was 80,000 florins. Joseph, who saw no reason why an archbishop should be a millionaire, deprived Migazzi of the Watzen diocese. The prelate complained to the Hungarian Council; a magnate, he argued, could not be deprived of his property. 'If he is a Hungarian magnate,' was Joseph's retort, 'I am the Hungarian king. I know the rights of the magnates in my kingdom, and I also know mine.'

Migazzi lost the 80,000 florins, but likewise his love for the emperor. The archbishop would not of course fight his sovereign on sordid economic grounds. He took a loftier attitude. The Church reforms, he told the emperor, were against the conscience of the clergy. Joseph knew that the conscience was worth, in this case, 80,000 florins. 'Conscience! Conscience!' the emperor jeered in a letter to Migazzi.

> Were the bishops more scrupulous in the matter of having cumulative benefices, money extortion, persecution of honest and protection of evil persons? When after the miscarriage of some shady deal a bishop can relieve his conscience . . . by kneeling before the crucified One, he may likewise place under the cross his hypocritical conscience-worm.

When ordinary protests were of no avail the pope decided personally to dissuade the anti-clerical emperor from pursuing his erroneous ways.

John Angelo Braschi, Pope Pius VI (1775–99), was an unusually handsome gentleman. The contemporary steel engravings show a fine face, a high forehead, an aquiline nose, soft eyes, and delicate hands. He was irascible and obstinate, but also kindly and generous. His great weakness was vanity. A descendent of an ordinary family, he wished to immortalize his pontificate and to make his race illustrious. To immortalize himself, Pius VI engraved his name and escutcheon on many Roman monuments, at a cost of some 200,000 crowns. His sole family arms consisted of wings, and to make it look imposing, Pius added an eagle, fleur-de-lys, and stars. As a result, 'those most pitiless mockers', the Italian populace, satirized the pope's escutcheon with a witty doggerel:

> Restore the eagle to the empire, to France her lilies,
> The stars to the heavens; the rest, Braschi, is thine own.

Early in 1782 Joseph first heard rumours that the pope intended to pay him the compliment of a visit. Joseph could not believe it. Since the Council of Constance (1414) no Roman pontiff had ever set foot on German soil. He wondered whether Pius would be rash enough to do that. 'We will see what will come of it,' the emperor said. In Rome, the imperial plenipotentiary, Cardinal Hrczan, reported, people mocked this new papal frivolity, but doubted whether even Pius would thus compromise his dignity. Soon after Hrczan's report, came a letter from the pope which disquieted the emperor. 'Most Beloved Son in Christ,' Pius wrote:

> with great melancholy we have had to see that all our urgent pleas and protests to Your Majesty not to disturb the oldest possessions of the apostolic see . . . were in vain . . . We are, Most Beloved Son in Christ, not minded to indulge with Your Majesty in the sort of quarrel which agitated the Middle Ages . . . Our spirit is far from such conflicts . . . We therefore burn with desire . . . to discuss with you, on a most friendly footing, as father with son, this and other subjects of innovation which had plunged us into deepest grief . . . We have decided to visit the court of Your Majesty . . . We implore Your Majesty to consider this our step as proof of our most high respect.

Joseph could hardly show himself less courteous than the Holy Father. 'Just as we would be delighted to see and speak to Your Holiness,' the emperor replied somewhat ambiguously, 'so we

are none the less sure that Your Holiness . . . plans to undertake
so long a journey . . . out of kindliness to us . . . We are strongly
convinced . . . that it is impossible . . . to persuade us to change
our enterprises.'

Pius would not take the hint. On the contrary, he was
delighted with Joseph's invitation. 'Our joy,' the pope wrote,
'is uncommonly great; it will give us an opportunity, Most
Beloved in Christ, to embrace you, to speak with you, to reveal
to your our innermost thoughts.' The emperor replied sourly,
'Most Holy Father, since we have heard definitely that you
intend to visit here, there is nothing left for us to do but again
express our readiness to receive Your Holiness with all due
consideration.' The emperor then offered the pope the hospitality of the *Hofburg*.

The pope left Rome on February 27th. 'Everybody in Rome
deplores this papal trip,' Joseph wrote to Leopold, 'and the
choice of persons he is taking with him.' While the pope was
trudging through the snows and crossing the dangerous Alpine
passes, the emperor in Vienna was pondering how to treat this
very distinguished and extremely unwelcome visitor. 'He will
find me, I hope,' he muttered, as he wrote down his thoughts,
'a respectful son of the Church, a polite host, a good Catholic in
the widest sense of that word, but at the same time a man above
phrases . . . firm, sure and resolute in his principles, and pursuing the good . . . of the state without any other consideration
whatsoever.'

But as the pope neared Vienna – the trip took about three
weeks – Joseph became less sure and more irritable. The emperor was then suffering from inflammation of the eyes and had
to wear bandages. The pain in his eyes and the intrusion of the
Bishop of Rome in the midst of mounting work and rising
difficulties shortened the emperor's temper. 'In times like these,'
he exclaimed, 'the pope's voyage is nothing but a silly prank
(*Schwabenstreich*) . . . He wants to appear as the saviour of the
Church, whereas no one thinks of doing it any harm.'

When the pope entered Görz, in Austrian territory, Philipp
Cobenzl was there to receive him. At each post-station His

Holiness was given an escort of a corporal and fifteen men, and at every lodging an officer and forty men. Of the three noble body-guards whom the sardonic emperor sent to do honours to the pope, one was a Catholic, one a Lutheran, and one a Calvinist.

As the pope entered Vienna, on March 22, 1782, a huge crowd of people received him with cries of jubilation. The papal cavalcade rode into the city in great solemnity. The church bells rang. Cardinal Migazzi had asked the emperor whether the bells might be sounded in greeting. 'Why not?' replied Joseph drily; 'are not the bells your artillery?'

They came to the Burg at three in the afternoon. The emperor helped His Holiness to alight from the carriage, and led him into the large reception hall which was specially decorated in violet and silver. A splendid throne stood under a blue canopy. The court was assembled in state. At the head, grave and inscrutable, stood old Kaunitz. Was he thinking of Canossa?

The doors of the great hall opened. The tall, imposing pope, clad in white, with a red cape flung around his shoulders, made his appearance. The venerable pontiff advanced, spreading his arms in benediction. Everybody fell on his knees. Everybody, except Kaunitz. Joseph introduced the immovable chancellor to Pius. The pope graciously offered his hand to be kissed. Impassively, without so much as a smile, Kaunitz grasped the pope's hand, shook it heartily *à l'Anglaise*, and exclaimed, as if the pope were his jolly companion, 'With all my heart, With all my heart.' There was a suppressed buzz of excitement; it passed quickly. The emperor led the pope into the oratory where a *Te Deum* was sung and the holy sacrament shown. Ladies packed the chapel, anxious to see the handsome pope. Marshal Loudon shook his grizzled head and murmured: 'As one grows older one gets to see strange things.'

The pope dined at five, alone, as was his custom. His own cook prepared the meals; he tasted each dish before serving it to the Holy Father. The chamber where Maria Theresa had died was given to the pontiff as his bedroom; it contained an altar, many relics, and the crucifix which had been the great consolation of Emperor Ferdinand II.

The pope was given little chance to converse with the emperor on political matters. Joseph was still angry that his subjects had turned out one hundred thousand strong to greet this foreign potentate. That was almost disloyalty, he thought irritably. The first few days Pius spent visiting churches and monasteries, and receiving the faithful who were flocking to him in thousands. On Easter Sunday the pope himself conducted the celebrations at St Stephen's church, which was packed to suffocation. But Joseph was conspicuously absent. The ostensible excuse was eye trouble; the real cause was that the imperial throne was set lower than the papal. From St Stephen's Pius returned to the Burg, where, from a balcony he blessed the thronging faithful. It was an impressive spectacle. 'The eagerness of the common people to receive his benediction,' the British ambassador, Keith, relates,

> amounted to a frenzy. The course of the Danube was fairly choked by the crowd of boats which bore the floods of pious pilgrims, and the great market place was often found filled with shoes and hats lost in the scuffle by the assembled multitudes; who, by twenty or thirty thousand (some say 50,000) at a time, passed into the streets to the Imperial palace, at the balcony of which, repeatedly during the day, its illustrious guest was obliged to show himself, and distribute blessings to successive shoals of devotees.

The pope played his pontifical role majestically. The impression he made on the senses was tremendous. A cultivated and sceptical Austrian who was present says he could hardly keep back his tears at the scene. 'The pope,' he relates,

> with the thrice crowned tiara on his head, three cardinals and two bishops, all in full ecclesiastical vestments, came out on the balcony. The pope seated himself on a raised throne under a gold embroidered baldachin, and intoned the absolution, which 400 choir singers picked up. Then Pius rose from the throne, the tiara was taken from his head; he stepped forward, slowly raised his arms, swept the heavens with a measured gesture, and began his prayer in clear transfigured tones. Only sighs and sobs interrupted the absolute silence which reigned below in the kneeling multitude. He seemed more hovering towards heaven than standing. During the long prayer the bishops supported his arms. Finally he

lowered his arms, and again raised the right one in blessing in the name of the triune God. His Amen was answered with tremendous firing and thunder of cannon.

Pius's personal triumph was of little political value. Joseph sat in his chambers, nursed his eyes and his grudge. Let the pope impress the credulous mob; he, Joseph, was still absolute lord and was not the man to be taken in by magnificent benedictions. The emperor was a courteous host; showed the Holy Father the sights of the city; was all politeness and attention. But when Pius came down to business the emperor blandly apologized; he must, he said, first consult his Councillors.

The pope was persistent; the emperor must realize the error of his ways. A great Catholic monarch should not endanger his immortal soul. How could a Catholic sovereign tolerate other religions, permit the circulation of heretical writings, suppress monasteries? The Holy Father was there to save his beloved son in Christ from eternal damnation. Ah, it was not easy to argue with a priest, and reluctantly the emperor entered into a discussion.

> Very Holy Father [Joseph said quietly]: I know what Your Holiness came here for; I did not wish to oppose this trip, nor to deprive my states and my capital of the happiness of having the Vicar of Jesus Christ on earth. But, firm in my principles, I never change; what I have done, I believed myself able and duty-bound to do. All attempts to change my firm resolution will be useless. I will not take a single retrogressive step, and I urgently beg Your Holiness not to bring up the subject again; my ministers are forbidden to interfere. During Your Holiness's sojourn here and in my states I shall give my people an example of respect and homage due to the head of the Church.

'I shall not make an impression on your heart,' the pope answered prophetically,

> seeing that it is of brass; I will no longer light the torch of faith before your eyes to illuminate your spirit, seeing that you wish to gratify your blindness . . . Your soul is inflexible; I saw this with grief, in abandoning its destiny to God whose counsels you set at nought. If you persevere in your projects destructive of the faith and the laws of the Church, the hand of the Lord will fall heavily

upon you; it will check you in the course of your career, dig under you an abyss where you will be engulfed in the flower of life, and put a limit to the reign which you could have made glorious. Meanwhile my hands will be ceaselessly raised towards heaven in order to bring about your repentance, and if you are in the end struck by a thunderbolt I shall pray that it open your eyes and convert you.

Joseph listened coldly and with some aversion. Spiritual artillery was always distasteful to his blunt mind. He was puzzled as to what reply to make. He and the pope did not speak the same language. Their ideas, their aims, their backgrounds were so profoundly different that they did not have a common meeting point. Although the two sovereigns used the same tongue neither understood the other's words. 'I must sincerely admit,' Joseph confided to his friend Catharine II,

that the three hours which I had to spend with him [Pius] daily in talking nonsense about theology, and in conversing about things in words which neither of us understood, reached a point where we both remained dumb, and stared at each other as if to say that neither of us knew what it was all about; but it was boring and odious.

'Our negotiations,' the emperor told Leopold, 'in the end led to nothing.'

Baffled in every attempt, the Holy Father decided to swallow his dignity and pay a visit to the only man who had power to help him: Kaunitz. The chancellor was the only dignitary in Vienna who had remained aloof from all papal receptions since that memorable first day. Pius's attendants begged him not to humble himself; they considered Kaunitz as 'undoubtedly the most embittered and open enemy of the church, religion, and the Holy See'. But the pope, Pius's diary relates, 'paid no attention to those who tried to dissuade him, but wished to show by this act of goodness and extraordinary courtesy his Christian virtue'.

The pope went to Kaunitz's villa in Mariahilf. Instead of coming out to meet the Holy Father, the chancellor sent down his two sons to receive him, 'thereby', the pope said, 'the prince showed in what little respect he held the person of His Holiness'.

Pius, clad in a mantle of red velvet, was ushered into the chancellor's room. Kaunitz, in blue dressing-robe, neither advanced to meet his distinguished guest nor bent his knee. Pius may have been Holy Father to tens of millions of faithful, but to the Chancellor of Austria he was only John Angelo Braschi, an Italian plebeian. The crestfallen pope stood hesitant, then he nodded and removed his hat. Kaunitz returned the greeting and also removed his hat. The pontiff then covered his head. Not to be outdone, the chancellor also put on his hat. It was a dreadful insult, doubly so, as one of the witnesses of this strange comedy was the Protestant Dutch ambassador, Count Wassenaer, then Kaunitz's guest.

Kaunitz, giving the pope a penetrating glance from his icy-blue eyes, murmured something about having to put on his hat because he had a weak head. The delicate humour was worthy of Voltaire, but it passed the understanding of the dispirited pope. The pontiff began a discourse about the mortal dangers involved in showing disrespect to the Church. Unsmilingly Kaunitz interrupted the homily and asked the Holy Father whether he was interested in art. Not waiting for an answer, the chancellor took the surprised pope's arm and led him to his excellent picture gallery, discoursing volubly about the glories of his collection. The pope soon left, overcome with shame and humiliation. As he went out he murmured that he was *Tutto stupefatto*.

The visit caused a sensation. All the wits of Europe laughed. Gossip magnified Kaunitz's eccentric reception of the Holy Father into a hundred distortions. In Vienna the dinner tables hummed with the affair. Some said that the chancellor received the pope in a bathrobe and slippers. Other versions, which the historian Vehse has perpetuated, told how before the finest portraits Kaunitz 'unceremoniously pushed the Vicar of Christ, whom other mortals scarcely dared to look at, now to the right, and then to the left . . . handling him in the most irreverential manner'. There were those who delighted in relating how Kaunitz pointed out pictures of nude women to the stupefied pontiff. What a story Voltaire would have made of it had he been alive! The man who enjoyed himself most over these tales was Frederick the Great. 'Who knows,' he mocked to Las Casas, the Spanish ambassador, 'whether I might not at last have believed in the infallibility of the pope? But – then that visit to Vienna – !'

The Holy Father achieved nothing but a damaged reputation. When he left Vienna, on April 22nd, Joseph exulted. 'At last,' he said,

> I have packed off the pope . . . I am really delighted at his depar-
> ture, for in the last days the affair was beginning to be unbearable,
> in view of his wiles and wheedlings in his negotiations and dis-
> courses, and the truly ridiculous enthusiasm which he has aroused,
> especially among women. All the passages and stairs of the court
> were crammed with people; despite redoubled sentries, it was
> impossible to protect oneself from all the things they brought him
> to be blessed: scapularies, rosaries, images. And for the benedic-
> tions which he gave seven times daily from the balcony he had a
> throng of people so great that one can form no idea of it unless
> one has seen it; it is no exaggeration to say that at one time there
> were at least sixty thousand souls. That was a most beautiful
> spectacle; peasants and their wives and children came from
> twenty leagues around. Yesterday a woman was crushed right
> beneath my window.

'As concerns the question of Church and State,' Joseph revealed his sardonic mind in a brilliant flash, 'I believe that both of us will stick to our convictions. Everyone earns the bread he eats. He the pope defends the authority of the Church . . . and I the rights of the State which I serve.'

Catharine of Russia sympathized with Joseph. 'I do not envy,' she consoled him, 'Your Majesty's rare privilege, which you enjoy at present, of living next door to Pius VI. To speak frankly, I wish the pope were far away from Vienna. I do not know why, but I cannot think of his visit without disgust. To those who are not Catholic, an Italian priest is an object of aversion.'

'A priest like that one,' Joseph replied wryly, 'is a very incon-
venient commodity.' And the emperor gleefully related to his Russian friend that before Pius left he had to give him a 'written

M

certificate on the sound state in which he found my religion and that of my people.'

The pope went to Germany. He stopped at Munich (here the imperial ambassador, Lehrbach, was ordered by Kaunitz and Joseph to keep an eye on him), where he did not hide the failure of his visit but was generous in praise of the emperor. Quietly Pius returned to Rome. He was coldly received everywhere. At Cesena, his native town, the pope hoped to stay for three days. 'But the people,' a contemporary reports, 'called so loudly for bread instead of benedictions, that he left them on the second.'

In Rome the pope tried to defend his actions before the consistory; he spoke of 'the great spirit of Joseph, the emperor, of whose special affection for us we have so many proofs'. He wanted to give the impression that the emperor had compromised in some of his anti-clerical measures; but the consistory was cold and the populace on the streets mocked the kindly pontiff. The Holy Father generously defended the emperor. 'This prince,' he said, 'has a great fund of religion; he has assured me of it, and had proven to me that he is the best Catholic on earth. After the death of his mother, his Councillors have led him astray.' But the zealots and mockers gave Pius no rest. They pinned libels in the papal chamber. One of them contained the cruel words: 'What Gregory VII, the greatest priest, has founded, Pius VI, the smallest of all priests, has destroyed.' Under this Pius added in pencil: 'Christ's kingdom is not of this earth; he, who dispenses heavenly crowns, does not rob earthly ones. Let us render unto Caesar the things that are Caesar's, and unto God the things that are God's.' But the mockers still gave Pius no peace.

Irritated by the scoffers and zealots, Pius lost his temper and wrote a sharp letter to Joseph, threatening him with the ban. The emperor returned the missive with the comment that he was sure His Holiness did not write it, that it was the work of some nasty person, 'whom the Holy Father will promptly seek out and properly punish'.

For a while things were quiet. Then Joseph appointed Visconti, Archbishop of Milan. Pius refused confirmation. The implacable Kaunitz informed His Holiness that he would straightway convene a council of Lombard bishops, as in the early days of Christianity (for Kaunitz was no mean historian), and have the council act over the head of the pontiff.

Joseph – whose correspondence with the pope Kaunitz edited and corrected – did not want to break with Pius. Leaving the conduct of the state to his chancellor, the emperor suddenly left Vienna in December, 1782, and hastened to Rome. 'My surprise,' he wrote to Leopold whom he visited on the way, 'has succeeded marvellously; no one has recognized me. The papal courier took me for the King of Sweden' (who was then on his way to Rome). The emperor dropped in on the pope 'like a bomb', as he said, and embarrassed the Holy Father. Joseph's language was moderate and courteous; he wanted the pope's approval for the reorganization of the bishoprics and the founding of the parishes. The emperor won every point, and made a concordat with the pope whereby the secular government was granted the right to appoint Lombard bishops.

'I will say this for Pius,' Joseph told Cardinal Bernis; 'he is a good fellow. You would laugh if you had witnessed our conference. He often grew choleric, and sometimes angry; I let him fume, retaining my composure and firmness. As I said, at bottom the pope is a very good fellow, he has sense, but does not realize that times have changed.' And to Leopold the emperor confided: 'I think I have succeeded here; they have changed their false ideas about my religion.'

Pius was delighted with the outcome. To all who would listen he related the smallest particulars of his negotiations with the 'incomparable emperor', as he called Joseph. 'There is no one,' the Holy Father said, 'more eloquent or spirited than the emperor.' Pius had a sense of humour and insight all his own. 'The emperor,' he remarked whimsically, 'says everything that he wishes, but not all that he thinks.' And Joseph, on his part, did everything to make a good impression on His Holiness and on the Romans. He showed himself kind and simple and very devout. He visited all the churches in Rome. He won the sus-

ceptible hearts of the Romans with 30,000 scudi. Such a golden
shower was irresistible. '*Viva il nostro Imperatore*', the inhabitants
of the Eternal City shouted.

From Rome Joseph went to Pisa and was almost snowed
under on the road. The snow was about two feet deep, and he
travelled all night in order to avoid being frozen and buried
in the storm. In Pisa he thawed out, dried himself; but he found
the city monotonous. 'It is like Lent here: neither carnival, nor
balls, nor amusement.' The roads being frozen, the emperor
remained in Pisa several days. Here he received a letter from
Kaunitz, congratulating him on the concordat. 'Your Majesty,'
the chancellor wrote, 'has recovered the right which your
ancestors have abandoned for centuries, and the pope, as the
saying is, came away with a black eye.' The slang expression
was written by the solemn chancellor in German.

The powerful emperor could not enjoy his victory over the
papacy. He was freezing. 'The rooms have no guarantee against
the rigours of the season,' he complained to his chancellor; 'the
windows and doors shut so badly, and the chimneys smoke so
strongly, that one is colder inside  than outside. . . .' The
acrid smoke burned his eyes; the frost made him shiver. He
could neither read nor write. There was not even the consolation of a good opera. 'There are certainly no shows here of any
kind that would attract one to Italy,' he added; 'composition
and orchestral music, singers and dancers, all are worse than
mediocre.' Had he been a true son of his father, he might have
had a delightful time, for in Pisa there were beautiful women.

He found Genoa more interesting. 'I have been here since
the day before yesterday,' he communicated to Leopold on
February 17th,

and I have almost seen all the sights. They wanted to escort me,
but . . . I insisted upon retaining my absolute liberty. The port
is fine, large, but the mouth which is contracted for the protection
against the *libeccio* (south-west wind) is narrow. The stores of
Porto-Franco are well calculated to make Genoa the ladder of
commerce and at the same time not to lose the considerable income from the goods consumed in the city. The hospital could
have need of your care . . . for it is as squalid as possible, although

large and rich, somewhat like San Spirito in Rome. The poor-house (*Ricovero dei Poveri*) is big, but its appearance is execrable. Most of the inmates are girls and boys, and more than a hundred unfortunately married women; there are about fifteen hundred souls in all, but they die of hunger, of cold, of misery, and are wasted by filth. This is the vilest thing I have yet seen in Italy.

From Genoa the inquiring emperor went to Milan. Again he had to battle snow and frost. 'The palace,' he wrote,

is beautiful and commodious, the opera bad, the ballet, of which there are three, long and mediocre enough. I have not gone out yet, as I have been overwhelmed with business from Vienna . . . I give audiences three hours daily, and so far I have heard no complaints . . . except of the lack of specie; the silk factories are declining . . . The university building, constructed anew, is good, and above all, the botanical garden and the chemical laboratory are well managed.

It was carnival time in Milan; but the emperor attended only one ball, at midnight. The music was gay, the women beautiful. But Joseph would not amuse himself. There was too much to be done, time was pressing, life was short. He hurried back to Vienna.

## VI

Toleration and church reforms were incomplete without the liberation of the Jews, a people exposed for centuries to every discrimination and violence Christendom could invent. There were about 200,000 Jews in Galicia, almost 70,000 in Bohemia, and 80,000 in Hungary; about 10,000 were scattered in the various provinces.

Maria Theresa's hatred for Jews was as great as her loathing of Protestants. Jews were forbidden to own real property, to practice crafts, to hold any office. She perpetuated the laws which excluded Jews from certain provinces and confined them in limited numbers to ghettos. Only with great difficulty was the empress restrained from banishing the Jews from Bohemia. 'I know of no greater pest to the state,' she said, 'than this nation, on account of their cheating, usury, money-lending, reducing people to beggary, and carrying on all kinds of evil transactions which honest persons abhor.'

Joseph did not hate Jews. He considered Jews no more and no less, no better and no worse, than his other subjects. His first act was to abolish the disgraceful Jew-badge, the yellow patch. Benjamin Cadet of Strassburg appealed to the emperor to repeal the body-tax which Jews had to pay for existing; the tax brought in 14,000 florins to the treasury annually.

'This tax,' was Joseph's laconic reply, 'is to be stopped.'

The Catholic population in the Austrian lands was violently anti-Jewish. Even Joseph hesitated for a while to grant Jews toleration, fearing the fury of the pious. He was not the man to stop at anything, but in this case he proceeded with caution. In May, 1781, he outlined a project for the liberation of the Jews.

> With a view of rendering useful to society the large class of Israelites who inhabit our hereditary lands [he wrote], considering that their means of subsistence are very limited; that until the present they have not been permitted to extend these means; and considering that the first necessary measure to take is to turn them from the exclusive use of their own language – we ordain that all their contracts, notes, testaments, accounts, commercial books, in short, all such matters, legal or extra-legal, be written in the language of the land they inhabit . . . It is necessary, however, to accord to the Jews a term of two or three years to familiarize themselves with the language of the country, and to facilitate this study, there ought to be established a school in each synagogue . . . under the inspection of professors, without the Jews being troubled in any way in the exercise of their ritual or dogma. . . .
>
> As to their civil life, the Jews could devote themselves to agriculture . . . They may also become entrepreneurs. Among the various crafts, they may exercise shoe-making, tailoring, masonry, carpentry, and generally those trades that have to do with building, including agriculture . . . If they know design, they may pursue that art; and finally, the free arts, such as painting, sculpture, etc. They should be permitted to form guilds, to work in factories, and in everything that has to do with machines . . . They should not be forbidden to work in spinning, weaving, and the manufacture of textiles. All humiliating distinctions, and all contraints hitherto imposed on the Jews . . . will be abrogated,

as well as all external marks whatsoever . . . Having judged it proper to consult the provinces on many points, I await their response concerning those matters which are not yet specified.

The response was not favourable; the Council of State opposed complete toleration for the Jews. Consequently, in January, 1782, the emperor issued a Toleration Patent for Jews living in Lower Austria, which contained a number of unfavourable provisions. The Jews were forbidden to maintain a separate communal organization in Vienna and prevented from erecting public synagogues in the capital. Their number in Vienna and in Lower Austria was to remain, as hitherto, limited. To settle in the capital or on the land special permission, based upon pecuniary qualifications, was required.

On the other hand ('in order that the Jewish nation . . . may become more useful to the state'), Jews were permitted ('we allow and command') to send their children to the public primary and secondary schools, 'to learn at least reading, writing, and arithmetic'. They could also, if they wished, erect their own schools. They were allowed to attend the higher schools, to bind themselves in apprenticeships to Christian masters, and to practice all the arts and crafts. Full liberty in commerce (*Grosshandlung*), banking, and industry was granted them. Big Jewish merchants were permitted to dress like gentlemen, and even to wear swords. The emperor commended the Jews to all his subjects and officials, urging the latter to respect them in their persons and rights, and never to show them contempt. Insult or violence offered to a Jew, the emperor warned, 'will be sternly punished', for the Jews must be considered as 'fellow-men'.

Similar Patents were promulgated for Bohemia, Moravia, and Silesia. In Bohemia Jews were limited in number, but they became active in the rising industries. Of the fifty-eight Bohemian textile factories, fifteen were in Jewish hands. The Jewish community at Prague retained its privileges, being an almost independent *Judenstaat*. In Hungary Jews were allowed to lease estates and practice crafts, even on the land, but were not permitted to wear beards.

Galicia presented a special problem. Maria Theresa had deprived Galician Jews of most of their economic privileges, including the rights of settlement and marriage. Even Joseph was hard on the middle-class Jews, hoping to make them agriculturally productive, without, however, giving them land on which to settle. Brody, in east Galicia ('at the extreme end of my frontiers'), had 18,000 Jews and Joseph, passing through there in 1787, humorously dubbed it 'this modern Jerusalem'.

Less than five months before his death, Joseph finally issued his Toleration Patent for Galician Jews; it contained provisions similar to those granted the Jews in other provinces. At the same time all Austrian Jews were made liable to military service, like the rest of the population. 'The Jew,' Joseph decreed, 'as man and citizen should be under the same obligations as others. It will not be an insult to his religion when he is free to eat what he wishes, and to do on Sabbath what necessity demands that a Christian do on Sunday. This is to be observed in all the lands.' For the first time in history Jews were compelled to serve in a Christian army.

Both Jews and Christians resented the military service, the former because it meant a violation of many sacred taboos, and the latter because they considered it a disgrace to serve with Jews. The customary military oath ended with the words, 'So help me God and the holy Gospels through our Lord Jesus Christ.' In deference to Jewish feelings, Joseph changed the oath for Jewish soldiers to read, 'So help me God to eternal life, through the promise of the true Messiah, his laws, and the prophets sent to our fathers.' The Jews, controlled by their very orthodox rabbis, opposed the emperor's reforms, fearing that the secular schools would lead the young men away from the Talmud, and that military service would impair their orthodoxy: making them *Goyim*. The rabbis, not to be outdone by the priests in fanaticism, sent a deputation to Vienna to protest against the compulsory military service. Whereupon the Jews of Trieste issued a ringing declaration against the rabbis:

> The monarch wants to raise Israel from the dust and make it competent for learning and agriculture. We are, like other

nations, to make use of trades, arts, and sciences, and also, like the others, to be employed in the army, to take up arms against the enemies of our fatherland. He puts more confidence in us than any other monarch before him. What, then, does he demand? That we love industry and hate slothfulness! Laziness brings human energy and abilities to stagnation; it is a corruption of the land. When indolent hands refuse to work, how can one live? From the sweat of others? To strive for the possessions of others is contrary to that one of the ten commandments which, according to the Talmud, outweighs the nine others.

How can we, then, utter anything against the command of that benevolent man, who takes our side and our children's side so paternally? How can we justify such a thing before God? Should not, then, the divine proverb which says: Man is born to work, be fulfilled? Should we be ungrateful to him who has loaded us with favours, who shows us so much confidence? God forbid that we should, by our conduct, bring upon us his just inclemency.

Although many pious Jews emigrated to avoid conscription, at the end of 1788 there were about 2,500 Jews in the army. Joseph may have been irritated by the Jewish protests, but he was convinced that his decrees would in the long run prove beneficial both to the Jews and the state; and he was right, as the long list of distinguished Austrian Jews in the nineteenth and twentieth century proves. The emperor, with a rare sense of delicacy, sternly forbade compulsory conversion of Jews. When Fischer, the censor of Prague, proposed that anti-Christian passages should be eliminated from the Talmud, as was ordered by the Council of Trent in 1581, Joseph ordered him not to mutilate the book.

The Jewish reforms, wrote Barthélemy, the French envoy at Vienna, 'arouse a universal cry of disapproval . . . The great facilities accorded to the Jews are considered as a sure ruin for the hereditary states'. Most vehement were the Christian merchants who feared Jewish competition, and the priests who hated the Jews for having given them their Saviour and religion.

Even without the Jewish reforms the emperor had a sufficient number of violent and powerful enemies; liberating the Jews required courage of a kind which no contemporary monarch possessed or wished to possess. Joseph knew that in granting civil rights to the despised people he was adding so much more dynamite to the supercharged atmosphere of hostility. 'My chief aim,' he said in his own defence,

> is education, enlightenment, and better training for this nation. The opening up of new sources of income, the repeal of the hateful constraints, the abolition of the insulting badges on clothes – all this, as well as rational education and the extinction of their language, will serve to weaken their own prejudices, and either will lead them to Christianity or improve their moral character and make them useful citizens.

And the cynical Frederick of Prussia, who liked neither Jew nor Habsburg, exclaimed: 'I am delighted. The emperor has had reason to ally himself closely with that nation. It is a long time since he has been titular King of Jerusalem!'

# CHAPTER 10

# Enlightenment

I

*Good God, even their souls are to be put in uniform! That is*
*the summit of despotism!*
                    Mirabeau on Joseph's school regulations

In the course of less than ten years, the emperor issued dozens of
decrees concerning the schools. In 1780 supervisors were appointed to make semi-annual visits throughout the provinces;
somewhat later district school commissioners were given the
same task, at a salary of 600 florins and 150 florins for travelling
expenses. The remaining monasteries were ordered to make
themselves useful by erecting schools. Provincial communities
were compelled to build schools wherever there were 90 to 100
children of age; the manorial lords, the villages, and the
parishes were to contribute one-third each to the construction
of the buildings.

More important was the educational compulsion. The emperor decreed that all children must attend school. Pious
Protestants and orthodox Israelites resented this kindness; nor
did the Catholics like to expose their children to secular education. To overcome parental hostility, Joseph ordered that those
who refused to send their children to the public schools pay a
double educational tax; poor parents, if they were recalcitrant,
were threatened with suspension of their charities. Finally the
emperor ruled that no one could be apprenticed to a craft unless
he had a school certificate.

The government founded a Textbook Publishing Company
and the books were made compulsory, at a low rate. Children of
soldiers and poor parents were given free textbooks. The curriculum in the lower schools was based on the *Trivium*: reading,

writing, and arithmetic. Of the 730,000 children of school age, 208,588 attended school, an attendance greater than anywhere else in Europe. The teachers' salaries were 150 florins annually.

The emperor was at least a century ahead of his time in his insistence upon education for women. In the special women's schools the feminine arts were taught: sewing, knitting, cooking, besides the regular *Trivium*. Where there were no women's schools the girls attended the boys' schools, but had to sit on separate benches and were forbidden to wear corsets, in order, one may suppose, that girlish figures might not distract the boys' attention. The convents were ordered to found schools to instruct women in higher studies, especially pedagogy; the graduates of these institutions had to serve the state as teachers, for a salary of course, for six years. Catharine of Russia found Joseph's educational system so admirable that she asked her ambassador at Vienna to send her the plans, as she wished to imitate Joseph in Muscovy.

Above the grammar schools were the *Gymnasia*, or 'Latin' schools. German Austria had 59 such institutions with 281 teachers (135 of whom were Jesuits) and over 9,000 students. The Gymnasium was divided into five classes, taking their names from the chief subject of study – the Principia, Grammar, Syntax, Rhetoric, and Poetry. To be admitted, a boy had to be twelve years old, possess a certificate of graduation from the lower (Normal) school, and have a knowledge of German. Joseph decreed that 'more geography, world history, and natural science' be taught. Even non-Catholics, including Jews, were admitted to the gymnasium. Impecunious students were given stipends and good scholars premiums. Examinations, oral and written, were strictly regulated by the emperor and rewards were given not only for scholarship but also for good conduct and good German. At the same time Joseph abolished the privileged aristocratic schools, the military institutions and the Theresan *Rittersakademie* in Vienna, because, he said, 'forty years of experience have taught that, despite the great expense, only very few really useful and able servants of the state are trained here'.

The emperor did not show himself so liberal to the universities. He did not want too many scholars. Society, he said, would not be the loser if some of those clever people devoted themselves to civic life rather than to intellectual pursuits. Possibly he was not wrong. At any rate, he considered the universities merely as institutions to train officials. He did not need erudites. The bureaucrats, he said satirically, 'can educate themselves, for no one yet became a scholar from the platform'. Consequently he favoured the juridical, theological, and medical faculties at the expense of the philosophical. He reduced all the universities to three: Vienna, Prague, and Lemberg, but that of Vienna lost its ancient jurisdictions and privileges, and was put on a par with the other two. The Universities of Innsbruck, Brünn, Graz, and Freiburg, were transformed into lycées to teach practical arts; in the lycées the medical, juridical, and philosophical faculties were reduced to two professors each and the courses were to last only two years. The German language was made compulsory in all the higher schools; conversation, lectures, and examinations were to be in that language. In the theological faculty, Latin remained the dominant tongue.

Unlike the lower schools, the higher institutions were given a large degree of intellectual freedom. Instructors were allowed to choose their own books and to be at liberty to teach what and how they pleased. The government was generous in the provision of facilities. Monastic archives and books were donated to the academic libraries; anatomical theatres for dissection were erected; and, in Vienna, the famous Josephinum was built for the training of military surgeons. In 1781–2 the educational budget amounted to 191,727 gulden for the universities, 23,241 for the lycées, 80,475 for the gymnasia, and 107,067 for the Normal schools. There were about 5,000 students in the universities and 8,000 in the gymnasia.

The emperor's great aim was to create a uniform state with right-thinking subjects. Hence his schools were formalized and rigid. Joseph did not want thinkers or free spirits; he wished to have disciplined subjects and obedient soldiers.

Thou shalt not send any money into foreign countries for Masses [read the political-moral catechism which the Emperor drew up for school use].

Thou shalt not appear at processions with costly flags, nor dressed with sashes, or high feathers in thy hat, nor with music.

Thou mayest obtain from thy bishop a dispensation for marriage, where there is no natural or religious order to the contrary.

Thou shalt not seek for any dignity of the court of Rome, without the permission of thy sovereign.

Thou shalt forbear all occasions of dispute relative to matters of faith; and thou shalt, according to the true principles of Christianity, affectionately and kindly treat those who are not of thy communion.

Thou shalt not in any wise use the crown of St Christopher, or other superstitious supplications.

Thou mayest marry the woman whom thou hast ravished, if she is willing to marry thee when she is out of thy power.

Thou shalt not keep any useless dogs.

Thou shalt not plant tobacco without the permission of thy lord.

What was lacking was: Thou shalt have no God but my God, and no prophet but me. But Joseph did not want to compete with the pope.

## II

Masonic societies flourished throughout the eighteenth century. Many distinguished persons joined the secret organizations, and when Pope Clement XII banned Freemasonry in 1738 the bull could not be executed in Austria because of the opposition of influential persons, including Joseph's father who was Grand Master of a Vienna lodge. One of the eight lodges in Vienna was called 'Saint Joseph', which made many people suspect Joseph was a Mason.

The repressive governments on the one hand and the winds of new doctrine on the other, explain the rise of secret societies in Europe. Where men could not assemble, write, or speak freely, they joined secret groups to express their views. The lodges became debating societies, oratory clubs, training grounds for the new generation of libertarians. Being secret, the societies were more dangerous to the established order than they would have been in the open; a dammed stream will break out in unexpected places.

Alongside the Masonic lodges there developed another secret organization, that of the Illuminati, whose influence was confined mainly to Catholic south-west Germany. The founder of the Illuminati was Professor Adam Weishaupt of the University of Ingolstadt. His programme was: 'Perfection of mankind, that is, higher cultivation for the attainment of pure morals and a many-sided moderate life; then the amelioration of civic and political life of the nations, and thereby the achievement of a universal spread of the highest possible earthly happiness.'

Candidates for the Illuminati order had to pass through many states of purification and trial before they could see light. Persons judged unsafe did not get beyond the lower seven grades and remained only the outpost of the order. The final secret of the society was revealed only to those who had passed through the last two grades, 'Magus' and 'Rex'. In the former religion was declared a fraud; in the latter the princes were denounced as usurpers. The aim of the Illuminati was, in the words of Weishaupt, 'to exterminate all parson- and scoundrel-regimes and the rulers, as the evil ones of the earth'. The society attracted many nobles and soon spread to Franconia, Swabia, the Palatinate, and Austria.

The Illuminati acquired extraordinary influence. By means of propaganda, writing, teaching, and personal contact they undermined the Church, won a large share of the control of the press, and made their way to the institutions of learning. Among the members was Charles von Dalberg, coadjutor of the arch-diocese of Mainz. Although the language of the Illuminati was at times violent, the aims were fundamentally educational. Since European governments were tyrannical, wasteful, and excessively stupid, there was nothing else for the educated and intelligent people to do but agitate in the only way open to them.

Every important city in the Habsburg empire had either a Masonic or Illuminati lodge. The Vienna lodge, 'True Concord', had its own temple and issued a journal. Among its members were the foremost literary and scientific men in the capital. There were Ignace Born, the metallurgist; Sonnenfels, the jurist and statesman; the poets Blumauer and Denis; the composer Josef Haydn; councillors like Greiner and Kressel; scholars like Eckel, Raczky, Retzer, and others. Practically all these men were loyal supporters of Joseph and his reforms. The emperor was, indeed, carrying out precisely those ideas which the Masons and Illuminati advocated.

The Freemasons [says the contemporary Caroline Pichler], carried on with almost ridiculous openness and ostentation. Masonic songs were published, set to music, and sung; Masonic signs were worn as *joujoux* on watches, ladies received white gloves from apprentices and journeymen, and many fashionable articles – such as white satin muffs bordered with blue – were named *à la francmaçon* . . . It was not unprofitable to join the brotherhood . . . One brother helped another . . . they supported each other everywhere, and he who did not belong, often met with obstacles.

In Joseph the sense of despotism was becoming aggravated with the years. Power always corrupts, and the emperor was no exception to the rule. He grew jealous of the secret and well-organized societies and, in December, 1785, he issued a decree regulating the Masonic brotherhoods. 'The so-called Free-mason societies,' Joseph wrote, 'of whose secrets I am informed as little as I care to know their tricks, are increasing and spreading even to the small towns; left alone, without supervision, they might become dangerous in their excesses to religion, order, and morals.' He unjustly accused the Masons of extortion (*Geldschneiderei*). He admitted, he said, that the societies were socially useful, but they must be regulated. Only one lodge was to be permitted in every provincial capital and meetings were to be announced to the police; the chiefs of the lodges were ordered to submit lists of their members to the authorities.

The Masons felt indignant. The emperor's contemptuous remark that he knew nothing and cared less about Masonic 'tricks' was not taken in good spirit by the brethren; distinguished Masons were hurt by Joseph's reference to money extortion. But they had to obey; the eight Vienna lodges were merged into two, with 180 members each.

## III

The Josephan epoch brought forth many scholars, artists, and scientists, not all of them Austrian, to be sure. Most of them had only a local, or at best German, reputation; but at least three artists, Haydn, Gluck, and Mozart, belong to mankind.

The centre of cultural activity was, of course, Vienna with its population of 260,000. The winds of doctrine blowing from the west, stimulated by the emperor, affected many nobles and the richer bourgeois. Some of the most distinguished aristocrats and prelates prided themselves upon their new ideas, and were not afraid of being 'modern'.

'In all branches of knowledge,' to quote the pious Caroline Pichler again,

> there was praiseworthy activity; one was allowed to think freely and so one thought well . . . A brisk cheerfulness penetrated even to social circles, displacing the former stiffness and obsolete forms. The theatre, under the direct protection of Emperor Joseph, contributed to this social gaiety. Our stage, under the leadership of the monarch, soon became the foremost in Germany . . . for the emperor on his journeys engaged the best talent.

For things spiritual, so-called, His Imperial Majesty had a pronounced contempt. He respected only the practical, the concrete. That the pamphleteers abused the privilege, and even attacked the emperor personally, did not concern him much. 'I am of the opinion,' was Joseph's motto, 'that it is necessary to let the world say what it wishes, provided that it lets me do what I please.'

Joseph took a certain grim delight in being abused. 'I have,' he said, 'a healthy skin; let whoever itches scratch.' When a pasquinade appeared accusing the emperor of Protestantism, he had the plates confiscated and republished thousands of exemplers, selling them at six Kreuzer a piece. 'I do not care,' Joseph said, 'if they speak well or ill of me; some will like it, others will not. What matters is that one should have no self-reproaches.' The chief of the Vienna archives, Michael Schmidt, who was at work on a history, Joseph admonished: 'Spare no

N

one, myself as little as others . . . Let posterity profit from the
errors of my ancestors and my own.' In that Joseph resembled
his ancestor Charles V, who refused a gift to the Italian historian
Paul Jovius with the comment: 'Just because he intends to
write my life I should be ashamed to bribe him by a pension.'

For literati Joseph had a royal scorn. He called them 'pen
cattle'. In the Voltairean epoch it was the fashion among
monarchs to dabble in literature. Catharine II prided herself
upon her prose and Frederick II wrote wretched poetry in
imitation of Voltaire. Such affectations irritated the forthright
Joseph. 'I do not know,' he told van Swieten,

> how some monarchs can occupy their minds with such trifles, as
> to acquire literary accomplishments, to seek out a sort of greatness
> in making verses . . . I conceive that kings ought not to be entirely
> unacquainted with the sciences; but that a monarch should pass
> his time in writing madrigals is, in my opinion, very unnecessary.
> The Margrave of Brandenburg [note the contemptuous use of
> Frederick the Great's family title] has become the head of a sect
> of kings who occupy themselves in writing memoirs, poems, and
> treatises. The Empress of Russia imitated him, studied Voltaire,
> and wrote dramas and verses to Vanhal; then some odes to her
> Alcides. Stanislaus Leszczynski [King of Poland] wrote letters of
> pacification; and, lastly, the King of Sweden letters of friendship.
> Their inducements to write are as singular as their productions.
> The King of Prussia began his academical occupations at Rheins-
> berg [Frederick's residence when he was crown prince] . . . When
> he became king he continued his learned engagements; immedi-
> ately a number of French champions assembled around him, and
> sang his victories in Silesia; that is to say, the conquests of a
> country which was defended by two regiments of infantry, and
> which he overran with 40,000 men. At a later period, his passion
> for making verses induced him to enter into friendship with
> Voltaire, which, however, was broken off, renewed, again dis-
> solved, and afterwards continued till the death of that watch-
> maker of Ferney.
> The Empress of Russia undertook it from pride; she wished to
> shine in everything; time and circumstances, love and friendship,
> and perhaps a portion of vanity, did the rest. Stanislaus was a
> good-natured man; he dreamed like the Abbé de St Pierre, and,
> if it had been possible, would, from his Lunéville, have com-
> manded peace to the whole world. His Majesty of Stockholm had

other motives; Gustavus had been treated in France with distinction, and after his return wrote such tender letters to Paris and to the Court of Versailles, that they could not help paying him a compliment, by saying that he was not only a king, but also an accomplished gentleman.

You see how I think on these matters. The illustrious Greeks and Romans are not unknown to me; I know the history of the German empire, and that of my states in particular; but my time never allowed me to make epigrams . . . I read for instruction; I travelled for the enlargement of my views; and when I patronize men of letters I do them more service than if I were sitting down with one of them to compose unmeaning sonnets.

Even in architecture the Josephan reign expressed the bare, economical, pragmatic spirit of the monarch. He cleaned up the city of Vienna, had the streets sprinkled and lighted, and planted trees on the glacis. But the public buildings, whether hospital or palace, resembled barracks, huge, square, block-like structures with heavy window frames. The new parish churches on the land did not resemble the traditional Gothic edifices. The countryside is still studded with Josephan churches: simple, bare, unornamented buildings with a poverty-stricken façade and a single small spire.

When Joseph was a boy of fifteen a child was born in Salzburg destined to eternal remembrance. Joseph had not been on the throne for five months when the twenty-seven-year-old Wolfgang Mozart arrived in the capital to make his fortune. Under the protection of the Prince-Bishop of Salzburg, Mozart immediately met some of the aristocracy, Galitzin, Thun, Cobenzl. 'My principal object now,' the composer wrote to his father a week after his arrival, 'is to introduce myself in some favourable manner to the emperor, for I am absolutely determined that he shall know me. I should much like to play my opera through to him, and some good fugues, for his taste lies in that direction.'

The emperor liked music but had no independent taste. He encouraged the young composer, however, not because he understood him but because he wished to flaunt the Austrian artist before the native patrons who preferred Italian operettas.

When Mozart produced his opera *Don Giovanni* in Vienna, th
audience received it coldly. The emperor was furious. 'It is ;
divine work,' he said to the composer whom he summoned t
his box, 'but it is not a morsel for my Viennese.' 'They neec
time to taste it,' was the composer's modest reply.

Mozart made a living by giving lessons. The court ladies, th
composer informed his father, 'pay me six ducats for twelv
lessons'. When he first came to Vienna, Mozart hoped that th
emperor would give him financial aid. But Joseph amused him
self by exhibiting the musician's skill. When in December, 1781
Clementi, an Italian pianist, came to Vienna, the military
minded monarch arranged a sort of pianistic duel between th
two musicians. 'The emperor,' Mozart relates the story,

> after we had complimented one another sufficiently, commandec
> that we should begin. *La Santa Chiesa Catholica*, said the emperor
> Clementi being a Roman. He preluded and played a sonata. Th
> emperor then said to me, *Allons d'rauf los!* (The command give)
> to an artilleryman). I preluded and played variations . . . I se
> clearly enough that the emperor is aware of my attainments i1
> the art of science of music, and wishes to do me justice in the eye
> of foreigners.

This was merely Mozart's modesty and hope for aid. But Josepl
never helped him. Mozart was becoming disillusioned. After ;
year in Vienna he lost hope for imperial patronage; his tone t
His Majesty became less humble. When *The Abduction from th
Seraglio* was performed, Joseph, who wished to display his know
ledge of the noble art, said to the composer in a patronizin;
tone, 'Too beautiful for our ears, and much too many notes
dear Mozart.' 'Just as many, Your Majesty, as necessary,' wa
the proud reply.

'How do you like Mozart's music?' Joseph once asked a con
noisseur named Dittersdorf.

'Very much,' said Dittersdorf.

'Some prefer Clementi. What is your opinion?'

'In Clementi's music there is much art and depth; in Mozart'
besides art and depth, also extraordinary taste.'

'That's what I say,' commented Joseph. 'What is your opinion of Mozart's composition?'

'He is indubitably a great original genius.'

'True,' was the imperial answer. 'But I think in his operas he uses too many notes, of which the singers complain much. I compare Mozart's composition to a golden snuff-box made in Paris, and Haydn's to one made in London. Both beautiful, the former on account of its simplicity and exceptional polish.'

Finally, the emperor made the snuff-box musician a chamber composer at the annual salary of eight hundred florins.

# CHAPTER II

# Economics

## I

*Hasten everything that brings me nearer to the accomplishment of my plans for the happiness of my people.*

Joseph to Gebler

'The peasant,' Joseph said, 'who bears the greatest burdens has a preferential right to the protection of his king.' When his lamented mother was still alive the emperor hoped that the manorial lords would voluntarily free their serfs from all feudal obligations. He expected a great deal from such a liberation. 'It would bring,' he reasoned, 'priceless advantages to the state, the manorial lords, and the peasants, by increasing population, industry, and general harmony. Happy moment this, which love of humanity and duty has made me ardently hope for for years.' It was idle hope.

The largest part of the arable land was held by the privileged classes, the clergy alone owning about one-third of it. In Bohemia 14 princes, 172 counts, 79 barons, and 95 knights owned estates whose value amounted to 193 million gulden. The soil-bound serfs worked these lands under the whip of the stewards. The lords' motto was: *Rustica gens, optima flens, pessima ridens* (The peasant is best when he cries and worst when he laughs). He had few occasions to laugh.

Less than a year after his accession to the throne, on September 1, 1781, Joseph issued an edict abolishing serfdom. The decree contained fundamental principles which, on the wings of the French Revolution, were to spread around the world. The six articles of the law guaranteed the subjects the right to free marriage, migration, work, occupation, and property. The freedmen were put directly under the protection of the state and, by the Penal Decree (*Strafpatent*) issued at the same time,

the manorial lords were deprived of the right of criminal
jurisdiction over their peasants. The lords could no longer
impose money fines, nor inflict punishment. A peasants' advo-
cate was appointed in every provincial capital to protect the
rights of the freedmen.

The edict, however, had certain drawbacks. The emperor,
having some regard for property rights, did not entirely deprive
the nobles of some servile obligations due to them. Robots and
fees, it is true, were regulated but not entirely abolished. A
supplementary law provided that peasants could pay in instal-
ments for the land they held, and their right of ownership,
control, sale, and exchange was guaranteed. 'The main question
for the state,' Joseph said,

> is whether peasant property should be inherited as a whole or in
> fragments. Strong peasant estates, composed of large families,
> are, for all purposes of state, more suitable than small holdings.
> It would therefore be proper to declare the estates as unalienable
> and indivisible, so that always only one son, be he the oldest or
> youngest, should be the proprietor.

Large estates, however, could be divided up among the heirs.

To enable the peasants to compete, in some degree, with the
big landlords, the emperor encouraged the improvement of
agriculture. The government instructed the peasants how to
treat sick cattle, provided for the preservation of forests, ordered
the peasants to fence their holdings so as not to waste time in
watching the cattle, compelled them to plough with horses
instead of oxen, encouraged horse-breeding, and offered premiums for the best horses, bees, and field produce. At the same
time, although it is hard to see the relevancy, the peasants were
forbidden to bake gingerbread cake; it was bad for the stomach,
the emperor said.

## II

In the eighteenth century Mercantilists held that national commerce and industry should be protected by all possible governmental means, and that the more money a country had the

richer it was; Physiocrats believed that agriculture was the basis of all wealth – verities which only a dour Scotsman could question. Emperor Joseph believed in both principles.

The ideas of the Mercantilists were popularized in Austria by a savant named Hornegg who wrote a book called *Oesterreich über alles, wann es nur will* (Austria first, if only she wishes to). The book contained ideas clear to Joseph, although he did not need the qualifying clause in the title. Adam Smith's pioneering work appeared in 1776, but it took a long time before it reached the continent, and the emperor probably never heard of it.

Money, an ancient Roman emperor said, has no smell, and the eighteenth century agreed with him. Noble princes and divinely ordained monarchs were not fastidious in financial matters. Even the pious Maria Theresa permitted lotteries in her dominions. In ten years, from 1759 to 1769, they brought in 21 million gulden, of which 3 million were pocketed by the court, for the Emperor Francis, Joseph's father, was the lottery farmer. In Brunswick the government held the lottery in lease and imprisoned the winners who had the presumption to claim the money.

There were other ways of raising money beside legalized gambling. Duke Charles of Württemberg, who controlled the salt monopoly, forced his subjects to buy large quantities of salt, and cheated them in the process by watering the goods. In Fürstenberg every subject was compelled to buy the official calendar, or pay a ten-thaler fine. Every Baden-Durlach inhabitant had to deliver twelve sparrows to the authorities, or pay four Kreuzer per bird. The cleverest system of extortion was the Prussian. Five hundred articles, including tobacco and coffee, were withdrawn from free circulation and made a state monopoly; the customs officers were hard-bitten Frenchmen who were paid higher salaries than the ministers of state – for the great Frederick despised his countrymen. Frederick, likewise, clipped the coin.

The most popular German method of raising cash was to sell soldiers. From the time of Richelieu to Louis XIV, German princes received 300 million francs for this human cattle; and from 1750 to 1772 the same noble rulers pocketed 137 million francs for selling their subjects. In diplomatic language the money was called a 'subsidy'.

The princes found life pleasant, but expensive. They needed money, but were divinely and ecclesiastically forbidden to work. Long ago a great theologian had established it as a universal truth that God had created society in an economically triune image; the head, the arms, and the feet. The head was the sovereign, and he was to rule; the arms were the nobles, and they were to fight; the feet were the common people, and they were to work and support the upper part of the body. The feet were never consulted.

A prince could not be expected to be a miser. Charles VI, Joseph's grandfather, who was always impecunious, had to have fifteen buckets of wine to bathe his parrots, could not get along without 4,000 guldens' worth of parsley for his kitchen, and provided his courtiers daily with gallons of Tokay. Charles's income was 25 million gulden, of which 14 million went to the support of the army which never won a war. In Prussia, Frederick William I had an income of 7 million thaler and spent 6 million on the army. His son Frederick the Great was personally scrimpy, but devoted 60 per cent of his income to the army, averaging two and a half thaler per head of population. In Saxony one diverting military encampment cost one million thaler; a celebration of the marriage of the Saxon crown prince ran to four million; and Countess Cosel, one of the innumerable mistresses of Augustus the Strong, cost her lover 20 million thaler. The income of the Palatinate was three million Rhenish gulden. A small state? Alas! The Prince Palatine, Charles Theodore, spent 200,000 gulden on the opera, 100,000 on the stables, 80,000 on the chase, and 120,000 on castles and gardens. His court consisted of 2,000 persons; a driver received 250 gulden in salary, and a professor of philosophy 200 gulden. Charles Theodore had a magnificent army of 5,500 men, of whom one-fourth were officers, commanded by twenty-two generals.

Charles Eugene of Württemberg had a court of 2,000 persons; when he went travelling it took 600 horses to haul the precious princely cargo. This mighty ruler of the great state of Württemberg spent 300,000 to 400,000 gulden on a single celebration. While Emperor Joseph always wore a simple military uniform, and Frederick the Great's wardrobe was sold after his death for 400 thaler, Count Brühl, the Saxon minister, possessed one hundred silk bed robes.

In the midst of the petty German princes' extravagance, Joseph stands out as a man of decency and principles. He had rich lands in his empire. His provinces produced almost everything needed for self-sufficiency. The Hungarian mines yielded annually seven million guldens' worth of gold and silver, not to speak of copper, iron, mercury, and marble. Galicia possessed the richest salt mines in Central Europe. Lombardy produced silk and Bohemia textiles. Inner Austria was rich in wines and mines, and agricultural products were grown in almost all the states of the empire.

The emperor tried to make his lands wealthy and self-sufficient. Unfortunately his economic ideas were confused. On the one hand he feverishly encouraged commerce and industry, and on the other he restricted enterprise. He attempted to break the tariff barriers among his provinces; failing that, he made the tariff fairly uniform in all the Austrian lands. His redefinition of the usury laws relieved banking enterprise of a serious burden. He permitted jewellers to deal in notes and credit papers. To facilitate transport, imperial posts were established throughout the dominions and a highway, the *Via Josephina*, was built across the Carniolan mountains from Carlstadt to Zeugg, thus giving commerce access to the Adriatic.

Alongside the small producers, employing only three or four apprentices, large factories now rose in the cities. Capitalist production brought a revolution in fashions. People were encouraged to make more frequent public appearances, and balls were sponsored. This required new clothes. Soon poor women dressed like ladies, and even servant girls looked as if they were daughters of officials. The public masquerade balls (*Redouten*) became, under the pressure of a rising capitalism, veritably democratic: people were admitted not on the basis of their social status but on their appearance, for the emperor himself was a sartorial democrat.

So eager was Joseph to foster industry that he crippled the ancient craft guilds and encouraged immigration in order to increase the labour supply. He prohibited emigration, for the same reason. The authorities were ordered to be especially careful to prevent artists, craftsmen, and skilled workers from leaving the country. To increase the hours of labour, the emperor ordered that people should work on the abolished holidays. Workers in the fields, factories, shops, and ships were exempted from military conscription.

The emperor aided the emerging capitalist class and raised industrialists to honours and dignities. He abolished the law, passed by Maximilian II in 1572, whereby only nobles and knights could acquire estates. Joseph not only humiliated the nobles by taking away their rights to levy tolls and tariffs, but also by ennobling rich bourgeois. He had good precedents. Had not his great-grandfather, Leopold I, ennobled chamberlains, and his father, Francis I, made nobles out of business men? Now Joseph raised bankers to the aristocracy. Banker Fuchs was made a baron; banker Fries, a Protestant, was created a count. The Prague banker, Paul Casati, and the Frankfürt money lender, Jacob Gontard, were both elevated to the baronage. That was bad enough; but when the emperor baronized a Jew, the whole aristocratic and clerical world was in uproar. The Jew was Joseph Michael Arnstein, a banker; Arnstein's wife, the beautiful Fanny Itzig, presided over one of the most cultured salons in Vienna. Joseph liked the lady, found the husband useful, and saw no reason why Arnstein should not have a title.

Rich bourgeois who were not ennobled were shown special favours by the emperor. Once in Prague, Joseph led a bourgeois woman into aristocratic society. The good lady was properly snubbed, but the emperor outsnubbed the snobs: he danced the first and only dance with the untitled woman. The old aristocracy was further enraged when the emperor issued a sumptuary edict restricting enormous wedding and funeral expenses; these splendid celebrations – joyful or funereal – were a waste of money. 'I wish to persuade my people, and especially the nobles,' Joseph said, 'that men ought to eat to live and not live to eat.'

The emperor's economic ideas, however, were not clear. He favoured the capitalist class, but was hostile to capitalist production and technique. He forbade spinning and other machines because, he said, 'it would deprive thousands of their livelihood'. More interesting was his veto of a credit bank. 'The suggestion for a Credit Bank or *Caisse d'Escompte*, or whatever you call it,' he told the Councillors who proposed it, 'is worthless and dangerous, and the whole idea must be given up forever.'

In his protective policy Joseph was more consistent. He systematically pursued the Mercantilist idea of a high tariff. 'Hitherto,' he told a councillor, 'the state has lost annually 24 million gulden in commerce; it has been almost a special intention of the Austrian government to support the manufacturers and merchants of the French, English, and Chinese.' Austrian merchants, he said, were nothing but agents of the English, French, and Dutch. Therefore, in 1784, he decreed a 'general prohibition of foreign merchandise', in order, 'to encourage home production'. A high tariff on foreign goods, he pointed out, would 'force the national consumers to use native products'. Among the prohibited articles were cloth, woollens, linen, glassware, crockery, porcelain, silk, and cotton goods. Violation of the law was punishable with confiscation and heavy fines. Even colonial goods – sugar, coffee, and indigo – were prohibited. The Mercantilist monarch forced the doctors to declare that coffee and chocolate were harmful. But the rigour of the tariff law made smuggling both widespread and profitable.

Certain prohibited articles could be imported for private use, at a payment of 60 per cent of their value. When the tariff decree was issued there were large quantities of foreign goods in storage; the merchants were given a limited time to sell their goods, after which the property was confiscated as contraband

and destroyed. In 1785, 30,000 guldens' worth of cloth, linen, and velvet was publicly burned; the next year 70,000 florins' worth of goods were consigned to the flames.

The tariff made Austria a hermetically sealed land, except for the occasional gusts of air let in by the smugglers. In this respect Austria became almost as bad as Prussia; but Joseph never went as far as Frederick in making the prohibited articles a state monopoly. The tariff caused many hardships and indignities. At the frontiers, women had to undress before the inquisitive customs officers. Joseph allowed no favouritism. When August Gottlieb Meissner, a professor of philosophy, was called from Dresden to the University of Prague, he petitioned that his books, clothes, and personal goods be let in duty free. 'Let him pay the toll like everybody else,' the emperor replied; 'and then the money may be refunded to him.'

The result was a certain amount of industrial activity – even nobles began to build shops and factories on their estates – which the emperor subsidized. Fairs began to flourish in the empire, especially at Lemberg and Prague. But as usual with protective tariffs, there was a great drawback. Native manufacturers, lacking competition, were interested more in sales than in quality. The public had to pay outrageous prices for shoddy goods. The bankers and industrialists, however, grew rich under the special protection of the well-meaning monarch.

Although Austria had no fleet, and was unable to compete with the English and Dutch, the ambitious monarch founded an East India Company at Trieste. A few scattered factories were established along the coasts of China and West Africa; in India, Hyder Ali gave Joseph a stretch of land on the Canora coast as well as permission to colonize the Nikobar islands. But by 1787 the Danube River merchants and the East India Company went bankrupt; the company had to sell its ships at auction.

In 1784, Austria concluded a commercial treaty with Turkey and won protection from the sultan against the Barbary corsairs. A trade agreement was made with the Emperor of Morocco guaranteeing free commerce between the two countries. One month after the signing of the preliminary articles of peace between the American colonies and England, Joseph wrote to Mercy at Paris that in the future 'commerce with America ought to be of the greatest importance'. He had ordered, he said, Prince Starhemberg at Brussels to pay special attention to the subject. 'The Low Countries,' the emperor added,

> appear to me to be the best situated to profit from the advantages which a free America will present. I am curious to know if the new United Provinces will make any overtures to me about having a minister or at least a consul; I would not be at all displeased if they did. Franklin is supposed to have written to Doctor Ingenhouse to come to Vienna; this will perhaps be the best occasion to establish connections with America.

Ambassador Mercy went to see John Adams at Paris. 'While I was writing,' Adams reported to Secretary Livingstone, 'the servant announced the imperial ambassador . . . We fell into conversation of an hour. We ran over a variety of subjects, particularly the Commerce which might take place between the United States and Germany, by way of Trieste and Fiume, and the Austrian Netherlands.' The desire to establish commerce with America led Joseph to attempt to open the Scheldt and his subsequent trouble with Holland.

Russia was another country with whom Joseph established commercial relations. Although as early as 1782 Vorontzov, president of the Commerce Commission, was of the opinion that 'the equality of Russian and Austrian productions would not result in a considerable trade between the two empires', a commercial treaty was ultimately concluded between Joseph and Catharine. The agreement was fundamentally more political than economic. Both countries promised each other special protection on the Danube and the Black Sea; the two empires were preparing for war against Turkey.

The emperor's strictly Mercantilist activities did not interfere with his Physiocratic principles. Imbued with the idea that land was the source of all wealth, he speculated on how to establish a tax system based upon this theory. 'A fair and just tax system,' he wrote in 1785, is undoubtedly the greatest fortune of a country . . . Land is the only source, whence everything springs and whither everything flows back . . . The soil alone should support the state . . . This assumed, it follows of itself that there should be complete equality between noble and peasant, and between crown and church lands, and each should be proportionately classified according to surface, fertility, and location . . . Is it not foolish to believe that the lords had owned the land before there were subjects, and that they apportioned their property among the latter? It would be equally absurd for a monarch to imagine that the land belongs to him, and not he to the land, and that millions of people were created for him, and not he for them, to serve them.

So he proceeded to issue a Tax Law, in 1785, equalizing all taxes, on the basis of the land possessed by the owner, and ordered that all the lands in the empire be surveyed.

Legions of scribes, copyists, and surveyors descended upon the provinces. Joseph thought the job would be completed in six months. It took four years. Vienna was swamped with millions of sheets of paper, at the expense of about 120 million gulden, which the grumbling landowners had to bear. All lands were registered, the communal fields were surveyed, and the products tabulated. There were not enough trained surveyors; the emperor ordered the peasants, under oath, to measure their own fields. The survey and registration were to take place on the fields in the presence of judges, committee men chosen by lot, and the landowners or their proxies. The hasty work resulted in an inaccurate cadastre.

Joseph's aim was a single tax. Food and salt taxes were to be abolished and industry was to be entirely free; only the land was to be taxed. For this purpose it was necessary to have a register of all the real property the fertility, and the income. A titanic task. In Hungary the survey aroused hostility, as the nobility objected to the registration, feeling that the emperor should mind his own business; the army had to be called out.

'There is neither equality nor equity among the hereditary provinces,' Joseph told Gebler who was in charge of the Tax Commission,

nor among individual proprietors; this can no longer continue.

> With this view I give you the necessary orders to introduce a new system of taxation, by which the revenue requisite for the wants of the state may be collected without augmenting the present taxes, and at the same time the industry of the peasant be freed from all impediments.

The tax decree, drawn up on February 10, 1789, is the most important document of the Josephan reign. It literally destroyed feudalism in Austria. 'In the future,' the patent read,

> all payments are to be based solely and entirely on a fundamental tax on land and soil. In this matter it would be against fairness and the best accepted principles to have any consideration for the status and qualities of the owner, and to make any distinctions; hence a thorough equality is to be observed henceforth . . . The aim of the state, to encourage the owners of the soil through a relatively equalized land tax so that they may carry out their duties of citizenship without hindrance . . . can never be achieved without relieving their burdens. Much as we are removed from the idea of encroaching upon the property rights of the manorial lords . . . our duty demands that we set a limit to the imposts paid to the lords by their subjects.

This was perhaps the most revolutionary decree concerning property before the French Revolution.

The edict established definite tax norms. Of a gross income of 100 gulden, the peasant should keep 70. The remaining 30 gulden were to be divided up as follows: 12 gulden and $13\frac{1}{3}$ Kreuzer to go to the government as a real estate tax; the rest, 17.46, to be paid to the manorial lords and the parish as tithes. The law provided that in the future there were to be no *corvées* (forced labour); 'money is to be the sole and unalterable scale for payments of feudal obligations, and neither the manorial lords nor the clergy may demand anything else but cash'.

The tax decree not only tended to destroy feudalism, but also the nobility. The privileged orders, facing ruin, broke into demagogic fury against God's representative on earth. In Hungary the nobles rose in revolt. 'Peasant God,' the embittered aristocrats dubbed the emperor, and that was the greatest insult they could hurl at their enemy. The Tax Law went into effect in November, 1789.

Despite his economic activities, Joseph did not succeed in balancing the budget, mainly on account of his heavy military expenditures. In 1787, the income was 92½ million gulden (not including the revenues from the Netherlands) and the expenditures 85,700,000; but the preparations for the war with Turkey consumed 112,600,000. From 1787 to 1790 military expenses amounted to 252 million. At the time of the emperor's death there was a deficit of 22½ million and a national debt of 370 million gulden.

Joseph's work in the economic sphere was fundamental, nevertheless. Austria's population had increased by almost two million, or 18 per cent, in nine years; horses increased by 9 per cent, and oxen by 5 per cent. The emperor left Austria much improved and with a fairly thriving industry. 'Factories,' a contemporary reported,

> have increased, in the villages wooden hovels are disappearing and many brick houses are taking their place. The roads are improved, and there are schools even in small places . . . Not less noticeable is the appearance of the cities. In many places wooden houses are not tolerated, on account of the danger of fire. In some localities public parks are fostered and also paving and lighting.

The tireless emperor found Austria a feudal country and left her a modern state – with brick houses. His successors reaped the advantage: Francis II was able to fight Napoleon, and Metternich to dominate Europe for four decades.

# CHAPTER 12

# Empire

## I

*Deeply convinced of the integrity of my intentions, I have the strength to hope that after I am dead, posterity, more favourable, more impartial, and consequently more just than my contemporaries, will examine my actions and goal before judging me.*

Joseph to Kaunitz

Since the Middle Ages the German land, torn by strife, disrupted by factions, and burdened with a national inferiority complex (which frequently burst out, and still does, in brutality) was the hunting-ground of military racketeers, political adventurers, and unfathomable philosophers. In such a land, where food was heavy, beer intoxicating, and the people both meek and industrious, everyone could help himself. And everyone did – especially the French and the Habsburgs.

Joseph would have liked to have been a real Emperor of Germany, but even he was not foolhardy enough to try to revive the ancient power of the Caesars. Failing that, he took what advantage he could from his title. His brother Maximilian was elected Archbishop of Cologne. Vienna tried to win any vacant episcopal see for the Habsburgs or their friends, often with success.

Germany was a network of privileges and prerogatives; the barbed wire fences of ecclesiastical and secular laws made entanglement unavoidable at every step. When, in 1783, Joseph deprived the Roman nunciature in Vienna of its rights, the pope sent a nuncio to Munich. The archbishoprics of Mainz, Cologne, Trier, and Salzburg considered the new nunciature an encroachment upon their own privileges, and took the field against the pope.

Again the ghost of Febronius rose to plague the pope. When the book *De statu ecclesiae* came out in 1763, the Prince-Bishop of Speyer wrote to Count Pergen in Vienna that 'the author deserves to have his head laid at his feet because he asserts many principia haeretica'. But in 1786, the Rhenish and the Salzburg archbishops, who were encouraged by Joseph's example, and who wished to free themselves from Roman domination, discovered that Febronius's work was useful. They met at Ems and drew up a virtual declaration of independence from the papacy. 'The pope is and remains,' according to the *Ems Punkuation*,

> the highest authority in the Church . . . but the privileges, which do not spring from the first Christian centuries, but are based on the false Isadoran Decretals and are disadvantageous to the bishops . . . can no longer be considered valid; they belong among the usurpations of the Roman curia, and the bishops are entitled, since peaceful protests are of no avail, themselves to maintain their lawful rights under the protection of the Roman-German emperor. There should no longer be any appeals to Rome . . . The orders should take no directions from foreign superiors, nor attend general councils outside of Germany. No contributions [Peter's Pence] should be sent to Rome. Every bishop may legislate, dispense, and establish foundations in his diocese. Vacant benefices should not be filled by Rome, but by a regular election of native candidates. The Pallium fees and similar contribution should be abolished by a church council held in Germany. A German national council should regulate these and other matters, and institute an improvement in church discipline.

Had the bishops supported this bold programme, a national church, similar to the Gallican, would have been established in Germany. Joseph was not unwilling. 'The four archbishops of Germany,' he wrote to Leopold, 'have sent me their complaints and projects for the reformation of the abuses . . . I replied and urged them to combine with their suffragan bishops, in order to shake off the yoke by common accord.' Leopold's answer was that this was the time 'forever to shake off the despotic yoke of the Roman curia in German'. But Joseph was sceptical. He thought, he informed his brother, the moment opportune for the great coup to liberate the German church from the chains of the Roman curia; but whether they will do it, despite my authorization and encouragement, I doubt. The majority of these lords know nothing about their business; they are blindly guided by their subordinates whose interests and views are different from theirs. A national council will never finish, and it would certainly occupy itself with things other than ecclesiastical reforms.

He was right. Nothing came of the whole affair, for the bishops were afraid to put themselves at the disposal of the archbishops; they preferred the distant overlordship of Rome to the immediate sovereignty of German princes.

In one instance, where Joseph did made a sincere effort at reform, he failed. There were two courts in the German Empire: the *Reichskammergericht* at Wetzlar, whose judges were appointed by the imperial estates, and the *Reichshofrat* at Vienna, controlled by the emperor. Both courts were notorious for their corruption and venality, particularly the one at Wetzlar, where Goethe once practiced. The *Reichskammergericht* dragged cases for centuries. One case lasted from 1549 to 1734; another, between Brandenburg and Nuremberg, started in 1526 and was not ended in Joseph's time. In 1784 Prince Salm-Salm wrote to Cobenzl, thanking him for bringing a 'two-hundred-year old case' to a conclusion. By the time the German Empire was dissoved (1806) there were 60,000 unfinished cases.

When Joseph attempted to galvanize the courts the princelings emitted a long cry of protest, accusing the emperor of autocracy and encroachment upon their rights. Joseph, the titular emperor, could do nothing. The commission which he appointed to speed up cases, dabbled for nine years, with a result that instead of seventeen there were now twenty-five judges. In his own court at Vienna, the emperor ordered that abuses cease and corrupt judges be dismissed; the magistrates adhered to the rigid forms of the law and leisurely continued taking bribes.

Joseph, knowing that this imperial label was mockery, played with the thought of relinquishing the ancient title of Holy Roman Emperor and calling himself Emperor of Austria

– as did Francis II in 1806, under pressure from Napoleon. Up to 1786 Austrian ships bore the imperial German flag. In the February of that year the emperor ordered that his vessels henceforth fly the Austrian flag – white and red, topped by the Hungarian crown. He went no further, for he was soon engulfed in disaster.

Joseph was a self-conscious Teuton. Unlike his Prussian rival, Joseph spoke, wrote, and thought in German. He antagonized Slavs and Magyars by his insistent attempts at Germanizing them. Where Frederick despised and loathed things German, especially the native language and literature, Joseph strove to establish a German theatre and encouraged the study of the German tongue. 'Gladly,' Joseph replied to an appeal of Coadjutor Dalberg of Mainz,

> do I accept your offer to submit to me your views concerning the means of achieving the general welfare for Germany, which I readily call our common fatherland, because I love it and am proud to be a German. Like you, I have often occupied myself with the thought of how to make Germany happy; I agree with you entirely that the only means to do so is a close union between the emperor and the German body politic. But to get there – that is the philosopher's stone. It is the more difficult to find, as it requires the uniting of various interests . . . which leave Germany in confusion to their own advantage . . . In every society, whatever its nature, there must be a common aim, but the word patriotism, which is so commonly used, must have exclusively a real significance; whereas the interest of the moment, the vanity if individuals, and political intrigues confuse . . . and subject everything. If only our German patriots would think patriotically; of they had neither Gallomania nor Anglomania, neither Prussomania nor Austromania, but a point of view peculiarly their own, and borrowed from no one; if only they could see their own interests! But they are nothing but the echo of a few miserable pedants and intriguers.

## II

While Joseph was helpless in Germany he had authority in his hereditary dominions, Hungary, Bohemia, Galicia, and Belgium. Hungary had an ancient constitution and her nobility iron-bound privileges. The nobles were exempt from taxation; 'peasants and strangers alone are obliged to contribute to the public expenses' (Art. 18). The feudality could be judged only in a court of peers or by a 'legitimately crowned king, according to Hungarian Laws'. The laws were made by the Diet, composed of prelates, barons, magnates, nobles, and free cities. A statute of 1687 provided that before his coronation the king – of the Habsburg house – should confirm all 'customs, privileges, and prerogatives' of the Hungarians.

Of the 5 million Hungarians, 40,000 were nobles, but only about 4,000 were magnates who owned and ruled the land; the rest of the inhabitants were mainly serfs. The land drooped under the burden of the worst medieval-feudal abuses and was handicapped by obsolete laws and archaic institutions, designed to keep the privileged classes firmly in the saddle. Maria Theresa feared the belligerent feudality and did nothing in the way of reforms. In the absence of a strong bourgeoisie, and with what little instruction there was monopolized by the clergy, Hungary little intellectual life.

The life of the serfs was pitiful. On one of his trips to Hungary Joseph found on a field eight dead children who had perished of hunger; near by lay twelve more at the point of death. The emperor sent the starving children to Vienna, ordering that they be fed and educated. On the same trip Joseph, filled with pity and indignation, noticed an old man working in a chain-gang in the mines.

'Why do you work here?' the disguised emperor asked.

'I found a dead hare,' the prisoner said laconically, 'and took it home with me. I was seen, and so here I am.'

'Are you charged with nothing else?'

'Nothing, sir.'

'Who is your chief? I want to speak to him in your favour.'

'Oh, no,' the old man exclaimed; 'please don't. A traveller, even as humane as you, once had the same intention, and . . .'

'Well?'

'Sir, after he left I was given fifty lashes.'

Joseph verified the facts, freed the old man, and had the

overseer horsewhipped. It was well meant, but petty; not the superintendent, but the system was to blame. And Joseph knew it.

From the beginning of his reign the emperor antagonized the Magyar nobility. He refused to be crowned, largely because of his hatred for the feudality. It was a fine gesture, but a costly one. The nobility retaliated by refusing to recognize Joseph as their king. In the Catholic churches prayers were offered, not for the king – such did not exist – but for the emperor. Some Magyar nobles, it must be admitted, liked and sympathized with the monarch. 'Joseph,' Baron Orczy said publicly, 'is such a great sovereign that both civilized and primitive people admire him; he overshadows the old Caesars; happy is he who lives under him.'

Regardless of consequences, Joseph applied his reforms to Hungary. As in the other Austrian dominions, Lutherans, Calvinists, and Greek Orthodox were allowed to worship freely and to build churches, though without steeple or bells. Non-Catholics were granted the right to hold office and to possess property. Although the Catholic clergy refused to marry mixed couples unless they agreed that their children be brought up in the true faith, the emperor ordered that offspring of such unions should follow their father's religion if they be male, and their mother's if they be female. The Hungarian counties (*Comitati*) sharply opposed these acts of toleration as contrary to the Hungarian constitution.

Many Catholics, who had once been forcibly converted, deserted the faith and became Protestants. In 1783 Hungary had only 272 Protestant communities; in 1784 there were 758. The Council of State wished to stop this drift, but Joseph forbade any coercion, 'because', he said, 'the free exercise of religion is designed to bring peace to the soul'.

Despite strong protests of the Hungarians, the emperor proceeded to suppress 140 monasteries, to reduce the number of canons and prebendaries in the cathedrals, and to found new parishes in the rural districts. He established a system of free primary education, put the University of Pest under government supervision, and established seminaries at Buda, Erlau, Agram, Pressburg, and Pest. The magistrates of Pest were so pleased that they offered to put up a monument to the emperor. 'When I shall have removed all ecclesiastical and civil abuses,' Joseph replied;

> when I shall have awakened the inhabitants to activity and industry; when I shall have caused commerce to flourish, and shall have provided the country from one end to the other with roads and navigable canals, as I hope will be the case; if the nation will then erect a monument to me, I may then, perhaps have deserved it, and will acknowledge the honour with gratitude.

Hitherto only the more pious had protested. But when Joseph began to centralize and Germanize the country he created a storm. In April, 1784, the emperor had the crown of St Stephen – sacred to Hungarians as a national symbol – brought from Buda to Vienna, and thereby excited national indignation. To aggravate matters Joseph ordered that German and not Latin was to be the official tongue of Hungary, 'because Latin has been banished by all enlightened nations as a dead tongue'. Those unable to speak German were barred from office. The emperor insisted that he did not wish to Germanize Hungary, but merely to facilitate the carrying on of administrative affairs. The Magyars feared that the decree meant that only Germans would be appointed to office; the Comitati protested vehemently.

The Hungarians refused to accept the German language, which threatened their national spirit. The Germans, they said, formed only a fraction of the population, and there was no reason why Magyars, Wallachians, and Transylvanians should accommodate themselves to a Teutonic tongue. One deputy pointed out that of the 50,000 taxable persons in Hungary only 100 understood German. Joseph, however, insisted that German was 'the universal language of my empire', and ordered the Magyars to learn it. 'I am Emperor of the German Empire,' he told a Hungarian magnate; '. . . the other states . . . are provinces, which, together with the whole state, form one body, of which I am the head.'

In the fall of 1784 a peasant rebellion broke out among the Wallachians in Transylvania. The Wallachians, who claimed to be descendants of the Romans, were in a more depressed condition than the three other racial groups: Szeklers, Hungarians, and Saxons. An ex-soldier named Hora led the insurrection. He had had an audience with Joseph to whom he complained against the president of the local tribunal. When Hora returned from Vienna a local judge had him horsewhipped.

The injured soldier, a man of intelligence and social conscience, began to rouse the peasants. In the presence of several thousand of his countrymen Hora read an imposing looking document (which later proved to be a simple legal paper), purporting to be an order from the emperor to free the serfs. An attempt was made to arrest him but the peasants rescued him.

The Wallachians began to plunder and burn manorial property. Castles were put to the flames all along the border up to the Banat. Within a week 120 nobles were killed. The regular army repulsed the peasants from one city and executed thirty-four of their number on the spot. But the revolt could not be quenched; the authorities became panicky and waited for orders from Vienna.

A true reformer, Joseph hated revolution. 'We have a very disagreeable event,' he informed Leopold; 'Wallachian peasants, instigated by a rascal who carries an order and a patent pretending to come from me, have gathered and are burning the houses of the Hungarian seigniors, and also killing.' To 'suppress this frenzy', Joseph ordered the army to advance against the Wallachians, but cautioned the troops to act with discretion. A prize of 300 ducats was put on Hora's head and an offer of pardon was issued for the rebels.

The peasants continued their revolt, hurling nobles out of their castles, impaling them on pitchforks and spears, mutilating their bodies and burning their houses. In the revolutionary conflagration religious fanaticism was aroused; the non-united Greek orthodox slaughtered Catholics and Protestants.

The infuriated nobles retaliated in kind. They felt wrathful towards the emperor, whom they accused of fostering revolution. Despite Joseph's order that no one should be executed before the arrival of the emissaries from Vienna, the magnates, wherever they caught a rebel, promptly impaled, beheaded, hanged, or broke him on the wheel.

Hora withdrew into the mountains of Hunyad and issued a proclamation. There were to be no more nobles, the revolutionary leader announced; everyone should be eligible for the imperial service. The nobility was to make contributions to the public treasury like the common people; and most important of all, the nobles' lands were to be distributed among the peasants.

Hora dreamt of uniting the Wallachians in Hungary with those in Wallachia and founding a Dacian kingdom; for a while, in fact, he called himself *Rex Daciae*. But his royal dreams were cut short. After several skirmishes, the army began to surround the stronghold of the Wallachians. Hora generously advised his followers to take advantage of the general pardon and desert him. It was too late. He and Klotska, his lieutenant, were betrayed by some of their men, and, in Joseph's words, 'taken by surprise in the woods'.

The prisoners were taken to Carlsburg, and in the presence of 2,000 captives, Hora was broken on the wheel and his body torn in four. Before his own brutal execution took place he was compelled to witness the same fate inflicted on his colleague Klotska. Of the 2,000 prisoners, 150 were impaled. Altogether the insurrection resulted in the destruction of 62 villages, 132 manors, and cost 4,000 human lives. 'In Transylvania,' Joseph announced, 'everything is passed and finished.'

Portraits of those who were executed still hang in the Wallachian peasants' cottages.

The peasants uprising gave the Magyar nobles an excuse to oppose the emperor's reforms. Here was proof that Joseph's ideas tended to inflame the 'canaille'. The Hungarian nobles suspected their monarch of sympathizing – which he did not – with the Wallachians, and resisted his conscription measures;

the lords were not going to supply troops to a sovereign who did not protect their property. 'Around the Hungarian gentlemen,' Joseph wrote to Leopold, 'I again have to twist the rope; they oppose conscription with unreason and impertinence. It is possible that I shall be obliged to deliver them an exemplary blow which will finish their arrogance.' He dismissed a Hungarian ringleader, Count Nicolas Forgàch, from office and sent a battalion of infantry to enforce the conscription law.

That was only the beginning of the magnates' opposition. Vienna's interference with Hungarian laws was bad enough, but when the emperor began to threaten their economic bases they revolted. The belligerent Magyar feudality contributed relatively little to the Viennese treasury, a condition intolerable to the emperor. 'The prerogatives and liberties of an aristocracy or commonwealth,' Joseph told a prominent Hungarian noble, 'consist in all lands and republics the world over, not in their *not* contributing to the public burdens, but, on the contrary, in a greater outlay, as is the case in England and Holland.'

No sooner had the Hora uprising been suppressed than Joseph issued a decree abolishing serfdom in Hungary. 'Since our accession,' the proclamation read, 'it has been our tireless care to foster and establish permanently the happiness of our people without regard to status, nationality, or religion.' He realized, he said, that the best way 'to improve agriculture and encourage zeal', was to grant personal freedom – 'which belongs to all men including serfs by nature and by right' – and assure the right to hold property. The law declared that serfdom 'which burdened the serf with eternal obligations and tied him to the soil', was 'definitely abolished' – 'We order and command that in future all subjects [serfs], without regard to their religion or nationality, be free in their persons, and be everywhere regarded and considered such'. The law gave the freedmen the right to marry at will, to study, to learn the arts and crafts, and to practice them everywhere. Peasants were given absolute right to dispose of their property as they pleased and, like their fellows in the rest of the empire, could seek the protection of the district officials.

It was all very well on paper. But shortly after, the Magyar nobles rose in revolt against the emperor. The law could not be enforced; the Josephan decree did not go into effect until 1836. To some extent, the same conditions were true also in the other provinces; feudalism was not effectually abolished in Austria until the revolution of 1848.

Simultaneously with the serf law the Hungarian administration was transformed. The local courts were changed into royal courts and the kingdom was divided into ten administrative circles, at the head of each of which was a royal commissioner; the Comitati (counties) which had hitherto been independent administrations were subordinated to these circles. This aroused the bitterest kind of hostility, for the privileged classes considered the county government the bulwark of their liberties.

But the greatest blow to the entrenched interests was the abolition of the immunity of the nobles and clergy from taxation. When the surveyors went down to Hungary to measure and register the lands in preparation for the new tax law, opposition became fierce and there was talk of revolution. The emperor, however, had too many troops in Hungary; around Pest alone there was an army of 80,000 men. The magnates bided their time.

The new system of taxation, Joseph told a Hungarian noble, 'prevents the nobility from making an arbitrary increase for their own profit . . . The peasant, who is obliged to bear the greatest burdens . . . has also an especial claim on the protection of his sovereign; and this, Sir, in your country is viewed with dissatisfaction'. Joseph mistook silence for consent. 'My affairs in Hungary,' he informed Leopold, 'progress laboriously, but always smilingly; I permit grumbling, but I arrive at my goal a little slowly though always surely.' He was mistaken.

### III

In Galicia, newly acquired from Poland, Joseph was more successful. Unlike Hungary or Bohemia, Galicia had no cultural tradition. The Polish peasants were slaves and their masters, the nobles, had neither much honour nor humanity. The potentially rich land was sunk in mud.

What the province needed most was an industrious peasantry. Under Maria Theresa steps had been taken to attract merchants and artisans from Germany, as the only native tradesmen were Jews; Vienna wished to encourage the immigration of Germans, even Protestants. Joseph wanted to attract skilled workers and subsidize them; he urged that the land be settled with German farmers. But Maria Theresa's religious intolerance prevented much activity in this direction.

In 1781 the emperor issued a Patent of 'Liberties and Immigration' for Galicia. The province was granted religious toleration and other liberties, 'in order to encourage commerce, industry, and the produce of the soil, to export them abroad, and to bring money into circulation'. Merchants, artists, and artisans were given civic rights and freed from military service. Skilled immigrants were offered timber for buildings, land for gardens, fifty florins for the purchase of tools and materials, and six years exemption from taxation. Peasants settling on crown lands were granted free houses, stables, agricultural implements, ten years exemption from taxation, and six years dispensation from servile duties.

One year later the economic director of the city of Sandomir, acting on his own initiative, sent an agent to southern Germany to round up 300 families. The agent carried with him a glowing description of the low price of Galician land and the cheapness of foodstuffs. In the new 'Eldorado', the emissary announced, one could buy a pound of beef for about two Kreuzer, an ox for from twelve to fifteen florins, a cow for six or seven florins, a pig for two or three florins, a chicken for six Kreuzer, a goose for twelve, and a duck for eight. To the poverty-stricken south Germans this sounded like the 'Promised Land'.

The idea of bidding for immigrants struck Joseph as good. He published an appeal to the effect that 'in our kingdoms of Hungary, Galicia, and Lodomeria we possess much unsettled, vacant, and deserted land, which we are minded to colonize with Germans, especially from the upper Rhine'. About

38,000 responded and settled in Galicia, and 7,600 made their homes in south Hungary, at an expense to the emperor of four million florins. In south Germany many villages became depopulated.

The immigrants sailed down the Danube, generally from Ulm. The journey was difficult and expensive for the poor people, and many became discouraged when they reached Vienna. One family of four spent 148 florins to reach Lemberg. But the eagerness to find a decent home spurred on thousands. A Swabian peasant was asked by a Viennese how he could undertake so long a journey into a foreign land. 'Ei,' drawled the peasant in his inimitable dialect, 'überall wo's Herr Göttle huset, do kan no allwil a Schwäble sein Plätzle haben' (A little Swabian swallow can find its nest wherever the dear little lord God is).

The 'little lord God' was not particularly merciful to the immigrants. The government was careless in preparations; houses and implements were not ready. The difficult journey, the poor food, the bad climate, all had a deleterious effect on the colonists; many fell ill, and there was no doctor to tend them. When more immigrants came it was found there was not enough fiscal land; many were compelled to return to Germany.

Joseph's aim was to establish small villages to serve as models for the native peasantry. He did his best to send down cattle and implements, and urged the governor to hasten in the erection of buildings. From March, 1786, to February, 1787, 531,000 pecks of grain were shipped to Lemberg. The officials were ordered to educate the peasants in farming and cattle raising, to teach them how to take advantage of the fallows, meadows, and grazing land, how to treat sick cattle.

Commercially the emperor was no less active. Rich in natural resources, especially salt, and cut through by the Vistula and San Rivers, Galicia was ideally located as a trading carrier, particularly in relation to Danzig. It was likewise contiguous to Hungary and Silesia, with their mines and agricultural products. Joseph tried to acquire free trade privileges for Galicia from Poland, and asked Catharine to bring pressure to bear on the Warsaw government. The plan almost succeeded, but Frederick of Prussia was too alert; he meant to keep Poland weak and to control her commerce himself. Despite Frederick's opposition, however, the Vistula between Poland and Galicia was made free; but this did not prevent the King of Prussia from cutting off Galicia from the Baltic. The anti-Austrian policy of Prussia, particularly a tariff war in 1785–90, was a blow to Galician cattle-raising and linen industry. Galician products had to be shipped through Lithuania, through Trieste, and through the Black Sea.

At the end of Joseph's reign Galicia had started on the road to civilization. Towns grew, factories were erected, roads were built, and the population increased. In 1786 the Lemberg Fair, which had been practically dead, had over a thousand visitors.

The beneficiaries of Joseph's activities were undoubtedly the common people, the peasants. About 1785 a Czech peasant wrote a poem to the 'great and illustrious father of our dear Country'.

Rejoice with me you nations and listen to the many truths and thanksgiving, that I am going to tell you, in praise of the wisdom from which sprang blessing and joy in our country, and which has done away with many sufferings.

When our great monarch, Joseph the Second, succeeded to the throne as the ruler of our country, he reigned wisely guided by wisdom, love and righteousness, all over the world; but especially over his dear subjects.

As an eagle tries to soar towards the sky, so his heart longed for righteousness and wished to do away with many wrongs, and this hope strengthened his heart.

He hoisted the flag of the Imperial Eagle, visited all the departments of state in person, and degraded many officials whom he found unworthy of their office.

His zeal for justice was not to be deceived, his sharp eye saw in the darkness, he made many changes among the evil-livers and well rewarded the righteous.

He walked among his subjects with a loving heart, and enchanted all of them with his kindness. People laid before him the wishes and desires of their hearts, and all found support in his mighty spirit of goodwill.

Many a poor tradesman could have found his fortune had he sought it in another district, but could not leave as he must redeem his bondage from his lord. How grateful then were they to their sovereign, when they were permitted to go freely wherever they could find their living.

This good-hearted monarch considered all the taxes, for he wished to tax all equally, and found out him who tried to conceal his riches or to speak falsely about his estates, and also him who oppressed his fellow-men.

Oh, who would not submit to such good teaching, the aim of which was to survey the land. God was pleased with our sovereign's penetrating eye, with his judgment, his zeal for learning and his enlightenment.

The numerous schools which he built show with what attention this loving father sought to awake his peoples to better morality. Mindful was he that teaching should progress, especially that little children should learn.

In old times people spent long in learning, yet when they grew up knew not why they came into the world. And, even if they learned to read, understood not what they read, and remained in darkness as before.

Take my thanks, O mighty sovereign, for thou lovest the simplicity of my speech more than fine art. I invoke the blessing of our Lord and His protection for our dear Emperor – Joseph the Second!

# IV

It was in Belgium that Joseph met his first great defeat. That country had a charter of liberties, known as the *Joyeuse Entrée*, which dated back to the thirteenth century; it fixed the constitution, the tribunals, the magistracies, and the privileges of the citizens – even amusements were not omitted from the document. An unusual clause provided that in case the sovereign infringed upon a single article in the *Joyeuse Entrée*, his Flemish subjects had the right to refuse him all service and obedience until he redressed the wrong.

The privileges were reaffirmed by formal treaty before the Habsburgs took possession of the country in 1715. According to that agreement, the Catholic religion was to be preserved; the decisions of the Council of Trent were to be observed;

> the bishop and his successors in dignity, the bishopric, the diocese, the church and cathedral chapter, the abbots, the abbeys, the priories and all their chapters, cloisters, churches, hospitals, convents (*béguinages*), the chamber, the schools for the poor and other seminaries, foundations, pious and communal establishments for both sexes, likewise all ecclesiastics both regular and secular, in general and in particular, present and future, will be maintained in all their pre-eminences, jurisdictions, immunities, privileges, benefices, exemptions, tithes, dignities, houses, movable and immovable goods.

Here were iron-bound medieval privileges, hoary with age, bred in a bone of burgher and noble. In Belgium Joseph was nothing but a constitutional monarch.

The constitutions of the seven provinces making up the Austrian Netherlands – Brabant, Luxemburg, Limburg, Flanders, Hainault, Namur, and Gelders – varied in form, but represented the privileges of the upper classes. At the head of each provincial administration was a corporation composed of powerful nobles, wealthy burghers, and great prelates.

Brabant was the most important province. Here was Brussels, the capital, and also the first church of the land; and here at Louvain the most important university was to be found. The Council of Brabant, like the *Parlement* of Paris, had the right of confirming the monarch's edicts. In the more commercial Flanders the nobility was disfranchised; and in Gelders the clergy had no political representation. Generally, however, the clergy were politically, morally, and economically all-powerful. The ecclesiastical hierarchy was composed of one archbishop and seven bishops ruling over more than one hundred rich abbeys and a mass of monasteries; their landed property at Brabant was estimated at 300 million gulden.

'Particularism' reigned in each city and in each province, although even under Maria Theresa attempts were made to break down the exclusiveness. The central government threatened the old constitutional traditions by means of the Councils

P

of Justice and the fiscal bureaux. The Theresan administration introduced an 'official aristocracy' which began to encroach upon the privileges of the haughty nobility.

The nobles were supreme in the rural districts, but in the large cities the lesser bourgeoisie, including the artisans, formed a strong Third Estate. The workingmen, were of course, excluded from the urban corporate organizations which were dominated by the guilds. The great mass of the people, workers and peasants were entirely without political influence; they were 'outside the social organism'.

In 1750 Charles of Lorraine, Maria Theresa's brother-in-law, was appointed Governor of the Netherlands. Like his brother Francis, Joseph's father, Charles was commercially minded and did something to foster Belgian industry. Under him the canal from Bruges to Ghent was completed. A highway was built from Limburg, through Liège, to Aachen. Weaving and cloth manufacturing were revived in Limburg, Tournai, Ghent, and Courtrai. Thousands of workers were employed in the Antwerp silk and lace industries. Pottery, glass, and porcelain were produced in Hainault and Namur. In the Charleroi area, where steam pumps had been used in 1730, coal mining began on a larger scale.

Charles of Lorraine was liked by the upper classes. He was a kindly, easy going, simple mannered gentleman and a patron of the arts. Maria Theresa had advised him not to exert himself or disturb others. She had told him to content himself with being 'the first cock in the village and let things go as they go'. He was, however, too intelligent a man entirely to obey this dictum, and did what he could under the circumstances, which was hardly enough. The feudality and the ecclesiastical hierarchy remained undisturbed. Charles' activities were not sufficient to create a new bourgeoisie. Medieval conditions prevailed throughout the provinces. The army was neglected. Taxation and the administration of justice were based upon privileges. Sale of offices was the universal custom, and there was no check on the social abuses that such a system engendered.

The stimulus which Joseph gave to reforms in Austria under

the co-regency also had their repercussions in Belgium. The penal code was modified; the use of torture by the courts martial was abolished (in 1784 Joseph did away with torture altogether); houses of correction were established. The co-regent likewise made an attempt to secularize education. After the suppression of the Jesuits, the administration took over their colleges and organized secondary schools on the Austrian model. As early as 1755 the decayed University of Louvain was brought under government control, new chairs were founded, and a university press was established. In 1769 the Imperial and Royal Academy, an official literary society, was founded for the purpose of publishing learned works.

Before she died Maria Theresa, knowing Joseph's aversion for his family, made him promise to appoint his sister Marie Christine and her husband, Duke Albert of Saxe-Teschen, Governors of Belgium. 'Madame,' the emperor coolly wrote to Marie Christine in January, 1781:

> it is with the utmost pleasure I discharge the obligation, which a promise to Her Majesty, the late empress, imposed upon me, by my offering Your Highness and your beloved consort the dignity of Governor of the Austrian Netherlands . . . The Netherlands have advantages over many other countries in Europe: They have rich citizens, a high noblesse, and a flourishing commerce . . . To render the cares of your government easy, I have associated with you Prince Starhemberg, who fully possesses the qualifications of a minister, and who will assist Your Highness in every affair.

Joseph knew nothing about the character of the Flemings or the Walloons. He seemed to have had only a dim idea of their constitutions and privileges; what he knew of these he considered merely, as he said, 'antediluvian rubbish'. Hence he blithely began to apply his reforming edicts to those ardently Catholic and reactionary provinces. His Patent of Toleration (November 1, 1781) aroused the fiery wrath of the clerics. Four weeks later he shocked the clergy by making the monasteries independent of the pope; seven days afterwards the churchmen were stunned to hear that they could no longer appeal to Rome in questions of marriage dispensations. Hardly had the clergy recovered from these rapid-fire reforms, when the emperor ordered the suppression of certain monasteries, as in Austria, and the application of their revenues for useful purposes. Shades of the *Joyeuse Entrée*!

Neither the governors of the Netherlands nor Prince Starhemberg were consulted by the emperor. Starhemberg retired and was replaced by Count Lüdwig Belgiojoso, former ambassador to London. Belgiojoso was an able person, who, in the words of a contemporary, 'though he loved pleasure, could devote himself to business'. But he had as little knowledge of Belgium as his sovereign. His cabinet was composed of hostile conservatives, the chief of whom, Secretary of State Crumpipen, Belgiojoso trusted, not knowing that the Belgian was intriguing against him.

The opposition, as was to be expected, came from the powerful prelates, led by the papal nuncio, Zondardari. Other opponents were the Primate of Belgium, the Archbishop of Malines, and the Bishop of Antwerp. Joseph expected the hostility of the high ecclesiastics, and since the people as a whole seemed to be passive he was determined to pursue his reforms to the end.

'It is necessary now,' the emperor told Marie Christine, 'to go to the provinces which you rule, where so much bigotry reigns, where studies and schools are in such an evil state and the clergy itself is so ignorant.' And he began to transform the external religious life. The *Kermesse* (local festival) was ordered to be celebrated on the same day everywhere; votive pictures and processions were forbidden; altar usage was changed. A general seminary at Louvain was established for all Belgium; control of instruction was taken away from the bishops, because, Joseph wrote, 'the children of Levi should no longer have a monopoly on the human mind'.

The pious Seminarists made a little revolution of their own. They issued a manifesto, demanding that the government put the seminary under the bishop, that they be granted separate living quarters, not too early breakfast, the right to receive guests and to go out visiting, 'better beer, tobacco and bread, and an orthodox dogma and discipline'. Surprisingly enough,

Belgiojoso took this nonsense seriously and instead of sending the pupils back to school, he made martyrs of them by ordering out three battalions of infantry and one regiment of dragoons with six cannon against the 300 youngsters. This stupid action caused extraordinary excitement in the land; it aroused the clergy and many laymen. The government exiled the clerical leaders.

Ignoring the agitated state of the land the government proceeded to transform the administrative life of the Netherlands. The provincial Councils of State were abolished, the Privy Councils were done away with, and the Secretariats of State ceased to exist; they were replaced by a superior body under the name of 'Council of the General Administration of the Netherlands', of which the chief minister was to be a plenipotentiary appointed by Vienna. Instead of the provincial Estates, five deputies for each province were to be elected and confirmed by the government. As in Hungary, the old provincial boundaries were annulled and replaced by nine regions, each administered by an intendant. The old corporations were deprived of their judicial privileges and a new judicial system was created. There were to be sixty-four tribunals of the first instance, two councils of appeal, and a supreme council of revision. All special jurisdictions – territorial, feudal, and ecclesiastical – were destroyed.

These reforms were admirable in themselves; they gave the Austrian Netherlands an order and unity which had hitherto not existed; they abolished feudal and special privileges. Years later, when Belgium was finally an independent state, the Josephan institutions were taken as the bases for the new administration. But the Belgians, used to self-government even though corrupt and venal, resented having reforms imposed upon them by force.

The Estates promptly protested. 'The *Joyeuse Entrée* have sometimes received changes and modifications,' Brabant declared in January, 1787, 'but in such cases they took place with the wish and consent of the Estates. If then it is . . . the determination of His Sacred Majesty to introduce . . . some changes incompatible with the *Joyeuse Entrée* . . . the remonstrants . . . dare supplicate respectfully . . . that the changes do not take place without the formal consent of the three Estates of the province.'

Joseph ignored the mild protests; he would brook neither opposition nor delay. 'I hope,' he wrote to Marie Christine, 'that the Council, when it begins to function, will be well appointed and led, will facilitate all other arrangements; the intendants in the provinces are of great importance, likewise the reforms in justice and in studies. One sees what ignorance and fanaticism can do to the human spirit.'

The administrative measures went into effect in the spring of 1787. The immediate effect was deflationary. Hundreds of people lost their positions, among them aristocratic dignitaries, bourgeois councillors, clerical office holders, lawyers, and procurators. All classes had some grievances; the country folk feared compulsory conscription; burghers hated the new penal code, for they did not relish the idea of equality before the law which gave the dis-franchised workers equal rights. Agitation, instigated by the clergy, began all over the land. Joseph, not realizing the extent of the discontent, told the minister: 'Either receive the protests, or seize by the head the first one who opposes the highest will.' The emperor invited the troublemaking Bishop of Malines to Vienna and told him cordially:

> My dear bishop, from your conduct I see that you have no conception of the present system of the theologians and the general seminaries. Hence I summoned you here to teach you better. I have called the Councillors and Ecclesiastical Commissioners . . . to show you our arrangements and to instruct you; have them show you everything and explain to you what appears doubtful. Then return to the Netherlands and preach the Gospel there.

In a land where class lines were sharply drawn and where the upper strata existed on ancient prerogatives, egalitarian reforms were bound to cause trouble. At every step the new administration violated some dear privilege. The outbreak occurred when the government arrested a merchant who had defrauded the state treasury, and sent him to Vienna in irons. The corporations of Brussels complained that this was a breach of the *Joyeuse Entrée*. Passions flared up. Belgiojoso's windows were smashed and there were riots in the streets. The Estates of Brabant refused to vote taxes until the government redressed the grievances.

The new executive council decided not to carry out the reforms and to withdraw all innovations which violated the *Joyeuse Entrée*. The Estates insisted that the whole judicial system was unconstitutional and should be abolished. Joseph was then away in the Crimea, and Marie Christine, who was not in sympathy with her brother's radical ideas, not knowing what to do, allowed herself to be intimidated. On May 31, 1787, the government promised the abolition of all hated reforms. There was jubilation in Brussels. The lawyer, Henry van der Noot, formed a corps of volunteers, ostensibly to maintain order, and with national cockades pinned to their caps, the patriots marched through the streets shouting '*Vive l'empereur! Vive la Joyeuse Entrée!*'. There was certainly a contradiction between the two slogans.

# CHAPTER 13

# Diplomacy

## I

*The Emperor seems to prefer the glory of terror to that of justice.*                    Thomas Jefferson on Joseph

In contrast to his internal reforms, Joseph's foreign policy was violent and crude, worthy of a medieval robber baron, and in this he did not differ from his contemporaries Frederick and Catharine, except that they were successful. His foreign policy not only brought his empire to the verge of ruin and himself to an early death, but destroyed his reputation in the eyes of posterity which forgives violence only when it terminates in success. *Die Weltgeschichte ist das Weltgericht!*

The long duel between Spain and the Low Countries ended in 1648 when the northern part, the Dutch republic, was officially declared independent; the ten southern provinces – now known as Belgium – remained in Spanish hands. It was a great victory for the opulent Dutch, for not only did a pan-European congress ratify their independence, but the Treaty of Münster (1648) closed the Scheldt River to the southern Catholic provinces, effectively cutting Belgium off from the sea. The shrewd Dutch burghers acquired a stranglehold on Scheldt-borne commerce and prevented foreign ships from sailing down south into Belgium.

After protracted dynastic and imperialistic wars which convulsed Europe for more than a generation the powers decided that it was time to rest. A settlement was reached at Utrecht in 1713 and Emperor Charles VI, Joseph's grandfather, was given, among other things, the Spanish Netherlands, henceforth known as the 'Austrian Netherlands'. Two years later Charles made an agreement with England and Holland – the

Barrier Treaty – permitting the Dutch to occupy certain barrier fortresses and recognizing the closing of the Scheldt.

Charles VI and Maria Theresa had both lived up to the Barrier Treaty; they had enough trouble on their hands elsewhere, and were too cautious to upset the *status quo* which might have brought them into conflict with the western powers.

Joseph wished to open the Scheldt because it would help Belgian business. Kaunitz coolly told the emperor that 'at bottom we do not have any right to the thing'.

The emperor thought he might take advantage of the war in which the western powers were involved, but Kaunitz again pointed out with exasperating logic that a treaty obligation could not be violated except by war. 'I am very much obliged, my prince,' Joseph replied drily, 'for your very just and well reasoned reflections, but there is a proverb: *chi non risica non rosica* [he who does not risk does not eat]; often the most unlikely things succeed.'

An opportunity soon presented itself. In October, 1783, some armed Dutch soldiers crossed into Belgian territory to catch a deserter. The imperial troops retaliated by seizing two forts occupied by the Dutch. When the Dutch Estates-General protested, they were told that the emperor did not recognize the Barrier Treaty but that he was willing to negotiate.

'This impertinent closing of the Scheldt,' Joseph wrote to the ambassador, Belgiojoso, 'is most disgraceful to a power like mine.' And he instructed Mercy at Paris to ask the French minister to help Austria bring the project to a successful conclusion.

The French intervened mildly; in April, 1784, a conference was opened at Brussels, where the Austrians demanded the demolition of certain forts, the suppression of the Dutch navy guarding the Scheldt, and the handing over of the city of Maastricht. 'I flatter myself,' the emperor told Belgiojoso, 'that if we remain firm, press the thing, and seize the opportune moment, we will succeed in liberating the Scheldt from its shackles.'

When the sturdy Dutch appealed to France, Joseph transferred the imperial army from Breda to Maastricht, and ordered two ships to guard the mouth of the Scheldt at Antwerp. 'I do not believe,' the emperor said, 'that the Dutch . . . will risk insulting them (the ships), and by this we will obtain the point which we could not perhaps achieve through negotiation.' Simultaneously Joseph issued a declaration that henceforth the Scheldt was to be considered open and that any obstruction on the part of the Dutch would be taken as an act of hostility.

But the Dutch did not allow themselves to be browbeaten. They dispatched a fleet to Antwerp to block all entry to the disputed river. Joseph did not believe that the Dutch would fight and was not himself prepared for war. 'I never thought of making war on the Dutch,' he explained to Belgiojoso when he asked for detailed maps of Holland, 'and, hence, have never prepared any maps.'

In Vienna, Kaunitz did not agree with his sovereign that the affair would pass so simply. The old fox had played the high game of international politics for forty-five years and knew every groove, wrinkle, and dot on the political horizon. The struggle over the Scheldt, in his opinion, was not even worth the trouble. 'Austria,' the chancellor said with rare bluntness, 'which has neither a navy nor construction docks, neither can nor will ever be able to carry on any but a very mediocre commerce, and this she could do through other ports.' The opening of the Scheldt, he said, was 'more an affair of honour than of interest'.

Joseph dispatched the brig *Lüdwig* to break the Dutch blockade at Antwerp. The Hollanders bombarded the imperial ship with cannon. The emperor was then in Hungary. When Kaunitz received the news of the shooting he wrote to Joseph laconically: 'But they did shoot.' Joseph hastened back to Vienna, but it was October and too late to start hostilities. Another imperial ship, *Erwartung*, was surrounded by the Dutch near Antwerp and compelled to return to Ostend.

Joseph appealed to Catharine to use her 'powerful influence' against anyone who would try to interfere and 'kindle the fire

of a general war in Germany'. The reference was to the watchful and hostile Frederick. 'I have ordered my minister at The
Hague,' the czarina replied cordially, 'to present an exhorta-
tory note to the Estates-General in order that they might come
to their senses.'

So long as Germany was not affected Frederick would not
meddle. 'As for me,' he said,

> I am neither the ally of France nor of Holland. I have not guaran-
> teed the Treaty of Westphalia; hence no engagement obliges me
> to do anything. I well believe the Dutch would like me to fight
> for them; but I do not love to be a Don Quixote, and chiefly to
> hazard my country and to expose it to the incursions of the
> Austrians and perhaps even the Russians, in order to palliate the
> imprudence of the republicans, who, thinking only of how to
> enrich themselves by commerce, have made no alliance with any
> sovereign in Europe. They always do tomorrow what they should
> have done the day before.

Frederick asked the Dutch ambassador how things were going.
'Very well,' was the reply; 'we shall hold our own against the
emperor.'

'Nonsense,' said the king cynically. 'I know exactly what will
happen. You will give a tip to His Imperial Majesty, and there
will be an end of the matter.'

Holland was isolated, except for France. The men who had
thwarted Joseph before were still in power at Versailles. Joseph
and Mercy stormed Marie Antoinette to use her influence with
Louis. The French queen did her best; her clan feeling was as
strong as that of any member of the Bonaparte family. She
lectured the king and cabinet, she meddled with diplomatic
instructions, she stopped the couriers and intercepted their
dispatches. 'You would be astonished and surprised,' Marie
Antoinette wrote to Joseph,

> if you could see the odious dispatch of Vergennes. I have blocked
> it in the Council for two weeks. I have delayed the departure of
> the courier for seven days. That is all I can do . . I blush to
> confess that after the king saw the minister his tone changed . . .
> I shall continue to urge and shall not cease my insistence. I hope
> that you will immediately destroy this letter, for it is a veritable
> confession.

The French public justly suspected the queen of Austrian sympathies. 'In affairs which personally concern my dear brother,' she said, 'I shall never fail him.' Mirabeau came out with a pamphlet sharply attacking Joseph's ambitions. What the French did not know was that Marie Antoinette had no political influence on her husband. 'When I reproach the king with not having told me of certain affairs,' the queen almost pathetically explained to her brother,

> he does not become angry; he has an embarrassed air, and some-times he answers naturally that he had not thought of it . . . The king's natural mistrust has been, from the very first, strengthened by his governor, since before my marriage. M. de Vauguyon had intimidated him . . . and his black soul had frightened his pupil [Louis] with phantoms invented against the House of Austria. M. de Maurepas . . . has thought it useful for himself to maintain the king in the same ideas. M. de Vergennes follows the same plan . . . I have clearly spoken of it to the king more than once. Sometimes he has answered me humorously, and, since he is incapable of any discussion, I am not able to persuade him that his minister was deceived or deceiving him. I do not blind myself as to my influence; I know that, especially in politics, I have no great ascendancy on the spirit of the king.

Joseph, who had so often scolded his sister, now addressed her in most affectionate terms. 'My dear and charming queen,' he called her. He had no intentions whatever, he said, of destroying the Dutch republic, but he must bring it to reason. 'I am waiting impatiently to hear what he [Louis] intends to do, and the tone he will assume on this occasion *vis-à-vis* the Dutch, as my ally and friend.' Louis, Marie Anoinette replied, thought that under the circumstances Joseph was justified in sending an army to the Low Countries. But, the queen con-cluded, Vergennes said nothing; 'that silent tranquility makes me a little uneasy'. On that very day, the inscrutable Vergennes drew up a secret memoir, in which he pointed out that, from a military standpoint, Holland must keep and defend Maastricht; the loss of that city, he said, would mean a separation of Holland from France and the dependence of the republic on Austria.

The French ambassador at Vienna declared that France was at the point of making an alliance with Holland. Joseph decided to increase his army in Belgium to 60,000 men. But the imperial troops had no artillery and no pontoons. The Dutch began hostilities by opening the sluices at the Scheldt forts and flooding the Belgian land. The excited Belgians prepared for war and voted an extraordinary sum of money; Joseph's war, they realized, was their war.

What was France doing? Lafayette, who had just arrived from America, summarized the situation as seen from Versailles. '[I] am so lately arrived in Paris,' he wrote in English to General Greene,

> that I had better refer you to your Ministerial intelligences – in consequence of Austrian demands upon the Dutch, and the gun these have fired at Fort Lille, 40,000 men were sent to the Low Countries by the Emperor and a second division was in motion the same way when France gave orders for two armies to get in readiness, the one probably in Flanders and the other in Alsace. Holland is gathering some troops, the greater number purchased in Germany, and will have at the utmost 30,000 men in the field. Count de Maillebois an old and able French general has been demanded by them. Russia seems friendly to the emperor, and although the Stateholder is a friend of the King of Prussia, while the patriots are wholly attached to France yet Prussia will no doubt side in Politicks with France: and the Stateholder will command his own country's troops. A grand plan is spoken of whereby the Emperor would endeavour to obtain Baviera (*sic*), and in return give the Low Countries to the Palatine house a bargain which centres and increases the imperial forces. Under those circumstances negotiations cannot but be very interesting. Although the Freedom of Holland, and the Protection of German Princes are very proper objects for France to support, yet a war with the emperor must be peculiarly disagreeable to court. It will certainly be avoided, if consistent with the Liberties of Holland, with faith and Dignity. And upon the whole, I strongly am of opinion no war will take place, at least for this year. The appearance of things however is still warlike enough.[1]

Joseph accepted Louis's mediation, but insisted that a Dutch

[1] MS. letter in the William L. Clements Library, Ann Arbor, Michigan. Quoted by special permission of Dr. R. G. Adams.

deputation come to Vienna to apologize for firing on the imperial flag, and that unless the Scheldt was opened by May 1, 1785, he would begin hostilities. Meanwhile Marshal Maillebois took over the command of the Dutch forces. 'I am just now told the account of an intended surprise against Mastrick (Maastricht) is mentioned in the Hague Gazette,' Lafayette wrote to Greene on March 16, 1785:

> But although warlike preparations are going on, negotiations have not been one instant interrupted, and according to all probability they will end in some arrangement whereby the Dutch will give up much less than they were likely to lose. They are divided into two parties, and very warm on both sides. The patriots are decidedly attached to France. The Emperor's plan to give the Austrian Low Countries to the Elector of Baviera (*sic*), and get his electorate in return, has been opposed by the Elector's nephew and heir, the Duke of Deux Ponts, who is in the French service. I think therefore this will be quickly terminated, to the very great credit of Count de Vergennes.[1]

Joseph, intimidated by Dutch belligerency and French hostility, was by no means inclined to war, but he persisted in his demands; he must have Maastricht or a compensation of 12 million florins. Maastricht, the old Roman *Trajectum ad Mosam*, was a powerful fortress, provided with great dikes; at the point where the city was located the Maas River was 155 metres wide. Possession of the fort meant effective military control over Belgium. Neither Holland nor France was willing to see Austria hold this strategic possession.

The conference opened at Versailles. Vergennes represented France; Mercy, Austria; Berkenrode and Brantzen, Holland. Joseph was already beginning to yield. It was no longer a question of opening the Scheldt, but of 'compensation' to the imperial honour. The negotiations dragged through the spring and summer. 'The political world,' Jefferson, from Paris, wrote to Charles Thomson, 'is almost lulled to sleep by the lethargic state of the Dutch negotiation, which will probably end in peace. Nor does this court profess to apprehend that the

---

[1] MS. letter in the William L. Clements Library, Ann Arbor, Michigan. Quoted by special permission of Dr. R. G. Adams.

emperor will involve the hemisphere in war by his schemes on Bavaria and Turkey.'

Two Dutch plenipotentiaries went to Vienna to offer the emperor an apology for firing on his flag. Joseph interrupted their statement with a friendly compliment, accepted the Dutch apology, and promptly sent a courier to Paris to conclude peace. Then he went on a tour to Italy, leaving his governor of Belgium without instructions for two months.

At Versailles the plenipotentiaries haggled about the money compensation. The summer passed, and no conclusion was reached. The Austrians asked for twelve million florins; the Dutch were willing to pay only eight million. Early in September Joseph secretly authorized Mercy to accept six million. If the negotiations had lasted longer, he would have yielded altogether. But Vergennes, to avoid war, decided upon a settlement of ten million, the Dutch to pay eight million and France two million. Had Vergennes known of Joseph's willingness to accept six million he would not have been so generous with his country's bankrupt treasury.

'Your prayers,' Joseph mockingly wrote to his sister Marie Christine, 'have softened the hearts of the Dutch, have opened their purses.' He yielded so readily because he realized France would not permit him to free the Scheldt; 'the rest', he said, 'is not worth the trouble'. As for the money needlessly extorted from Holland and France, he ordered that 500,000 florins of the first payment of 1,200,000 be used to indemnify those who had suffered from the inundation, 'farmers, cultivators, and peasants to come first, as being the most needy, then the seigniors'.

The Dutch fiasco was damaging to Joseph's political reputation. 'I am beginning to think,' Frederick mocked, 'that this prince is very inconsequential; he drops his projects as soon as he meets with serious obstacles.' Frederick would never have acted with such recklessness and levity.

In Belgium and France there was bitterness; both had spent money in vain. Contemporary French tracts violently attacked Marie Antoinette for the payment of the two million florins to Joseph; the overtaxed French public accused the queen of enriching her brother. The great revolution was not far off, and the French remembered their grievances against the queen. Joseph was compelled to defend his sister. 'I am not unaware,' he said, 'that the enemies of my sister Antoinette have dared accuse her of having given me considerable sums. I declare, ready to appear before God, that this inculpation is a horrible calumny.'

## II

The acquisition of Bavaria never left the minds of Joseph and Kaunitz. By the Treaty of Teschen, Austria had renounced all claims to the south German land, but Joseph planned to acquire Bavaria by giving Belgium in exchange. It was a sound and statesmanlike idea. Belgium was far away and, in the face of Holland and France, not easily controllable; Bavaria, on the other hand, was contiguous to Austria and the Bavarian people were, like the Austrians proper, Catholic and German. A union of Austria and Bavaria would have meant an effective balance against Prussia in Germany.

Kaunitz thought that the Bavarian revenues, 'although poorly administered by its rulers, should not only be equal to those of the Low Countries, but they even might exceed them by about a million'. Joseph wished to have a comparative report on the Low Countries, 'the military forces, resources, and debts'.

But would the Bavarian Elector, Charles Theodore, consent? The Elector was sixty, shy, dull, intimidated; he had no legitimate children and did not love his legal heir, the Duke of Deux Ponts. Charles Theodore was willing to strike the bargain with Joseph, although when the news was broached at Munich it 'caused an indescribable sensation'.

Vienna needed Russian aid in case Prussia should oppose the project. Joseph told Catharine that if she would help him he would 'devote himself to Her Majesty' with all his forces. The exchange being 'doubly agreeable' to the czarina, she replied that she wished 'to co-operate efficaciously'. She instructed Romanzov, her envoy at Frankfürt, to influence Deux Ponts to accept the project.

To Marie Antoinette Joseph wrote that the exchange was 'of the greatest importance for the fatherland and your family, and at the same time will procure real advantages to the monarchy, and make for ever indissoluble the bonds of alliance which subsist between us'.

But Louis XVI hesitated to help his brother-in-law. He was not sure, he told Joseph, that the exchange would be so easy. The emperor, expecting support, was hurt. He expressed his grief in a long and tender letter to his dear sister. If only Louis, he said, would help him in the exchange, the French king 'would never have any reason to repent it'; Louis would then find Joseph ready 'on all occasions to back his desires and views'. Without ceasing to be a good King of France, Joseph concluded, Louis 'can show me that he is also my ally, my friend, and my brother-in-law'.

Marie Antoinette was helpless. 'It will be impossible for me,' she confessed, 'to make him [Louis] . . . come to a decision by himself . . . But when the moment appears to me essential, I shall try to see Vergennes with the king, and engage them.' But Vergennes raised difficulties. The queen wished to face the minister in the presence of the king,

> in order that he should not distort nor exaggerate what I should say to him . . . Vergennes has communicated to all the ministers of the Councils the report which he has made on the proposition of the exchange. I do not know whether this is a new manoeuvre of duplicity on his part, but from what the king has told me, his report is more conciliatory than the opinion of some other ministers . . . My dear brother ought to be sure that, whatever happens, my zeal and activity in this matter will never abate.

The phlegmatic king did not let himself be influenced by his vivid wife. He saw no reason for making his obstreperous brother-in-law more powerful than was strictly necessary. Louis informed the emperor that the proposed project 'would form a change of the greatest importance in the position of the Germanic body . . . would derange the system of equilibrium which has been the most essential object of the Treaties of Westphalia'. The language was diplomatic, but the intention unmistakable.

R

Louis proposed, not without malicious intent, that Joseph consult the King of Prussia!

In Germany itself the diplomatic struggle became more complicated. Charles Theodore insisted upon an unconditional exchange of all his Bavarian possessions for all of Joseph's Netherlands; but Joseph thought this was not fair. Bavaria had 800 square miles and 1,400,000 inhabitants; while Belgium had 700 square miles, 1,800,000 inhabitants, and an income of 7,600,000. Joseph wished to withhold Luxemburg and Limburg, in order to exchange the latter for Salzburg. The Elector would not agree, although the Belgian revenues exceeded the Bavarian by one million. Austria finally offered him the Palatinate, Jülich and Berg, and proposed to let his natural son, Prince Bretzenheim, become Grand Prior of the Order of Malta with the permission to keep the Order's estates in Bavaria. The Elector loved his son and agreed; but, he said, the plan must be submitted to the Duke of Deux Ponts, because 'his approval thereof is necessary'.

The impecunious Deux Ponts did not like the Austrians. For a while he thought himself a very important figure. France showed him deference and cordiality; Prussia flattered his vanity and gave him money. Russia was more blunt. Count Romanzov, Catharine's ambassador, submitted an agreement to Deux Ponts and asked him to sign. The Bavarian Elector, the articles read, was to turn over his land to Austria and to become King of Burgundy. 'Furthermore, the Elector is to receive . . . one and a half millions, the duke [Deux Ponts] one million, and his brother Prince Maximilian half a million gulden for their approval.' Romanzov told Deux Ponts that Charles Theodore had already agreed to the bargain, and that the 'Russian empress demands, in the name of her ally the German emperor, the duke's approval, and advises him to give it, as the proposition is very advantageous to him and to his house'.

The duke asked eight days to think it over; he wanted to hear what France would say. Romanzov said bluntly that whether 'the duke agrees or not, the thing will take place anyhow'. The Russian was wrong. Deux Ponts' answer, prepared by the

Prussian minister Hertzberg, came in a few days. 'He would rather,' Deux Ponts replied in Prussian language, 'be buried amidst the ruins of Bavaria than agree.'

Joseph considered the duke's answer, 'inconceivable, insolent and ridiculous'. Deux Ponts' hostility, the emperor said, 'feels more like Potsdam than Versailles'. Potsdam or Versailles, it was the same thing. The project had to be given up.

Twice the Prussian king had thwarted the ambitious Habsburg in Germany, but it was necessary to consolidate the victory. The time was ripe, for Josephs' activities had antagonized the German princes. 'I insist,' wrote Duke Charles August of Weimar to his protégé Goethe, 'that we German princes must build up an army in order to secure our lands and our persons from the yoke of Joseph II.' Other 'particularist' princes sympathized with this aim.

Frederick took advantage of the anti-Habsburg sentiments and put himself at the head of a union of German rulers – the *Fürstenbund*. The articles of the league were drawn up by a Hanoverian politician, revised by two Prussian ministers, and signed on July 23, 1785. Saxony was the next to join and soon all the secular and ecclesiastical princes – except Württemberg, Oldenburg, Hesse-Darmstadt, Cologne, and Trier – became members of the *Bund*. The aim of the union was: 'The preservation and strengthening of the German imperial system according to the laws . . . and for this purpose to have a thorough understanding and to maintain a confidential correspondence.'

The Austrian government tried to deny the importance of the *Fürstenbund*, but the blow to Vienna had struck home. Frederick carried on a vicious propaganda against Joseph; Catharine had to urge the Prussian king to restrain himself.

Blocked in Germany, the *Drang nach Osten* became a political necessity for Vienna. With Prussia no reconciliation seemed possible. When Frederick died in August, 1786, there was a feeling of relief at the *Hofburg*. 'As a soldier,' Joseph told Kaunitz, 'I regret the loss of a great man who has been epoch-making in the art of war. As a citizen I regret that his death has arrived thirty years too late.' The emperor wrote in the same strain to Leopold: 'The death of the King of Prussia leaves no other regret than that he has lived so long.'

Joseph had little hope that Frederick's successor would be any less hostile because, he said, 'since Hertzberg was the soul of everything, it will be necessary to expect the worst'. Still the frustrated emperor wished to have peace with Prussia. The experienced chancellor, however, realized that there was no room in Germany for both Habsburgs and Hohenzollerns; between the two dynasties there was bound to be war. 'Nothing would be more desirable,' Kaunitz pointed out to the Austrian ambassador at Berlin shortly after Frederick's death, 'than to have the new king at peace with us. To achieve this, we have to conceal our claws carefully, so that, when we are challenged, we may strike more surely. This and nothing else must be the whole goal of our policy, because the solid and permanent union of our state interests with those of the Prussian court is merely a pious wish.' Austria's aim should be, the chancellor said, to act so as 'to divert the new king from warlike intentions, and thereby to unbend the springs of the Prussian machine; then, with the necessary time and circumstance, to burst forth with all possible force'.

Joseph accepted this view, although reluctantly. Prussia remained a persistent enemy, instigating rebellion in the Austrian lands, until the French Revolution and Napoleon forced the Teutonic powers to unite against the common enemy. For a generation, in the next century, Metternich succeeded in holding Prussia in leash. Bismarck finally finished what Frederick had begun. Austria, again ousted from Germany, was forced once more to turn to the Balkans. What Joseph had begun ended in World War I, with the destruction of his empire, and the annihilation of his dynasty in 1918.


# III

Between Vienna and St Petersburg there had been an almost uninterrupted friendship since the time of Peter the Great. Only Catharine II and Maria Theresa, two German women endowed by an inscrutable Providence with unlimited power, were hostile to each other, an enmity from which the Prussian king had gained most. In the last year of his mother's reign, Joseph had decided to rectify this error; his visit to the czarina in 1780 was a step in this direction.

The flirtation between the two sovereigns continued for the next nine years. As Catharine warmed to Joseph she grew more hostile to Frederick. After the emperor's visit, the pro-Prussian Panin was replaced by the pro-Austrian Osterman in the conduct of foreign affairs. When in 1781 the czarina sent her son Paul and his wife to Vienna, she forbade the couple to visit Potsdam. Catherine disliked Frederick but she despised his successor, the future Frederick William II, whom she mockingly dubbed *le gros Gu*.

'It is necessary,' Joseph said, 'to take advantage of the Byzantine fantasies of the empress, as her weak side, in order permanently to secure her friendship.' He cultivated Catharine's fellowship assiduously. The numerous letters the two sovereigns exchanged have the flavour of a sentimental juvenile romance *à la Rousseau*. But there was hard reality behind the diplomatically tender phrases. 'With Russia on our side we can achieve everything substantial and useful,' Joseph wrote in cipher to Ambassador Cobenzl at St Petersburg; 'without her, hardly anything.'

'Her friendship, her esteem,' the emperor flattered the czarina, 'are sufficient for my *amour propre*; I desire nothing else but to continue to merit them.' Ruling was a difficult job, Joseph told Catharine, and he begged her, who was 'a master in the art of ruling,' to give him publicly, 'a mark of her esteem.'

Joseph developed the technique of handling the susceptible woman to a fine art. Not that the astute czarina was deceived; she herself was no mean player of the game; of all the contemporary sovereigns, only Frederick of Prussia was her match in craft. But Catharine and Joseph had similar ambitions; to have a distinguished man pay assiduous court to her and at the same time be able to take advantage of his proffered aid, was a gift not to be despised. In corresponding with Cobenzl, his plenipotentiary in Russia, Joseph, who knew that Catharine intercepted the mails, had Kaunitz carefully read and revise all that he wrote. Kaunitz was given permission to 'add or delete' whatever he wished. 'It is necessary to realize,' Joseph told his chancellor,

> that we have to deal with a woman who cares only for herself and no more for Russia than I do; hence one must flatter her. Her vanity is her idol; persistent good luck, exaggerated homage, and the envy of all Europe have spoiled her. One must therefore howl with the wolves; provided that the good is achieved, it matters little under what form it is obtained.

Catharine may have been prodigiously vain, but she was also a hard-headed business woman. Joseph may have fatuously thought that he could obtain everything by flattery. It was Catharine who took advantage of Joseph. Before making an alliance with him, she demanded of the emperor that he exert his influence with the Turks to carry out the Treaty of Kutchuk-Kainardji (1774), and that he intervene with the pope in favour of the Greek Catholics, because 'as chief of the Greek church it will be my duty . . . to recommend the true believers.' Joseph hastened to obey the request: 'It is an honour which she [Catharine] does me,' he said. The emperor was, indeed, ready to do any kind of service for the czarina. Catharine wished to know his attitude about Poland; she must be sure of Austria on her western frontier. Here, too, Joseph showed himself eager to be her friend. 'I can well assure Your Imperial Majesty,' he wrote her, 'that on my honour I neither have nor can have any design in regard to Poland which does not perfectly conform to yours, our interests being perfectly the same on the subject of preserving that species of anarchy and impotence which results therefrom.'

The letters between Joseph and Catharine disquieted both Potsdam and Versailles. Maurepas and Vergennes, Mercy informed Joseph (March 3, 1781), regretted 'to see renewed the intimate connection between Your Majesty and Russia'. France feared for the Ottoman Empire. Frederick, despite his excellent espionage system, could find out nothing certain, but he felt the wind was blowing against him. 'The emperor,' he said, 'weighs heavily on my seventy-year-old shoulders.'

By means of two letters exchanged between Joseph and Catharine on May 21 and 24, 1781, an Austro-Russian defensive alliance was secretly formed. The contracting powers mutually guaranteed each other's pacts and conventions made with Turkey from 1704 to 1779. In case of war with the Porte, the two bound themselves to support each other with an equal number of troops and not to make a separate peace. Joseph promised that, in the event of an attack on Russia he would 'regard such an aggression not only as a *casus foederis*, but also a common cause', and would go to Russia's aid. The fateful alliance was aimed directly at Turkey and indirectly at Poland.

For over a year Frederick knew nothing of the treaty. In 1782 he could still say of Joseph: 'We are struggling now as to who should win over Russia.' And the emperor considered the alliance with Catharine 'a mortal blow to my irreconcilable enemy, the King of Prussia'. When Frederick found out what had happened he swore a sharp oath and grimly thought of his dragoons.

In Vienna it was summer and the flowers in the Augarten were in bloom. Emperor Joseph and Sir Robert Murray Keith, the British ambassador, were strolling through the park. Only recently the emperor had promised 'my empress, my friend, my ally, my heroine' always to support her, especially in the Crimea, a sun-drenched land which Catharine coveted. Keith knew nothing of this, but he was curious to know what Joseph thought of the czarina. The emperor was in an expansive mood; his reforms were going well; he had great plans. Keith was his friend, a gentleman of humour and discretion. One could talk to him, but the Englishman must realize that the imperial words were 'most secret and confidential'.

> The great Art [the emperor said], is to enter into the Empress's Character, and to humour it. She is no doubt a Princess of distinguished Genius, but she cannot do everything. Whoever has to deal with her must never lose sight of her sex, nor forget that a woman sees things differently from one of our sex. I speak

from experience in saying the only way to keep well with her is *ni de la gâter ni de la heurter de front*; to give her her way in matters of little consequence, to render every necessary Refusal as palatable as possible, to let her perceive a constant desire of pleasing, yet at the same time a firm adherence to certain essential Principles . . . The singular Misfortune of the Empress is that of having no Person about her who dares to restrain, even to repress effusion of her Passions. Count Osterman [the vice-chancellor] is *un homme de Paille*; he does nothing, and has no weight. As to M. Besborodko [the First Secretary], he is an Upstart; he was a low scribe, a mere Interpreter, under M. Romanzow, and he retains the Sentiments of that class of Men.

'It is an unhappy thing for Princes,' Keith remarked piously, 'that they are forced to give their confidence to men of low Birth, sordid Education and loose or timid Principles; but has not the Empress Prince Potemkin for a Confidential Counsellor?'

O, yes [replied Joseph]. . . . He has a little knowledge, joined to great Indolence, and even the Empress affects to treat, or at least to speak of him as a Scholar of her own Politicks, and consequently as a man who is more likely to need a Guide than to become one. It is a favourite Phrase of hers to say, '*Il est mon élève. C'est à Moi qu'il doit toute la connaissance des affaires*'.

'Does it appear, Sir,' Keith asked, 'that Prince Potemkin's Weight and Influence are diminished?'

'Not at all,' the emperor answered, 'but in Politicks they have never been what the World imagined. The Empress of Russia does not wish to part with him, and from a thousand Reasons, and as many Connections, of every sort, she could not easily get rid of him, if even she harboured the wish of doing so.'

Catharine entertained a Grand Project which she communicated to her imperial ally. It was nothing less than a partition of Turkey. Russia was to get Ochakov, the territory from the Bug River to the Dniester, Moldavia, part of Wallachia and Bessarabia, and was to found a Greek empire at Constantinople with Catharine's grandson Constantine (so named for this purpose) as emperor.

An excellent plan, Joseph replied; but Prussia, France, and Spain would oppose it. The two Bourbon courts, he pointed out would render Catharine's 'measures and operations null or at least very difficult by their fleets' in the Mediterranean and the Black Seas; while 'my provinces of the Low Countries, those in Italy, and those which I have on the Rhine, would find themselves exposed to all their land forces'. Joseph urged the necessity of coming to an understanding with France and of detaching Saxony from Prussia. France could be won by an offer of Egypt. As for Catharine's Greek empire at Constantinople – her 'Byzantine Fantasies', as Joseph privately called it – 'only the events of war could decide that, and if they are successful, there will never be any difficulty on my part'.

As for the price of his co-operation in the Grand Project, the emperor asked for the city of Chotim, 'in order to cover Galicia and Bukowina'; a part of Wallachia; the territory along the Danube from Nicopolis to Belgrade, including Vidin and Orsova, 'in order to protect Hungary'; a strip of land from Belgrade to the Adriatic including the Gulf of Drina; 'and finally the *terra firma* possessions of Venice, as well as Istria and Dalmatia', to furnish the 'sole means of making the products of my states valuable'. The Danube commerce was to 'remain perfectly free to my subjects, both to the mouth of the Black Sea and the Black Sea outlet at the Dardanelles'. This would have given Austria possession of the northern Balkans and command of the Adriatic. The emperor concluded by urging the importance of winning over France and Saxony; 'without them I will find myself absolutely unable to serve Your Imperial Majesty'.

Joseph wrote to Mercy to interest France in the design by holding out Egypt as a bait. 'That rich, fertile, and commercial province,' Joseph said, 'if it became a French colony, would in short time enable France, by means of the port of Suez on the Red Sea and the opening of good and assured communication against the Isthmian brigands, to become the mistress of all the commerce of the Persian Gulf and the great Indies.' The emperor wanted to know Mercy's frank opinion and also whether France would prefer war with him in order 'to conserve the Ottoman Empire and prevent the possibility of its destruction'. France was then at war with England and Joseph explained that possession of Egypt would be 'a palpable blow at English commerce', a situation of which France should be glad to take advantage.

The emperor also consulted his cool-headed brother Leopold. What did the Grand Duke of Tuscany think of the scheme of partitioning Turkey? Leopold was sceptical. Catharine's project, he told his brother, was 'so vast that I venture to doubt its success; I believe that the Turks are not yet so disunited and enfeebled among themselves, nor the Russians sufficiently strong . . . to attempt to destroy them entirely'.

'I find,' was Joseph's answer, 'your ideas perfectly just.'

Catharine refuted Joseph's objections. He should not 'needlessly worry' about Prussia. She agreed to many of his demands, but hesitated granting Venetian possessions, for the partitioners might need the republic's co-operation. The czarina hoped the emperor would prepare for the war.

Joseph was afraid to plunge into the venture. He dreaded the hostility of Prussia. Frederick, he knew, would never permit him to enlarge his territories. Austria could not rely on France. Russia might or might not be an effective ally. The adventure was much too dangerous.

Austria was in a dilemma. If the astute czarina started war with Turkey, Joseph would have to show his hand. The problem troubled Kaunitz even more than the emperor. The chancellor reasoned logically that Austria could not remain passive, for the hard-won friendship of Catharine would 'turn into hatred'; nor could Vienna oppose Russia's war on Turkey, for the same reason. The inexorable conclusion was that Austria would have to fight the Turks.

The czarina was preparing to seize the Crimea, and still Joseph hesitated. A year passed; the emperor would not budge. When France, uneasy at Catharine's machinations, asked the emperor to intervene, Joseph replied: 'I assure you I will not hesitate to tell Catharine all that is necessary to prevent her from making war on Turkey. But that woman has an uncommon head, and nothing stops her. It is true that inconsistency often takes the place of reason.' A few days later Joseph told Catha-

rine that he would help her. 'Well now!' the czarina exclaimed
to her councillors. 'You see now that I was right and that I
alone know my true friends!'

Kaunitz urged his sovereign to march an army into Turkish
territory. 'You well realize,' Joseph explained to Leopold,

> that this would absolutely force the Porte to war, while the
> Russians do not desire it, and the French fear nothing so much
> as war and preach patience to the Turks. In fine, I alone would
> have the whole Ottoman mass on my back, and very probably
> also the King of Prussia, and perhaps even the Bourbon courts
> in the Low Countries, on the Rhine, and in Italy; and for this
> end to risk losing everything to gain a miserable strip of desert in
> Bosnia or Serbia . . . Temporizing, I gain all; I am entirely pre-
> pared, and am enclosing a list of troops ready to be assembled in
> fifteen hours.

The emperor and the czarina both wished to slice up Turkey;
but while Catharine could take the Crimea without danger of
European intervention, Joseph could hope for no such luck.
France and Spain consistently opposed the destruction of
Turkey. 'France,' Joseph bitterly pointed out to Marie
Antoinette,

> has augmented her states by the acquisition of Corsica without
> the slightest jealousy having been manifested on the part of
> Austria . . . Certainly I desire the conservation of Turkey as much
> as the king [Louis]; but if she destroys herself by her miserable
> constitution, what is to be done? On this I have frankly and
> amicably asked the advice and opinion of my ally, and all I
> received for answer were reproaches and threats.

Catharine saved Joseph the painful effort of a definite decision
by occupying the Crimea without war. The emperor told his
ally that he would compensate himself 'in the next war' against
the Porte. Joseph congratulated himself on the outcome of the
Eastern crisis. He had gained no Turkish territory, but had
managed to retain Catharine's friendship and to show 'all of
Europe my distinterestedness'. He kept up his correspondence
with the czarina, in order, as Kaunitz said, that 'her sentiments
do not cool off'. Turkey could rest in peace for another four
years.

## IV

In the intervening years Joseph had applied his reforms, had antagonized all his provinces, and had almost fought a war with Holland. He had wanted to open the Scheldt and had failed; he had tried to acquire Bavaria and was humiliatingly defeated. He yearned for glory and Frederick of Prussia frustrated his aims. Would he be more successful against Turkey?

The peace between Russia and Turkey was precarious. In the summer of 1786 Catharine complained to Joseph of Turkish instigations in Georgia and announced her intention of making a grand tour through her southern provinces; she hoped that Joseph would join her. The invitation was added in a postscript, as an afterthought, and it piqued the haughty Habsburg. 'I find the invitation,' the emperor said to Kaunitz, '. . . very cavalier. I shall sleep over the answer, it will be short, but I will not omit letting the Catharinized Princess of Zerbst know that she should show a little more respect . . . when she wishes to order me.' In his anger Joseph wrote the czarina a rude letter, but the chancellor, fearing a rupture, begged him not to send it. 'Your Majesty understood how to win the personal friendship of this princess,' Kaunitz argued with the excited monarch, 'and you will know how to retain it . . . Who knows what advantages we can yet draw from it, when the time and circumstances are favourable.' The astute chancellor added that if he were only twenty-five years younger he would consider it an honour to accompany Joseph to Russia.

Reluctantly Joseph accepted the czarina's invitation. 'I am looking forward to the time,' he wrote her, 'with the liveliest desire . . . to undertake the journey in order to be a witness of the happiness with which your presence will fill your new subjects.' Her answer was no less sugary. 'My lord brother! My soul trembles with joy in the hope . . . of seeing Count Falkenstein again . . . I pray to heaven that it bless the undertaking and the journey, and above all the health of my most esteemed friend and most faithful ally.'

Catharine and her magnificent suite left Czarskoe Selo in January, 1787. She was attended by the chief personages of her court, and accompanied by the three foremost foreign ambassadors, Ségur of France, Cobenzl of Austria, and Fitz-Herbert (afterwards Lord St Helens) of England. Ségur remembered the instructions which Vergennes had given him: 'to seek means to make yourself personally agreeable to that princess and to those who have most influence on her'. The inevitable Prince de Ligne was also there. Potemkin was in charge of the expedition.

'The closer the moment approaches,' Joseph chirped to the perambulating czarina,

> when Count Falkenstein . . . may hope to have the happiness of seeing you again, the more his zeal and desire increase. Self-love . . . however, forces me not to conceal from Your Majesty that Count Falkenstein will appear to you, after the lapse of time, much deteriorated. A wig covers his head [Joseph was completely bald]; but, above all, it is the tension exacted by work as assiduous as it is exacting and often thankless, that has aged him and has largely driven away his gaiety.

After six years of intermittent work, Joseph looked indeed old and worn; there is a certain pathos in this confession of a vain man to the czarina who was growing more fat and complacent with the years.

When the snows began to thaw Joseph left Vienna. His trip, said the *Politisches Journal*, 'put all the European cabinets in commotion'. On the way to Cherson the emperor assured King Stanislaus August Poniatowski that he did not have 'the slightest demands on Poland'. Stanislaus bowed deeply, gratitude in his heart.

Catharine was at Kiev, a city whose palaces were of wood and whose streets were mud tracks, when she heard of Joseph's approach. In the presence of a flotilla of twenty-two galleys manned by a thousand marines, the plump empress boarded the imperial galley and sailed down the Dnieper. From her gilded cabin, lying lazily on downy cushions, she watched the miserable towns on the shore as they fired cannon in salute.

It was the middle of May when the mud-spattered Joseph arrived at Cherson on the Dnieper. The town was only six years old and inhabited by people from many lands, including Englishmen who dealt in hemp, potash, and lumber. Cherson's bank had 300,000 rubles and the fort 800 cannon.

The two royal friends met several days later. Catharine began to entertain sumptuously. The aim of the empress, Joseph wrote to Kaunitz, 'is to amuse herself'. He underestimated her feline guile. They sat at the loaded table, with eighty other guests, and while 120 musicians were playing, the monarchs smiled, nodded, whispered, and wondered who would be the winner in the next war. After dinner they talked politics.

'The empress,' Joseph communicated to Kaunitz, 'is dying of desire to begin with the Turks; she does not . . . listen to any reason, for her vanity has blinded her to a point where she believes herself capable of executing alone all that she wishes . . . I have taken care not to push this conversation too far, seeing that this was not the moment to make her listen to reason.'

Catharine did not take Joseph's objections seriously. She looked at him with smiling eyes, looked through him, saw to the bottom of his being; with extraordinary acuteness the clever woman detected his weak spots, realized that he was proud, sensitive, eager for glory, but also weak, vacillating, unintegrated. 'I have nothing to teach M. Falkenstein,' the czarina confided to her friend Grimm at Paris:

> he is formed already and will become a pretty skilful master, but the right noble apprentice . . . has far to go yet before he can become a journeyman. The poor fellow, one never knows what is in him. He stammers much and is so terse that nothing ever comes out of him. He is so reserved that those who have any dealings with him find him indigestible. It is said that he thinks well; that is possible, but one can also say that of a goose.

The imaginative Potemkin, with fine dramatic sense, had arranged the journey and the festivities to dazzle the czarina and her foreign guests. He put up idyllic huts, built fake towns, constructed wooden forts to delight his mistress. Joseph was not taken in. He told Lacy that the fortifications of Cherson were made of sand and turf, and that the Russians dared not fire their cannon for fear of making the walls crumble. Two vessels built in the Cherson wharves were made of wet wood and the sails were so rotten that the ships had to be demolished. 'Everything,' the emperor said to Ségur,

seems easy when one wastes money and human lives. We in Germany or France could not attempt what they dare do here without hindrance. The lord commands; hordes of slaves obey. They are paid little or nothing; they are badly fed; they do not dare to protest, and I know that in three years fifty thousand persons were destroyed in these new provinces by the toil and the emanations from the morasses, without their being lamented, even without anyone mentioning it.

Charles Joseph François Lamoral Alexis, Prince de Ligne, was an elegant gentleman of fifty-two. He knew everybody in Europe and could converse wittily on every subject. Catharine said that he was 'one of the most pleasant beings and the easiest to live with', and she made him a field marshal. Joseph, too, made him a field marshal. The prince had great wealth and everybody liked him. He lived through the French Revolution, the Reign of Terror, the Napoleonic wars, and died at the age of seventy-nine when the Congress of Vienna was dancing its way through the European shambles. A day before de Ligne died he said cheerfully, 'They have exhausted all kinds of spectacles to amuse the sovereigns; I am preparing a new one – the interment of a field marshal.'

Now in 1787 de Ligne accompanied Catharine and Joseph to the Crimea in the quality, he said, of a 'diplomatic jockey'.

Joseph met de Ligne as he was leaving Catharine. The emperor was moody. 'It seems to me,' he said, 'these people want war. Are they ready? I don't think they are; if they are, I am not. And what do they expect to get? I have just seen their fleets and their fortresses, and they are only sketched out to throw dust in one's eyes. Nothing is solid; it has all been done in a hurry, and very expensively, to humbug the empress.'

The cultured western Europeans felt themselves superior to the Russians with their barbarous display and crude magnificence. A subtle bond of understanding was established between the clever Ségur, the sophisticated de Ligne, and the liberal Joseph. Truckle as they might to the all-powerful czarina, these children of an older culture despised the crude Russians and the extravagant woman who ruled them. Ségur relates how the emperor, de Ligne, and he went for a walk and suddenly met a strong body of Tatar horsemen from Catharine's bodyguard. 'Admit,' said de Ligne, not without malice,

> that it would be a singular occurrence, and would cause an alarm in Europe, if the twelve hundred Tatars who are surrounding us here would decide to drag us head-over heels to the nearest port, and thence, with the eminent Catharine and the mighty Roman emperor Joseph, ship us all to Constantinople for the entertainment and pleasure of His Highness Abdul Hamid, Lord of the Faithful. There would be nothing immoral about such a trick, for without scruples they could abduct two monarchs who, by violating all treaties and international law, had robbed their land, dethroned their prince, and put their liberties in irons.

The frank de Ligne's comment may have made Joseph squirm; fortunately for the visitors the simple Tatars had not yet learned such European stratagems.

Royalty, courtiers, chamberlains, and flunkeys embarked on their flotillas and sailed down towards the Crimea. 'Never,' de Ligne relates, 'was there a voyage so brilliant and so agreeable. Our chambers are furnished with chiné silks and divans; and when any of those who, like myself, accompany the empress, leaves or returns to his galley, at least twelve musicians whom we have on board celebrate the event.'

Joseph was morose. He bluntly told the czarina he would not help her weaken Turkey. To his friends the emperor said that he would oppose Catharine's boastful inscription on the gates of Cherson, which read: 'Road to Constantinople.' 'What I want,' Joseph said to de Ligne, 'is Silesia, and war with Turkey will not give me that.'

The emperor was annoyed at all this pompous frippery, this

:ruel waste. The fat and bejewelled czarina went glittering
lown the Dniester, sparkling with witticisms, drinking costly
wines, entertaining sumptuously at a cost that must have been
staggering. Everything in Joseph's character resented the
scene; he became glum, smiled more and more wryly. De
Ligne was always there to amuse the two sovereigns, and little
escaped his sharp eyes. 'Their imperial majesties,' he relates,

> felt each other out now and then about these poor devils of Turks.
> They threw out suggestions and glanced at each other. As a lover
> of glorious antiquity . . . I talked about restoring the Greeks;
> Catharine of reviving the Solons and Lycurguses. I enlarged on
> Alcibiades; but Joseph II, who was more for the future than the
> past, and for the practical instead of the chemical, only said,
> 'What the devil should we do with Constantinople?'

Joseph was not interested in the prattle about antiquity; such
camouflage did not deceive him. He knew that Catharine
cared no more for Solon and Lycurgus than she did for the
Holy Grail. They both wanted large slices of Turkey, but
neither wished the other to get too much. Politics, however,
ancient or contemporary, made good conversation. Sometimes
their Imperial Majesties were frank. 'Rather than sign the
separation of the thirteen states,' Catharine once softly remarked apropos of the American Revolution, 'as my brother
George has done, I would have shot myself.' Joseph's comment
was more sincere. 'Rather than throw up my power,' he said
with reference to the calling of the Notables by Louis XVI, 'as
my brother-in-law has done by convoking and assembling the
nation to talk of abuses, I don't know what I would have
done.'

Potemkin secretly asked de Ligne to speak with Joseph in
favour of a Turkish war. 'I do not see exactly what he wants,'
was Joseph's irritable reply. 'It seems to me that when I do
as much as I did in helping them to get the Crimea, that ought
to be enough. What would they do for me if I should have war
with Prussia some day or other?'

Nevertheless he wished to remain in the good graces of the
czarina.

s

'How do you think I succeed with the empress?' Joseph asked de Ligne.

'Wonderfully, Sire.'

'Faith! it is difficult to hold one's own against the rest of you,' the emperor commented.

> There is, my dear ambassador [Cobenzl], out of gratitude, kindness, liking for the empress, and friendship for me, always swinging his incense-pot, into which you throw gains for the rest of us pretty often; M. de Ségur pays her his very witty and very French compliments, and even that Englishman lets fly from time to time some tiny shaft of flattery, so epigrammatic that it is all the more piquant.

On the first day of June the flotilla arrived in the Crimea. They disembarked in great confusion. There were few wagons to carry the baggage and no horses to pull the wagons. When the travellers finally began to move inland, there was, Joseph writes, 'a disorder of which one can form no adequate idea; some of the carriages are still on the water; everyone takes *Kibitques*, native wagons, to carry his baggage'. The carts broke down, and the steppes were strewn with mattresses, pots, pans, pillows. The food was rotten, cold, hard, tasteless.

They arrived at Baktshiserai, the ancient capital of the province and the residence of the Tatar Khans. The czarina occupied the Khan's palace which was furnished in oriental style; there Catharine stayed with her new lover who was, in the words of Joseph, 'a young man of twenty-six, practically without education, a child'. Prince Potemkin and his suite occupied the harem, which reminded Joseph of a Carmelite monastery. The emperor himself stayed in the apartment of the Khan's brother, and his neighbours were only old women, so that his ideas, he said, could not be rosy.

Having nothing to do, the curious emperor visited a neighbouring city inhabited by a Jewish sect. 'Some of them,' Joseph writes,

> are very rich merchants, other agriculturalists, but they hide their women like the Tatars. They have to content themselves with

one woman until she becomes either ugly or weak-eyed, and only then may they marry another. If this law were introduced in Vienna many women would begin to wear glasses in order to get rid of their husbands.

When, two days later, the party arrived at Sebastopol, Joseph received a disquieting dispatch. An insurrection had broken out in the Austrian Netherlands. Hastily the emperor retraced his steps and hurried back to Vienna.

# CHAPTER 14

# Insurrection

*There is one thing I do not understand about that quarrel: namely, this prince who converses with everyone, from the lowest to the highest, did not have the slightest indication of what went on in the Low Countries; that at the moment when resistance broke out he was unaware of the mood of the people.*

Catharine to Grimm

Hastening to Vienna Joseph wrote to Belgiojoso 'to have patience' with people as 'stubborn as the Flemings', but to remain firm; 'the use of force against madmen and fools should be undertaken with extreme caution'. The emperor was perplexed and bitter. Why were the Belgians revolting? Did he not mean well by them? 'I do not understand why,' he complained, 'against whom, how, nor for what all this is directed. Is it not absurd to suppose that because of a single change in the tribunals which concerns only the forms and does not affect the laws of the country, the citizens . . . will fire houses, pillage, and destroy one another?' He suspected that his plenipotentiaries had mismanaged affairs and ordered Belgiojoso to have the provinces send delegates to Vienna.

It took almost three weeks to reach Lemberg from the Crimea; he arrived there with 'bitterness in my soul'. His anger mounted. 'Never in my life,' he wrote to Kaunitz, 'have I felt a more just indignation . . . The government has lost its head entirely; it uses words like *the inevitable loss of the Low Countries*, in order to justify unheard-of actions which are entirely senseless.'

On the way Joseph received dispatches informing him of the whole extent of the disaster in Belgium. Marie Christine had yielded to the insurgents, Belgiojoso had lost his presence of mind, Kaunitz had on his own initiative tried to pacify the

Belgians by sending back the merchant who had been brought
to Vienna in chains. 'I am surprised,' the emperor raged at the
old chancellor,

> at the step which you have dared to take by yourself in sending
> Hondt back, without waiting my orders. In always yielding . . . it
> seems to me one has gained nothing . . . for when inflamed and
> insolent men see that one fears them, they dare everything . . .
> What you advise me, my prince is cowardice, and certain death
> would not draw that signature from me.

On the last day of June when the sun was setting the pale and
haggard emperor galloped into Vienna and hastened to the
Burg. Bad news awaited him. After the successful rising of
May 30th, students and burghers had armed themselves in
many Belgian cities and indulged in various excesses. The
government at Brussels seemed to have lost its nerve.

Would the emperor yield or fight? For three days he did
nothing but read reports, talk vehemently, argue with his
councillors. Worn and pallid, his hooked nose looking sharper
than ever, Joseph swore and threatened and breathed violence.
He would send a whole army and teach the rebels a lesson
which would remind them of the days of Philip II. Calm, placid,
logical, his blue eyes fixed coolly on the son of Maria Theresa,
Kaunitz reminded his sovereign that Belgium had a constitution which guaranteed its liberties, that this was not the
sixteenth century, that violence would only aggravate matters.
Joseph replied that he was still emperor, that he still had power
to crush rebellious subjects. In that case, the chancellor said
with a slight bow, he would ask His Majesty to permit him to
resign from office.

The cool nights brought calmer counsel. Joseph curtly
summoned Belgiojoso and Marie Christine to Vienna and
sharply criticized their conduct, which he called cowardly. To
undo the damage Belgiojoso and the governors had done, the
emperor wrote, there was only a single alternative: either the
plenipotentiaries and the deputies arrive in Vienna, 'or to put
myself on the royal square in Brussels at the head of fifty thousand men, and to destroy to the last vestiges the privileges,

constitutions, and the evil heads who have dared to forget themselves so far against me'. The direct invitation to the provincial Estates was couched in somewhat more moderate terms, thanks to Kaunitz's intervention.

General Count Joseph von Murray was ordered to take over the Belgian administration temporarily. 'You will be responsible to no one,' Joseph instructed the general, 'except myself, to whom you will submit your reports . . . and will receive further orders from me. My intentions are: absolutely to suppress the insolent steps which especially the citizens of Brussels have permitted themselves and thereby wrested from the government unheard-of and cowardly concessions.' Murray was commanded to concentrate his troops around Brussels and Louvain and should warn the population that in case of the slightest insolence there would be shooting, and not in the air or with blank cartridges; 'one must give a great example of sternness, so as to bring the great mass to reason, without regard for those who will be the unfortunate victims'.

The Netherlands were seething with excitement. There was a riot at Antwerp; numerous pamphlets and manifestos were circulated; petitions were signed. For the moment, Joseph informed the Estates, 'all new regulations will be suspended until the governors-general and the deputies of the provinces have arrived in Vienna, where an understanding for the common welfare based on the laws of the land . . . will be discussed'. But, the declaration ended with a threat, if 'this last act of my goodness towards you is ignored to the point where you refuse to come here with your grievances, your fears, your doubts . . . and you continue your shameful excess and your inexcusable actions, then you will have no one but yourselves to blame for the resulting consequences'. The emperor grimly told Kaunitz that he had no intention of repeating the cowardly action of Belgiojoso and Marie Christine or of imitating their 'stupid fear'. He ordered thirty thousand men to march towards Belgium.

The Estates met at Brussels and decided to heed the emperor's summons. Joseph grew suspicious; he thought the insurgents

simply wished to gain time. 'If the Estates think,' he said, 'that
I will be satisfied merely with their sending me a deputation
with compliments . . . they are very much mistaken,' and he
instructed General Murray to announce publicly that the
government would oppose the rebels *coute que coute*. If the
Belgians objected that to send foreign troops into the country
was contrary to the constitution, Joseph mockingly ordered
Murray to justify the action on the ground 'that I hold the
troops necessary in order to spare the artisans and citizens the
time which they now waste in playing soldiers and neglecting
their work to occupy themselves with public safety'.

The assembly at Brussels, angered by the movement of the
imperial troops, seized power. 'Now,' the emperor told General
Murray, 'it is no longer a question of capturing the spirits,
of conquering the terrain little by little, but it is absolutely
necessary to remain firm and to demand subjection and
obedience on all points.' The general could not concentrate his
army as quickly as the situation demanded. The insurgents
appealed to France for aid, but they sent deputies to Vienna
at the same time.

At the Foreign Office in London, Lord Carmarthen, feeling
England's isolation in Europe, thought he saw an opportunity
'to obtain the confidence of the emperor'. Ambassador Keith
was instructed to deliver to Joseph 'the very friendly sentiments'
of His Britannic Majesty, and 'his real concern for the actual
troubles in the Low Countries'.

Keith went to see the harassed emperor and repeated the
message. Joseph said that His Britannic Majesty's sympathy
gave him 'sincere pleasure'. He laid hold of Keith's arm and
said,

I am greatly obliged to the King . . . His Britannic Majesty knows,
by his own experience, that it is the unhappy lot of monarchs to
see their upright intentions frequently misapprehended. He has
seen the subjects of his distant dominions abandon their duty and
allegiance, from false notions of liberty, and through the instigations of factious, selfish, and artful men. What have they gained
– even by the success of their audacious enterprise? Only anarchy

and confusion. I have lately seen my subjects in the Netherlands on the very brink of open rebellion, from the frantic adoption of views . . . artfully and incessantly instilled into their minds by designing lawyers, bigoted priests, and a few men of higher birth, who are new-fangled dabblers in what *they* call patriotism. The feebleness of my government in the Low Countries had, by timid and unwarrantable concessions, in a manner encouraged the arrogant demands of my subjects . . . I hope to convince the Flemish that I meant them no harm, and that an equitable line ought to be drawn between legal prerogative and constitutional principles.

Keith wanted to know how the emperor would treat the delegation. Joseph was frank.

My language [he said], in regard to their possible resistance has been this: You say, gentlemen, that I am to lose the Netherlands for ever; I tell you . . . that my monarchy is indivisible and that I will risk the whole of it to preserve it entire. I should be truly sorry to order a single musket to be fired against any subject of my own . . . You threaten me with emigrations; I shall be sorry for them; but valuable subjects and industrious men do not emigrate, and your soil and your situation are in every respect too good and comfortable for you to abandon them lightly. The monied men, say you, will quit the country: no such thing monied men know their own interests, and I will make it clearly to theirs to remain where they are. You perhaps think you may indulge a little spirit of anarchy, and even try the weapons of rebellion . . . In relation to this last point, I make to you, gentlemen, this explicit declaration . . . If any province of my monarchy should ever wield against me the sword of rebellion, and that I should succeed in reconquering it . . . I publicly declare that I should look upon the entire property of every individual, of every rank and condition, who had taken up arms against my government, as irretrievably forfeited to the crown; and the whole laws, privileges, and institutions of that country, wholly and solely at my disposition and mercy.

These were the words of a man not sure of himself; more heat than determination, more indignation than understanding. Joseph was too human to be a tyrant; too much of an ideologue to be a successful Alba.

In the middle of August thirty deputies, representing all the provinces, arrived at Vienna. The delegation was introduced by Kaunitz to the emperor. What did the gentlemen have to say? The gentlemen were still loyal subjects; they had no wish to renounce their obedience to their lawful ruler. But His Majesty must restore the constitution, must reinstate the old courts, must not secularize the seminaries.

His Majesty told the deputies that he expected 'prompt and entire obedience'. The deputies looked humble but stubborn. 'The well-being of my subjects,' the emperor said, 'is the sole aim of my actions. I do not at all intend to overthrow your constitution; be convinced, then, that despite all your attempts . . . I repeat to you the assurance that I will maintain your liberties.' His Majesty asked to be introduced to each deputy in person. 'Gentlemen,' he concluded, 'the ceremony is over. You are no longer delegates; we are all citizens; you want to regard me as such. I will be easy to instruct myself, and you will not be angry to listen to me. When one has spoken to me, one has never found me unreasonable. Come and see me whenever and as many of you as you wish . . . Everyone is perfectly free.' The gentlemen smiled and bowed; the emperor smiled, nodded, walked out of the room.

Kaunitz showed the delegation a message to General Murray, wherein the commander was ordered to restore things to the condition they were on April 1, 1787, to collect the back taxes, to reinstate the officials who had been removed by the Estates, to dissolve the burgher corps, and irrevocably to open the general seminary. Was this a victory – and for whom?

At a second audience the emperor told the delegates that to show his goodwill to Belgium he would put Count Trautmanns-dorf in place of the hated Belgiojoso. The deputies asked His Majesty to visit their land. The emperor shook his head. 'Gentlemen,' he said, 'I wear a black cockade.'

The rebellious Estates refused to accept the emperor's compromise. When Murray tried to abolish the patriot corps the citizens of Brussels put up barricades. They prepared a huge demonstration. Murray was frightened; he did not want to shoot; he was afraid of not shooting. The general solved the dilemma by issuing a proclamation promising the preservation of the constitution and the restoration of conditions to the status before the reforms. On that same day Joseph sent a courier to Murray instructing him to disarm the patriotic troops. When the emperor finally heard what Murray had done – yielded without a fight – he furiously ordered the general's dismissal.

Trautmannsdorf took Murray's place; the military command was given to General Richard d'Alton. Trautmannsdorf acted like Murray. He was unacquainted with the Netherlands, and no sooner had he come to power than, on his own accord, he issued a general amnesty and ordered that the seminaries should not be opened.

The insurgents would not yield. They insisted that Murray's promises – which Joseph had never recalled – be carried out. Trautmannsdorf issued an ultimatum demanding unconditional execution of all ordinances published before April 1, 1787, within twenty-four hours. General d'Alton assembled his troops, marched them down the streets. The patriots glowered; they insulted a military patrol. The troops opened fire. Trautmannsdorf's ultimatum was accepted.

D'Alton's firm action delighted the emperor. 'I am charmed,' Joseph wrote his general, 'that the so-called patriots are beginning to realize the arrant folly of their wish to fight with me.' It was essential, the emperor thought, 'that the public realize that the military no longer lets itself be insulted.' He praised the general: 'I approve . . . everything which you have done in order to re-establish order.' Henceforth, Joseph instructed d'Alton, 'firmness as much as patience are necessary, and I recommend to you . . . never to forget to blend one with the other'.

His Majesty thought the troubles were over.

CHAPTER 15

# War

*Auf, Brüder! ins Gewehr,*
*hängt Säbeln an die Seiten,*
*puzt eure Flinten aus*
*und rústet euch zum Streiten.*
*Der rauhe Muselmann,*
*der Christen Sklaven macht,*
*Schleift seinen Säbel zu,*
*das alles blitzt und kracht.*

*Ein Joseph steht schon da*
*Mit unzehlbaren Heeren,*
*dem stolzen Muselmann*
*den Buckel abzukehren.*
*Ein Joseph, der sein Reich*
*so weit emporgebracht,*
*das er beim ersten Wink*
*die Feinde zittern macht.*

*Auf! wer noch Muth besitzt!*
*kasst euch nicht lange laden,*
*wir wollen unser Schwert*
*in Türkenblute baden*
*Folgt unsern Kaiser nach*
*und thut, was Russen thun,*
*der Türk bezahlte uns*
*so vielen Christen blut.*

War Song, 1788

'What are all these romances?' Joseph had asked de Ligne in
Russia. 'They want to go to Constantinople. What are we to
do with Constantinople?'

'Make it a Greek republic.'

'Don't you remember the joke of the late King of Prussia who
wrote to d'Alembert that the name of Constantine given to a
little grand duke meant that they would seat his little person on

the throne of Constantine? . . . But you may believe me that when we get there and have to take it, they will be more embarrassed than I. However, that woman is lucky.'

No sooner had the czarina returned from her magnificent journey to the Crimea than the Turks declared war on Russia. Promptly, and without declaration of war, Joseph invaded Turkish territory, regardless of the insurrection in the Netherlands and the incipient revolt in Hungary. He had the best army Austria possessed since Eugene of Savoy, and thought he would succeed in this international hold-up.

With the aid of his intimate friend, the inept Marshal Lacy, Joseph planned to draw a cordon from the Bukowina to Dalmatia, and transported six army corps of 200,000 men to achieve his aim. The main army was to be placed opposite Belgrade, two corps were to cover Slavonia and Croatia, and the rest to be spread over the Banat and Transylvania. This was the first strategical blunder, for the troops thus scattered over a distance of 180 miles were – it is obvious even to a layman – ineffective in an offensive campaign.

The six corps were commanded by mediocre generals; neither Coburg, nor Fabris, nor Wartensleben, nor Mitrofski, nor Dewins, nor Liechtenstein had any military talent. Joseph himself was the worst bungler of them all, second only to Lacy. The only man capable of winning a victory was Marshal Loudon; but the emperor, with a Stuart-like genius for choosing wrong persons, neglected that general in favour of Lacy.

The army was well equipped. There were 800 guns with 176,000 shells and 10,000 hundredweight of powder. The cavalry and transport had 56,000 horses and 12,500 oxen; a reserve of 6,000 cattle for food was held in Hungary. 'The imperial army,' wrote Lafayette to General Knox in 1786, 'is more substantial, more numerous than those (*sic*) of Prussia – but not so well exercised by far.' It did not matter; it was brains that were lacking.

The emperor was then a sick man; his stomach, he complained, was 'out of order', and he suffered from a 'dry cough' and a 'feeble and hollow voice'. He had varicose legs, running eyes, bad lungs, and erysipelas; heedless of the danger signals, he continued working incessantly. De Ligne reproached him for killing himself. 'What else can I do,' Joseph said bitterly, 'in this country, out of mind, without zeal, without heart in the work? I am killing myself because I cannot rouse up those whom I want to work.' Disease was undermining his constitution and clarity of vision. Greedy for glory, he was impelled by an inordinate desire for conquest, driven by an urge for which there is no other word than self-punishment. 'Hardly did I mend things a little in the Netherlands,' he confessed to Leopold in August, 1787, 'than this vexation arrives, a war in those damned lands with all their diseases, pests, famine, and for little gain.'

Having his army assembled, Joseph did not know what to do first. At Constantinople, the Vizier commanded all the *sandjaks* (administrative divisions: of which there were 288 in European Turkey) to prepare their contingents of men and horse by the end of February; the Turks hoped to gather an army of 500,000 but in January they had only 70,000. At Berlin, King Frederick William II thought he would like to play the role of mediator and offered Vienna his services. 'The House of Hohenzollern,' Joseph replied with Teutonic rudeness,

arrived at the summit of its greatness by the same means [conquest]. Albrecht of Brandenburg took from his order [the Teutonic Knights] the Duchy of Prussia, and his successors secured to themselves the sovereignty of that country in the peace of Oliva. Your Majesty's late uncle [Frederick the Great] took Silesia from my mother at a time when, surrounded by enemies, she had no other protection than the powers of her mind, and the fidelity of her people. What equivalents have the courts, which talk so much about the equilibrium of Europe, what equivalent have they to the House of Austria for the possessions she lost in the present century?

The blow in the Prussian king's face was to prove costly. Promptly Frederick William incited Sweden to declare war on Russia, thus hampering Catharine's campaign against the Turks and preventing her from aiding Austria. While Joseph was having his hands full in fighting the Turks, the King of Prussia instigated revolution in Hungary.

Half a year after the invasion, in February, 1788, Joseph formally declared war on Turkey. 'I regret,' he informed Kaunitz,

> that I am obliged to announce to you that the Ottoman Porte has declared war against Russia, my ally . . . Considering the treaties that exist between Russia and myself, I cannot leave the empress exposed alone to the dangers of war . . . I commission you to make known . . . my resolutions and dispositions against the Porte, and to send the circular dispatches . . . in order that the war between Austria and the Turks may be notified to all the respective courts in due form.

Hostilities began with the Austrian bombardment of Turkish-Gradisca and the seizure of Old-Orsova. When Joseph arrived on the battle-front in March, his army was ready to attack the fortress of Shabats on the Save River. His Majesty took over the command in person.

While the cannon were booming over Shabats and the invading Christians were issuing appeals to the native population, His Highness the Hospodar of Wallachia battled with his thoughts. He would not let the Germans entice his subjects with artful promises. He, the Hospodar, was still loyal to His Imperial Majesty the Commander of the Faithful, though himself a Christian and no Turk. The Hospodar composed a manifesto.

> We prince do announce and make known to you Christians, all *bojars*, chiefs, and all manner of folk, and at the same time order you, that you obey and remain loyal . . . to our emperor. Do not waver in this fealty and do not let yourselves be ensnared by the Germans, for the German is like a leaf on the water, and so is the Russian. The Russian once already started a war with our emperor, but it did not last long . . . Now the German wants to do the same. He scatters writings against us; he wants to make believe, that he will come to our land. But he cannot; his aim is only to sow the seed of dissension amongst us. Let him only come! But he is afraid; for our emperor is so mighty that even if all the emperors and kings rose against him they could not overcome him. And I too am mighty in men and steeds, like the other kings. Also God

is with me, because I am of the Christian, but not of the German, religion.

Up, therefore, you Christians! Up everybody in the name of God! Arm you as can! Snatch axes, guns, lances, or whatever comes to hand! Up against the Germans! Block his entrance! Stealthily he wants to break in, only to plunder. Then he will, like the Russian, flee; for the Russian, too, invaded our land, and where is he now? Do you not see that our emperor still rules even now? Entertain no suspicion against our lofty emperor under whom we have had prosperity until now! He, however, who, blinded by the German, distributes writings amongst you, will be eternally damned and excommunicated.

We command that you seize and destroy writings counter to our holy religion. He who will catch a person carrying such writings and deliver him to us, receives a gift of 300 lee, and will be raised from peasant status to *bojar* status; and I myself will place the robe upon him. He, however, who will permit himself to be used for the propagation of such writings, should be stabbed alive on the spot where he is caught. Remain true! Obey our orders! Therefore you will pay only the contribution imposed now; henceforth you will be free from all tributes. Up, up! Against the Germans, so that we can overcome them!

The little fortress of Shabats was bombarded for three weeks; it finally surrendered after the emperor had almost been killed by a shell. An attempt of the Austrian fleet to surprise Belgrade failed, for the doughty seamen could not see through the fog and passed the White City; they realized their error only when they were in front of another town.

The emperor settled down near Semlin and waited for Russian aid, which never came. He sat under a tent in that malarial country and worked at dispatches and reports which passed to and from Vienna; the imperial soldier, eating scantily and drinking nothing but water, worked over his piles of papers until midnight. He slept for a few hours on a hard cot, coughed, rose, muttered restlessly, coughed again, and went back to his papers. He was bewildered, nervous, tense; he dared not cross the Save to attack Belgrade. He breathed with difficulty and sputtered. Reports came that the Turks were mercilessly harassing the rear of his army. The emperor was afraid to move.

The heat was fearful. Epidemics broke out. Thousands died,

tens of thousands were in the hospitals. Between the summer of 1788 and May, 1789, 172,000 soldiers fell ill, of whom 33,000 died. May, June, July passed in inactivity and death. In July the epidemic was at its height; 22,000 men were in the over-filled hospitals. Turkish guerrillas gave the exhausted army no peace. In August Joseph contracted the disease that was soon to kill him, but he wrote to the French minister of foreign affairs in the tone of a maniac: 'The time has come when I appear as an avenger of mankind, when I take it upon myself to compensate Europe for the oppressions which it has had to bear [from the Turks], and I hope to . . . cleanse the world of a race of barbarians.'

The avenger of mankind fell victim to quartan fever; he could hardly breathe. 'I live,' he said, 'on a strict diet, taking salts and bitter tea.' Kaunitz pleaded with the emperor to save his life and leave the conduct of the war to his generals, as his ancestors had done. 'I will not leave my post of duty,' Joseph replied.

The army was dying; the emperor grew worse. 'My heart palpitates at the slightest movement,' he complained, 'which absolutely prevents any motion, either on foot or on horse.' He fatigued easily, had an irregular pulse, and he could not sleep.

The Austrian lands cried out in despair. The people and the army all clamoured for the old hero Loudon. Within man's memory Loudon was the only living Austrian who had won victories, even from Frederick the Great. He knew the Balkans. The emperor finally appointed the marshal to the command of the fifth army corps in Croatia.

In August the Grand Vizier Yussuf Pasha moved against Nish with 70,000 men, crossed the Danube and threatened the Banat.

Leaving half his army near Belgrade, Joseph took twenty-one battalions and thirty-two squadrons to defend the Banat. On the left bank of the Danube where the river is so narrow that a pistol shot can reach the other side, the Turks defeated the Austrians, drove them back, and gained command of the river.

The Danube was now open all the way to Belgrade; the road into the Banat lay exposed. It was imperative for Joseph to join General Wartensleben at Karansebes to block the advance of the Mussulmen.

Prayers were intoned in the Austrian churches;

O God! thou who confoundest the designs of warriors, thou who annihilatest the enemies of those who put their confidence in thy goodness, accord to us thy powerful protection. Come to the rescue of thy worshippers, scatter thy strength upon the waters, weaken thine enemies in order that we may praise and thank thee. God, our protector, throw a propitious eye on us, save those who fight for glory from all dangers which confront them, from all the evils which the infidels prepare for them, in order that, free in heart and soul, we may thank thee.

The Moslem prayers were more efficacious. 'Creator of all that breathes,' the children of the Prophet cried,

thou who, from the height of thy throne, seest the sun, the stars, and the world like twinkles, thou who couldst hold in thy hand the vast ocean even like a drop of dew, be favourable to us, hear us! Thou hast sent thy Prophet to earth, and we have followed thy laws. Why hast thou become angry with thy faithful Mussulmen? Why hast thou roused the wrath of our enemies, whose destructive chariots roll over the lands of our domination, and fly like a whirlwind of dust? Why hast thou permitted that their steeds grind, with a proud foot, the soil that is our heritage? Rise, Lord; disperse our enemies who are thine enemies; show thy people thy force as of yore, and we will land thee under the porticoes of thy sacred temple at Mecca.

Despite the rebuke, Allah did not turn His face away from His children.

What Allah did was this: He caused Joseph to break up camp at Szatmar and Slatina and march towards Karansebes. The night was moonlit and the Austrian columns marched in good order, protected by a detachment of hussars in the rear; the army had already crossed the bridge. The hussars stopped at the bridge and bought whisky from a Wallachian peasant. Some stragglers came over to buy a drink and the hussars chased them away. The angry stragglers retreated, began to fire their guns, and yelled *Turci! Turci!* The drunken hussars fired off their guns and also shouted *Turci! Turci!* Panic-stricken, the rear columns started firing aimlessly. Officers cried Halt! Halt! In the confusion the words sounded like Allah! Allah! Terror seized the transport workers; they began to drive their wagons and beasts wildly into the columns. Hell broke loose in the night. The whole army stampeded. The sick emperor was in an open carriage; the onrushing soldiers and horses dashed madly against it and hurled wagon and occupant into the river. Enraged, in an agony of despair, the emperor leaped on a horse and tried to stop the madmen, but in the shooting, yelling, and screaming no one recognized or heeded him. Wagons were overturned, the cannon deserted, baggage thrown away. Men fled in panic, screaming – 'The Turks are here; all is lost; save yourselves!' The moon shone brightly.

The Turks, aroused by the pandemonium, began to pursue the fleeing army. Only at dawn did the cavalry of Count Kinsky succeed in driving off the Moslem hosts. Over 10,000 men were killed and wounded in the panic.

Joseph's spirit was almost broken. 'I do not know,' he complained to Leopold, 'how I continue it all; sleep is entirely gone, and I pass the nights in the most distressing reflections.'

While the emperor was reorganizing his demoralized army at Lugosh the Turks were devastating the Banat. They burned several hundred villages, trampled the fields, carried off the cattle, and then hastily recrossed the Danube towards Belgrade. 'While we are waiting,' the impotent emperor exclaimed, 'the beautiful province is destroyed; they are burning everything.'

The Moslems again defeated an Austrian army and put up a great camp at Belgrade. It was autumn when Joseph hastened to meet the Turks, but the wily Moslems did not wait for their enemy; they withdrew to winter quarters and, the cold coming on, the emperor was forced to do the same.

Joseph was stricken with disease and humiliation. For the second time this would-be Frederick was defeated at war when he led his troops in person. He was too ill and his vanity was too deeply outraged to rejoice over the slow but inexorable ad-

ance Loudon was making in Croatia, freeing the Save River.
His Majesty would not admit his own shortcomings; he, of
course, was not to blame; it was the tardy Russians, distracted
by having to fight also the Swedes in the north, who were
responsible for his defeat. 'One cannot count upon effective aid
from the Russians,' the emperor told Kaunitz, 'but only upon
promises and pretty words; there is a lack of money, credit, and
energy, and the czarina occupies herself with the intrigues of her
favourites.'

The army retired to winter quarters and the dying emperor
left the battlefield for Vienna. In December he arrived at the
capital, suffering from 'heavy breathing, cough, and a dull
pain near the heart'. News was uniformly disastrous. The
Prussians were intriguing in Galicia and Hungary. In Vienna
and Austria there was sickness, cold, starvation. 'We are having
a fearful winter,' the emperor complained to Marie Christine,
'much snow and fierce cold, which is very bad for the march of
the regiments and the transports. What with the chaos, the
political commotion that has seized Europe, I cannot yet make
any prognostication as to what will happen.' The towns and
villages were full of starving people; the emperor was worrying
about the march of the troops.

From his sick room the emperor prepared for the campaign
in 1789. Heavy taxes were levied, new men were conscripted,
provisions were gathered. His Majesty was confident that this
time he would be victorious.

'In the spring,' he said,

the Russians will occupy Bender and move to the left bank of the
Danube; on the right bank of this river I seize Belgrade and
spread into Serbia. The conquest of Nish, Viddin, Sarajevo, and
up the Save River from Berbir (Turkish-Gradisca), Banjaluke,
and Konstantinovich, are undertakings which are completed by
August. Should the vizier meet me or the Russians on the Danube,
he would have to offer battle, and after he is defeated, I drive
him up to the mouths of the cannon of Silistria. In October, 1789,
I order a congress, after Osman's people beg the Giaours for
peace. The Treaties of Carlowitz and Passarowitz serve my envoys
as the bases for the negotiations, whereby I also appropriate

Chotim and a part of Moldavia. Russia receives the Crimean peninsula . . . Prince Charles of Sweden becomes Duke of Courland, and the Grand Duke of Tuscany [brother Leopold] King of the Romans. Then there is universal peace in Europe.

This was written five months before the French Revolution by a man whose heated fantasies were the expression of a body ravaged by half a dozen diseases.

In the spring, while the emperor at Vienna was dreaming about conquests, a new sultan, Selim III, ascended the throne of the Caliphs. Selim was twenty-eight; he girded the sword of the Prophet and called on all the faithful, from the ages of sixteen to sixty, to take up arms in defence of Allah. 'I will not put my sword in the scabbard,' the Commander of the Faithful said, 'until the aim of this war is achieved. It is a disgrace that we have allowed ourselves to be humiliated so far by the infidels.' His Majesty the King of Prussia offered Selim an alliance against the infidels.

The campaign started when the lilacs began to bloom and the fields sprouted green. Fortunately for Austria, Joseph was in bed in Vienna. In Croatia, Marshal Loudon seized Berbir after a short siege. The dying emperor appointed Loudon commander-in-chief of all the armies. The marshal spent the summer driving the Turks from the Banat and never stopped his inexorable march until he reached Belgrade; in a month the Moslems evacuated the city. Grimly Loudon dogged the heels of the Turks, past Semendria, past Passarowitz, past Orsova, through Serbia, through Wallachia. In a short time, and with the aid of the Russians, the Turks were driven from Moldavia, Wallachia, Serbia, and Bosnia. The campaign recalled the golden military days of Prince Eugene of Savoy.

The emperor was not in a position to enjoy the victory; he sent a diamond-studded Maria Theresa Order to Loudon, acknowledging his services. His Majesty was bitter, crushed by the consciousness of personal failure. He could neither eat, nor breathe, nor sleep.

# CHAPTER 16

# Revolution

## I

*Es dreht sich alles um und um in unser Capitolium.*
Vienna Drinking Song, 1790

While in the *Burg* at Vienna the emaciated emperor was spitting blood and struggling for breath, national passions swept Europe. The French Revolution was on so vast and dramatic a scale that it overshadowed revolutionary stirrings elsewhere in Europe. Yet even before the Estates-General met at Versailles, Poland was preparing to declare her independence from Russia, Belgium had virtually broken with Austria, Hungary was at the point of seceding from the Habsburg empire. Feudal Europe was disintegrating.

In Hungary and Bohemia and Poland Prussian agents were busy instigating revolt against Austria and Russia. As early as 1786 one Emerich Malonyai called on the Hungarians to elect a new king; Joseph condemned him to the galleys for ten years. Next year a petition of grievances, based on the ideas of Rousseau and old Hungarian juridical theory, was circulated in Transylvania. Soon after, a Piarist monk, Remigius Fanyó, drew up a plan whereby Frederick William II of Prussia was to become King of Hungary on condition that he turn Catholic; the Hungarians would send him 30,000 men to invade Vienna. An outline of the plot was submitted to influential Magyar nobles, Count Esterhazy, Count Anton Karolyi, Primate Count Joseph Batthyany, Emerich Dosza, Stephen Karasz. Esterhazy, and Karolyi, loyal to the emperor, sent Fanyó's plan to the authorities. 'The monk,' said Kaunitz, 'is crazy.' Fanyó was condemned to thirty years imprisonment; Joseph doubled the sentence.

Friedrich Jacobi, Prussian resident at Vienna, was the chief of the anti-Habsburg machinations in Hungary. What Frederick William II aimed at was to use Hungarian independence as a bargaining point with Austria to acquire the latter's portion of Silesia. In Hungary there was enough unrest and discontent to make Prussian plots dangerous. The emperor could not raise the military quota there; he found it difficult to collect provisions, for his money was worthless paper; deadly epidemics increased the bitterness and resistance. Jacobi took advantage of the situation.

The Austrian secret police were aware of what was going on; they intercepted all correspondence, unsealed the letters, made copies; but failed to incriminate Jacobi; the astute Prussian carried on his intrigues orally. Joseph said grimly he would 'uproot the evil'.

But the emperor was in a perilous situation. 'I cannot,' he told the czarina, 'make war with the Porte and the King of Prussia at the same time . . . I cannot expose the monarchy and my subjects to the risk of such evident destruction.' The desperate monarch begged Kaunitz to tell him what to do; he was even prepared to make an alliance with Turkey.

In March, 1789, Jacobi advised the King of Prussia to urge the Porte to distribute leaflets among the Magyars to the effect that the Turks wished to free Hungary from Joseph's yoke; Jacobi also informed his king that some Hungarians told him that they wanted Frederick William to march an army into their land. This letter was intercepted by Joseph's police.

Hungary as a whole, however, was not yet ready for the desperate step of secession. There was always the danger that Joseph might make peace with the Turks and turn his whole army against the unprepared Hungarians. But the nationalist excitement rose to boiling point, fanned by the events at Paris. In the autumn of 1789 an irresistible movement swept Hungary for the convocation of the Diet. 'Should the Hungarian nation,' the patriots, their eyes and ears on Versailles, asked, 'which knew how to maintain for a thousand years its liberties brought from Asia, be deprived of them in this enlightened century when other nations fight for their lost rights, and die out of the great family of nations?'

The sick emperor had no power to resist. Early in 1790 Joseph, at the urgent pleas of Leopold, revoked most of his hated reforms in Hungary. 'We have decided,' the dying man announced,

> to restore the administration of the kingdom . . . to the status of 1780 . . . We have instituted [the reforms] out of zeal for the common good and only in the hope that you, taught by experience, would find them pleasing. Now we have convinced ourselves that you prefer the old administration . . . But it is our will that our edict of toleration, the regulation concerning the founding of parishes, as well as those concerning the serfs, their treatment and their relation to the seignior, remain in force.

Even in the midst of reaction he saved the most fundamental of his reforms.

## II

Hungarian turmoil was allayed, but the revolution in the Netherlands could not be stopped.

The winter of 1788–9 was severe and there was widespread famine which added to popular discontent. The Estates, particularly of Brabant, refused to vote taxes. Trautmannsdorf announced that as the Estates had forgotten their duties of loyal subjects, their sovereign no longer regarded himself bound by the *Joyeuse Entrée*, and he threatened to dissolve the Estates and to confiscate the treasury and archives. 'I would,' Joseph informed Marie Christine, 'rather risk everything than to give way in points which are his good right.'

The administration proceeded to make good its threat. Troops surrounded the Estates of Hainault then in session and dissolved the body; the imperial commissioner issued a decree abolishing Hainault's privileges and replaced the officials with those loyal to the government. The constitutions of the Low Countries were suspended.

Then the patriots rose in armed revolt. They numbered 46,000 and had active agents in London, Berlin, and The

Hague. A central committee at Breda, Holland, guided the insurrection, organized and trained corps of volunteers. The government imprisoned many of the leaders and commanded the patriots to disarm. Clashes occurred between the imperial troops and the volunteers; the patriots seized Ghent and held it in the teeth of the imperial army.

Had d'Alton been given a free hand he might have defeated the insurgents; but Joseph was deadly sick, his mind in distress and full of vacillations. His brother and heir Leopold disapproved of force. The emperor talked about 'tearing out the evil by its roots', but could not decide upon drastic action. Then momentous events occurred in France. Joseph was frightened; he began to disapprove of d'Alton. The Belgian administration fell into confusion, and the insurgents were able to seize and hold most of Flanders.

The capture of the Bastille in Paris sounded like a bell in the night to the dying emperor. The events in France, he wrote to d'Alton, were 'as incredible as they are inconceivable'. He feared the revolutionary contagion would spread to his own army in Belgium and ordered that the pay be increased. He also asked d'Alton to recruit from the French émigrés.

Joseph followed the events in France with breathless interest, not unmixed with terror and rage. In July Louis XVI accepted the Paris revolution. 'Let me tell you,' Joseph said to Keith, '. . . that the King of France has acted very unwisely, not to use a harsher term, to have sown the seeds of the fructifying doctrine in his own dominions . . . he may expect inevitable growth of them throughout the whole of his future reign.' Prophetic words!

Because of the 'delirium which reigns in France', Joseph was afraid to employ harsh measures in Belgium.

> It is necessary [he instructed d'Alton], that the government do nothing, either by way of innovation or concession . . . In the most desperate case of a general explosion, the sole object of the army should be to concentrate in one or two points, to abandon all the small towns, to assemble all the money . . . at one place, which should always, in my opinion, be at Brussels.

The insurgents threatened Brussels. Trautmannsdorf revoked the reforms and urged Marie Christine and her husband to flee. As was natural, the patriots considered the concessions as a sign of fear and weakness. The Estates of Brabant refused to meet so long as the army surrounded them; Flanders declared its independence from the Habsburgs.

At Paris, the Declaration of Rights was adopted by the National Assembly. The revolutionists compelled Louis XVI to move to Paris where they could keep an eye on him. The National Assembly began to confiscate church property and to draw up a constitution.

At Vienna the dying emperor watched these events with bitterness. 'What these French do not do,' he exclaimed, 'to give themselves a good constitution, while they are destroying it! The same stupidity reigns partially in Brabant. The only difference is that the French intoxication is due to champagne, which is swift but passes quickly; while that of Brabant comes from beer, which is slow and obstinate.'

In conflict with his rival Trautmannsdorf, the disgusted General d'Alton marched out of Brussels, leaving behind him the treasury which contained three million gulden, the archives, and thousands of guns. The officials fled on foot. The imperial army was dissolved.

Joseph made a final effort to save Belgium. He begged his friend Philipp Cobenzl to go to the Low Countries on a personal mission. 'I will give you,' the emperor said, 'unequivocal power to come . . . to an understanding.' The emperor looked white as death; his face was fleshless and his hands trembled. He had only a few weeks to live. Cobenzl, who knew he would never again see his friend, could not restrain his tears.

The Belgium patriots were in full control; they declared the emperor to have lost all sovereign rights. The Estates of Brabant swore an oath of allegiance to the new Belgium union and summoned provincial deputies to Brussels.

Belgium was lost to Austria, mainly because of the blunders of the emperor. Despite his fire-eating talk, Joseph was too humane to systematically employ violence on a large scale against his subjects. The 'philosopher' on the throne was a dismal failure. 'These unfortunate conditions in the Netherlands,' he told Marie Christine, '. . . have crushed me. I cannot breathe, nor sleep, nor move; I spend the nights sitting up. For the moment, I believe nothing will help in the Netherlands. One must await events and the opportunity to reconquer the land. Full independence is declared and is supported by the three powers [England, Prussia, and Holland].'

'Your land,' Joseph exclaimed to de Ligne, a Belgian, 'is killing me; my death struggle began with the seizure of Ghent. What dishonours for me! I am dying of it.'

The consciousness of defeat finally broke Joseph's spirit. He knew that his family – his own brother and heir – resented his ineptitude and bungling. Leopold, in fact, was bitter and angry. 'Never,' he said, 'have I been consulted about the Low Countries.' When, in January, 1790, the Belgians formed their union, Leopold told his sister: 'I am inconsolable about the Low Countries; we have lost such a beautiful country, so necessary and useful to the monarchy, so lightly.' When Leopold II, after Joseph's death, tried to win back Belgium and unscrupulously cast aspersions on his brother's previous actions, one of Joseph's most virulent enemies exclaimed: 'It is true, we hate Joseph, but we despise Leopold.'

In France, the revolution was gathering momentum. The emperor in Vienna, with only a few days to live, sat up, his face a death mask, staring sombrely at the leaden winter sky. Ségur, the French diplomat, was announced and ushered into the room; he did not recognize the emperor because he was 'so cruelly changed'. Joseph remembered him from the Crimean trip and welcomed him with a wan smile. Ségur was moved and confused; he forgot how to address the emperor, calling him 'Monsieur le Comte'.

'You are a singular person,' Joseph said in a low voice, 'in the Crimea you always insisted upon calling me Sire, and in Vienna you absolutely wish to address me as Count Falkenstein.'

The two men spoke of politics. 'A general folly,' Joseph said, 'seems to have seized all peoples; those of Brabant, for example, are revolting because I have wished to give them that which your nation demands in a great crisis.' He stared dismally.

Ségur told the emperor that Marie Antoinette was in a critical situation and asked for a letter to Joseph's sister. 'Me, to give you a letter!' the emperor exclaimed. 'Everywhere the people are in arms; everywhere one sees brigands; others pillage chateaux . . . At the slightest suspicion a traveller is arrested . . . if one found on you a letter from me, I do not know what would happen to you.'

Ségur asked for a verbal message. 'Eh, what advice, what advice,' the sick man said brusquely, 'do you wish me to give them, when I see them surrounded by men who persuade them that with one regiment, a company of guards, some acclamations, and cockades put up in the midst of an orgy, one can stop and destroy a revolution? I commiserate with them; but, from this distance, I could not indicate any other means to extricate them from so bad a situation than much prudence and firmness; if they have both, everything will, perhaps, arrange itself; if they lack them, I have nothing to say to them.'

Marie Antoinette and Louis XVI had neither prudence nor firmness.

# CHAPTER 17

# Death

*The Emperor is at death's door, blazing up a little, like an expiring taper, but certainly to extinguish soon.*
Thomas Jefferson to John Hay, June 17, 1789

*Der Bauern Gott, der Bürger Noth*
*Des Adels Spott liegt auf dem Tod . . .*
*Imperando, et revocando vixit . . .*
*Menschenhass ohne Reue.*
Viennese satirical witticisms on Joseph's death

*Here lies Joseph II, who was unfortunate in all his enterprises.*
Joseph's own epitaph

The sick emperor was treated by Doctor G. A. Brambilla, founder of the *Josephinum* and the best physician in the capital. Brambilla prescribed a diet of goats' milk, which did no harm, but neither did it do any good. 'I am bedridden,' the patient wrote to Leopold, 'with a fever and pain in the side . . . The lungs, especially the left one near the heart, are much weakened.' Finding it hard to breathe, to speak, to write, or to lie down, he had to sit up in bed or in a chair.

The obstinate man never ceased working. Erysipelas broke out on his face; his lungs became weaker. Still he issued decrees, dictated, held consultations, read dispatches, gave orders. 'I cough, I spit, and respiration is always difficult. I take Seltzer water with goats' milk, but I do not see that it does me any good. This has lasted eight months now, and none of the remedies have wrought the slightest change.' He had few illusions about his illness, realizing that he had 'a malady of the lungs which is incurable'. Dutifully he took the 'decoctions' his doctors prescribed, drank the goats' milk in Seltzer water, but – 'I see very well that these gentlemen [the doctors] will not cure me again'.

Störck, one of the doctors, asked the emperor to be permitted to bring a number of physicians for consultation. Reluctantly Joseph agreed. 'They have examined me,' the patient relates, 'have deliberated, and finished by saying that I should continue the same decoction, and that my lungs are enfeebled and the heart also; they told me not to exert myself . . . *Voilà*, the result which signifies nothing; and what would one expect them to say, when they know neither the disease nor the remedy?' He became disgusted with the doctors and refused to take the 'essence of herbs' which they prescribed. He had 'pain near the shoulders', 'purulent expectoration', continued palpitation of the heart: 'The Aesculapians fumble, change medicines, but gain no ground.'

In the spring of 1789 he began to vomit blood. 'At first,' he wrote to Leopold,

> it was thought to be hemorrhoids, and leeches were applied, but the vomiting continues nevertheless, and even getting worse, seeing that yesterday I vomited almost three ounces of blood at one time . . . I continue spitting blood, but it is more black and clotted than red . . . respiration is more free . . . and the doctors find the pulse astonishingly good.

The symptoms lasted throughout April. 'I drink only cream of barley and broth . . . I take ass' milk . . . I eat no meat in order not to upset the stomach which ought to digest the milk.'

Soon the stomach virtually ceased to function. He had fever and cold chills alternately. Then came pain in the liver. 'I continue to take the same medicines; I purge and have my spleen lubricated twice daily.' The doctors prescribed quinine, but the fever kept returning. Despite the high temperature and an 'obstruction in the liver', the emperor continued to dictate several hours daily to his secretaries. When the physicians urged him to rest, he replied, 'Work has become such an unconquerable habit that it would be too painful for me to remain inactive.'

In June, he complained of being 'tormented by violent pains in the kidneys'. The Aesculapians did their best to relieve him.

By dint of injections, poultices, and other remedies the pain

ceases somewhat; I rise, but it always hurts there, and I have put
on a plaster . . . I observe the strictest diet; I eat neither meat,
nor vegetables, nor dairy products. Soup and rice are my main
nourishment. I do not leave my chamber; I do not open a window;
I am wrapped as I used to be when I went sleigh-riding. I get up
at eleven o'clock, go back to bed about six, and take about half
an ounce of extract of quinine daily; but with all this I still do
not see a relapse in the fever.

As if he did not have enough to die on, new complications set in.
He developed an anal abscess which had to be cut open. Then
he had to submit to another operation; it was 'a sinus in the
place which leads to the orifice and sphincter'. Dr Brambilla
'cut the sphincter in two'. The pain, Joseph wrote, was insupportable. Sleep left him entirely.

Towards the end of the year his stomach became bloated,
the fever and chills returned with new vigour. He sat up, tormented by pain and suffering from the thoughts of revolution
in Belgium, Hungary, and France, 'afflicted by all the horrors'
which Marie Antoinette was facing at Versailles. His anguish
was so great that he prayed for death: 'Any kind of an end would
be the greatest happiness.'

The flesh fell from the dying man and he looked like a
skeleton. To the fever, sleeplessness, suffocation, pain in the
lungs and kidneys a merciful Providence added dropsy. 'My
stomach,' he groaned, 'is so impaired that I have a real disgust
for food.' He could hardly breathe and to find relief he was
forced to lie prone with legs raised.

But in the storm of events he could not die in peace.

As the emperor lay dying his lands were torn by fierce class
conflicts. Few rulers have ever died amidst such articulate
execration. What splendid intentions he had had! Justice,
equality, wealth, security, happiness for his people – such had
been his dreams; for these he virtually gave his life. And what
results! The inheritance laws broke up families. The peasants
complained of lack of land. The prelates loathed the religious
and social egalitarianism. The nobles resented the new order

the result of which was, in the words of Joseph, that 'now many a nobleman is only a lieutenant'. The dissolution of the monasteries threw thousands of doctors, druggists, artisans out of employment. The tariff raised prices. The Turkish war with the resulting taxation threw the burden on the poor people and caused widespread distress.

Wits and pamphleteers were busy savagely castigating the emperor. Hatred and confusion reigned everywhere. Poor people were starving, but it was the aristocracy that was most articulate in its grievances. 'Everybody begins to economize,' wrote the Abbot of Seitenstetten from Vienna; 'horses and servants are laid off; even Prince Kaunitz has only eight courses served at his table. Prince Liechtenstein's war taxes amounted to 92,744 florins, and hence he is economizing. Since everything has doubled in price, and so many people are breadless, there will be real misery here this winter.'

Joseph was galled by the hatred which surrounded him. In his rage he once wanted, it seems, to revoke all his reforms. 'From a very trustworthy source,' writes the Austrian historian Beidtel, 'it is known to the author of this work that . . . Councillor von Spielmann often boasted that it was he who dissuaded Joseph from his decision to recall all his reforms, although the emperor thought the people deserved no better.' When prayers were ordered in the churches for the restoration of the emperor's health, Joseph said: 'I know it; but I also know that the larger part of my subjects does not like me.'

Leopold, his successor, was far off in Tuscany. Kaunitz could not bear the sight of sick people and although he lived only a short distance away, he never saw the emperor alive after 1787. 'Do you believe it possible,' Joseph asked Leopold early in 1789, 'that I have not seen him [Kaunitz] for almost two years?' At a time of the greatest crisis the two rulers of the empire had no personal contact.

Ravaged by pain and fever, Joseph kept on working, always dressed and wigged. In the evening his friends – Lacy, Rosenberg, Dietrichstein, Cobenzl – chatted with him in his room. He knew he was dying, yet he would not take his brother and heir into his confidence. 'I am informed about nothing,' Leopold complained; 'I know only the news from the gazettes.'

'I dare neither speak nor write,' Leopold wrote in invisible lemon ink to his sister, 'nor even think of sending anyone to the Low Countries. I am so much surrounded and spied upon by the dependents of His Majesty that I do not dare stir.'

In Vienna old Kaunitz was discouraged. 'It is frightful,' he groaned, 'how this despotic obstinacy has reduced the beautiful monarchy to such a state.'

By February, 1790, Joseph was at the end of his resistance; he knew he could not live much longer. Enclosing a medical diagnosis which his doctors, at his request, had drawn up (the medical report has been destroyed), the emperor begged Leopold to come to Vienna.

> I conjure you, my dear brother, both in the name of friendship for me and of duty . . . and the patrimony of our ancestors and that of your children . . . to come here as soon as possible. This is essential, and I could not die content unless I knew that the state is provided with a chief . . . You know my heart, my friendship for you; from this you may judge what a consolation it would be to me to see you before my death . . . There is no time to lose . . . At this moment . . . I entrust the [state] to your conscience, if doubts hold you back . . . I am eternally your faithful brother and friend. Joseph.

Leopold hesitated to accept the invitation. He knew his brother's temper too well to arouse his suspicions by appearing in Vienna. Nor would the grand duke accept the co-regency which Joseph offered him – 'as the empress did for me'.

Joseph began to make preparations for death. To his doctor, von Quarin, who tearfully told him that he would not live much longer, Joseph gave 10,000 gulden and made him a baron. Then the emperor wrote farewell letters to his friends. 'Nothing but the impossibility of writing these few lines with trembling hand,' he wrote to Marshal Lacy, 'would induce me to use the hand of another . . . I have seen your tears flow for me; those of a great and wise man are a noble apology. Receive my farewell. I embrace you tenderly.'

With his own trembling hand the dying emperor wrote fare-well letters to his brothers and sisters, none of whom was present. The only relative near him was his favourite nephew, Francis, son of Leopold and afterwards Emperor Francis II. On February 12th, Francis's birthday, Joseph gave his nephew a diamond-studded dagger, in memory of an uncle 'who will soon be no more'. Loudon, the marshal, and Haddick, the president of the War Council, were at the death-bed. 'Give me your old hand,' the emperor said to Haddick; 'I will no longer have the pleasure of pressing it.' The old soldier burst into tears. Joseph turned away his head. 'Adieu, my dear Haddick,' he said in a trembling voice; 'we are seeing each other for the last time.'

The sick man struggled on for five more days, talking and writing. 'I do not know,' he said to a minister, 'whether the poet who writes, "Fearful is the step from the throne to the grave", is right. I do not miss the throne; I feel at peace, but only a little hurt with so much painful effort to have made so few happy and so many ungrateful; but, then, such is the fate of men on the throne.'

He was not really serene, however. Bitterness was eating him. Three days before his own death, his favourite niece Elizabeth died in childbirth. 'And I live yet?' he cried out; 'Lord, thy will be done.' News came of an uprising in the Tyrol and the break with Prussia. 'I will permit them everything,' murmured the broken man, 'only let them allow me to be buried in peace.' Forty-eight hours before he expired he heard that the crown of St Stephen was being taken to Hungary. 'Now I see,' he said, 'that the Almighty is destroying all my works in my lifetime.'

On February 18th and 19th he made his final disposals. To his secretaries, servants, and poor widows he left 500,000 gulden. He signed eighty documents, and wrote letters to Kaunitz, Catharine II, and some women friends. Dressed in boots and gown, he continued dictating to his secretaries until ten o'clock in the evening of February 19th. At that moment Vienna was giving itself up to a lively carnival. 'The carnival,' a correspon-dent reported to his journal, 'is gay and undisturbed.'

U

At ten in the evening the emperor dismissed his secretaries and was laid in bed; he spent a feverish night. At five in the morning he woke up, looked for the sun which had not yet risen, asked for soup, called for his confessor, was seized with convulsions, and four minutes later he was dead. He was not yet forty-nine years old.

The body dressed in a field-marshal's uniform was laid out in the Burg chapel and was placed in the vault of the Capuchin church on the third day. The people of Vienna, shivering in the cold and suffering from high prices and heavy taxes, followed the funeral with imprecations. 'After the Turkish campaign,' people said bitterly, 'Joseph gave his officers a small cross, but his citizens the big one.'

At the news of Joseph's death Kaunitz said that the emperor had shown 'great and admirable qualities'.

Hungary celebrated gaily. The Cardinal-Archbishop of Gran sang a *Te Deum*. In Pest the whole city was illuminated and the German flag was publicly burned.

Only Prince de Ligne lamented the dead man. 'He is no more, Madame,' he wrote to Catharine of Russia, 'he is no more, the prince who did honour to mankind, the man who did most honour to princes. That ardent spirit is extinguished like a flame.'

# Appendices

# Appendices

# APPENDIX I

## STRUCTURE OF GOVERNMENT UNDER MARIA THERESA AND JOSEPH II

### COUNCIL OF STATE
#### (*Staatsrath*)

In control of four major Cabinet departments:

1. *Chancery* (*Hofkanzlei*), for administration.

2. *Exchequer* (*Hofkammer*), for finances.

3. *Council of War* (*Hofkriegsrath*), for military affairs.

4. *High Court of Justice* (*Hofrath*), for judicial affairs.

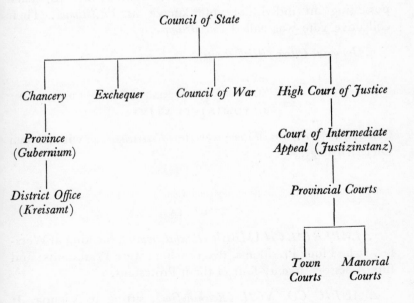

# APPENDIX II

## A. LEGISLATIVE

*IMPERIAL DIET* (*Reichstag*), consisting of three colleges:

1. *Electors.* They were nine in number, three spiritual (Archbishops of Cologne, Mainz, and Trier) and six laic (Count Palatine of the Rhine; Elector of Saxony; Margrave of Brandenburg; the Kings of Bavaria, Bohemia, and Hanover).

2. *Imperial Princes* (*Reichsfuersten*). There were about forty of them – Dukes, Margraves, Pfalzgraves, Barons, Bishops – each possessing an individual vote known as *Virilstimme*. Their collective vote was called *Curialstimme*.

3. *Imperial Cities* (*Reichstaedte*).

## B. ADMINISTRATIVE

*CIRCLES* (*Kreissen*). There were ten *Kreissen*, each with its own Diet (*Kreistag*).

## C. JUDICIAL

1. *IMPERIAL CHAMBER* (*Reichskammer*), meeting at Wetzlar. It had four Presidents, two of whom were Protestants; and fifty Assessors, twenty-four of them Protestant.

2. *AULIC COUNCIL* (*Reichshofrat*), sitting in Vienna. It consisted of one President and eighteen Councillors.

# Bibliography

# BIBLIOGRAPHY

Part of this book is based on unpublished manuscript materials found in the Vienna archives. For published sources, the author has relied largely on the publications – letters, documents, state papers – of the standard Austrian and German scholars, notably Arneth, Wolf, and Beer. Of special importance are the works of Arneth, particularly his 10-volume *History of Maria Theresa*, which in its scope and thoroughness, is a veritable encyclopedia of the epoch. Another fruitful collection is Frederick the Great's monumental *Politsche Correspondenz* in 35 volumes.

The few published biographies of Joseph II in German and French have been of limited utility, primarily because of a tendency to be controversial. The only English-language biography, that of J. F. Bright, published in 1897, is much too thin to be useful. As for contemporary memoirs that throw personal light on the subject, Austrians have produced few of them in the eighteenth century. The best are the French, written by aristocrats who were international in their interests and connections. M. F. Barrière's library of memoirs – *Bibliothèque des mémoires relatifs à l'histoire de France pendant le XVIIIe siècle* – is an indispensable collection of autobiographies.

The following list does not claim to be exhaustive. It does not, for example, include newspapers and pamphlets, of which there was a plethora in the Josephan period. But the author has tried to select the most important publications on the subject, to be found not only in Vienna, but also in the library of the University of Chicago, the Crerar and Newberry Libraries in Chicago, the Library of Congress in Washington, D.C., and the Library of the University of California in Berkeley. Only those books actually used are included in this bibliography.

## ABBREVIATIONS

*A.O.G.* – *Archiv für Oesterreichische Geschichte*

*B.B.M.* – Barrière, ed., *Bibliothèque des mémoires relatifs à l'histoire de France pendant le XVIIIe siècle*

*F.R.A.* – *Fontes Rerum Austriacarum*

*H.Z.* – *Historische Zeitschrift*

*K.A.* – *Kirchenrechtliche Abhandlungen*, by U. Stutz

*K.H.* – *Kwartalnik Historyczny*

*M.C.* – *Mémoires couronnés et mémoires des savants étrangers publiés par l'Académie Royale des Sciences et des Beaux-Arts de Belgique*

*Z.B.* – *Zeitschrift für Bücherfreunde*

GUIDE

The best bibliographical guide to Austrian history is F. Krones, *Grundriss der oesterreichischen Geschichte mit besonderer Rücksicht auf Quellen- und Literaturkunde* (Vienna, 1882)

SOURCES

BEER, A., 'Denkschriften des Fürsten Kaunitz', in *A.O.G.*, XLVIII (1872) 1*f*

HANDELMANN, H., ed., 'Vom Wiener Hof. Aus der Zeit der Kaiserin Maria Theresia und Kaiser Josephs II. Aus ungedruckten Depeschen des Grafen Johann Friedrich Bachoff von Echt Königlich Dänischen Gesandten (von 1750 bis 1781) am Kaiserlichen Hofe', in *A.O.G.*, XXXVII (1867), 459–67

*Joseph dez Zweyten Gesetz über einheitlichen Steuerfuss mit Belehrung, Formulare und Summarium*. Text in German and Latin, being a manual and guide for the land surveyors (Vienna, 1786)

KHEVENHÜLLER-METSCH, J. J., *Aus der Zeit Maria Theresias. Tagebuch des fürsten Johann Josef Khevenhüller-Metsch, kaiserlichen obersthofmeisters 1742–76*, edited by R. Khevenhüller-Metsch and H. Schlitter (7 vols., Vienna, 1907–25)

MARTENS, F. DE, *Recueil des traités et conventions conclus par la Russie avec les puissances étrangères*, II, *Traités avec l'Autriche*, 1772–1808 (St Petersburg, 1785); VI, *Traités avec l'Allemagne*, 1762–1808 (St Petersburg, 1883)

NEUMANN, L. and PLASSON, A., ed., *Recueil de traités et conventions conclus par l'Autriche avec les puissances étrangères depuis 1763 jusqu'à nos jours* (20 vols., Leipzig, 1855–1902)

*Politisches Journal nebst Anzeige von gelehrten und andern Sachen*. Journal published monthly at Hamburg, starting in 1786

*Recueil des instructions données aux ambassadeurs et ministres de France depuis les traités de Westphalie jusqu' à la révolution française:*
 *Pologne*, II (ed. L. Fargo; Paris, 1888)
 *Autriche*, I (ed. A. Sorel; Paris, 1884)
 *Russie*, II (ed. A. Rambaud; Paris, 1890)
 *Prusse* (ed. A. Waddington; Paris, 1901)

WERTHEIMER, E., ed., 'Zwei Schilderungen des Wiener Hofes in XVIII Jahrhundert', in *A.O.G.*, LXII (1881), 201–37. The documents here published are from the Paris archives (Ministry of Foreign Affairs), and are entitled *Portraits de la Cour de Vienne*, and *Tableaux des ministres et des principaux personnages de la Cour de Vienne ainsi que des ambassadeurs et ministres étrangers qui y résident*; they were written some time about 1770 possibly by the Marquis de Durfort.

CORRESPONDENCE

ARNETH, A. and FLAMMERMONT, J., ed., *Correspondance secrète du Comte de Mercy-Argenteau avec l'Empereur Joseph II et le Prince de Kaunitz* (2 vols., Paris, 1889–91). See the review in *English Historical Review*, VII (1892), 792–6

ARNETH, A., ed., *Joseph II und Katharine von Russland. Ihr Briefwechsel* (Vienna, 1869)

ARNETH, A., ed., *Joseph II und Leopold von Toscana. Ihr Briefwechsel von 1781 bis 1790* (2 vols., Vienna, 1872). The Vienna archives contain 575 letters of Joseph to Leopold for this period, and only 161 letters of Leopold to Joseph; it seems that the emperor destroyed most of his brother's correspondence

ARNETH, A., ed., *Maria Theresa und Joseph II. Ihre Correspondenz sammt Briefen Joseph's an seinen Bruder Leopold* (3 vols. for 1761 to 1780; Vienna, 1867)

ARNETH, A., ed., *Marie Antoinette, Joseph II und Leopold II. Ihr Briefwechsel* (Leipzig, Paris, and Vienna, 1866)

ARNETH, A. and GEFFROY, M. A., ed., *Correspondance secrète entre Marie-Thérèse et le Cte de Mercy-Argenteau, avec les lettres de Marie Thérèse et de Marie Antoinette* (3 vols., Paris, 1874)

BEER, A. and FIEDLER, J., ed., 'Joseph II und Graf Ludwig Cobenzl. Ihr Briefwechsel', in *F.R.A.*, II, liii-liv (1901)

BEER, A., ed., *Joseph II, Leopold und Kaunitz. Ihr Briefwechsel* (Vienna, 1873)

BEER, A., ed., *Leopold II, Franz II und Catharina. Ihre Correspondenz* (Leipzig, 1874)

*Briefe einer Kaiserin, Maria Theresia an ihre Kinder und Freunde* (Berlin, 1910)

BRUNNER, S., ed., *Correspondance intime de l'Empereur Joseph II avec son ami le Comte de Cobenzl et son premier ministre le Prince de Kaunitz* (Mainz, Paris, Brussels, 1871)

CALVI, F., ed., 'Lettere di Giuseppe II Imperatore', in *Curiosità Storiche e Diplomatiche del secolo decimottavo*, pp. 491–513 (Milan, 1878)

CORBERON, B. de, *Un diplomate français à la cour de Catherine II, 1775–80. Journal intime du Chevalier de Corberon, chargé d'affaires de France en Russie* (2 vols., Paris, 1901)

FREDERICK II, KING OF PRUSSIA, *Œuvres* (30 vols. and index; Berlin, 1846–57)

FREDERICK II, KING OF PRUSSIA, *Politische Correspondenz* (35 vols., Berlin, 1879–1912). The last volume was published in Weimar, 1912

GROT, J., ed., 'Pisma Imperatritzy Ekaterinyi II k' Grimmu (1774–96)', in *Sbornik Imperatorskoyo Russkavo Istoricheskayo Obschtschestva*, XXIII (St. Petersburg, 1878) [Letters of the Empress Catharine II to Grimm, in Collection of the Imperial Russian Historical Society]

GROT, J., ed., 'Lettres de Grimm à l'Impératrice Catherine II', in *Sbornik Imperatorskoyo Russkavo Istoricheskayo Obschtschestva*, XLIV (St Petersburg, 1885)

KRACK, O., ed., *Briefe eines Kaisers. Joseph II an seine Mutter und Geschwister* (Berlin, 1912)

Letters of Joseph, selected from *Briefe von Joseph des Zweyten, als characteristische Beiträge zur Lebens- und Staatsgeschichte dieses unvergesslichen Selbstherrschers. Bis jetzt ungedrückt* (Leipzig, 1822), in *North American Review*, XXXI (1830), pp. 1–26

MALMESBURY THIRD EARL, ed., *Diaries and Correspondence of James Harris, First Earl of Malmesbury, Containing an Account of His Missions at the Court of Madrid, to Frederick the Great, Catherine the Second, and at The Hague; and of his special missions to Berlin, Brunswick, and the French Republic* (4 vols., London, 1845)

*Recueil de lettres originales de l'Empereur Joseph II au Général d'Alton, commandant les troupes aux Pays-Bas, depuis Décembre 1787 jusqu'en Novembre 1789* (Paris, 1790)

SCHLITTER, H., ed., *Kaunitz, Philipp Cobenzl und Spielmann. Ihr Briefwechsel (1779–92)* (Vienna, 1899)

SCHUSELKA, F., ed., *Briefe Josephs des Zweiten* (3rd ed., Leipzig, 1846)

SMYTH, G., ed., *Memoirs and Correspondence of Sir Robert Murray Keith, K.B. Envoy Extraordinary and Minister Plenipotentiary at the Courts of Dresden, Copenhagen, and Vienna, from 1769 to 1792* (2 vols. in one; London, 1849)

TOYNBEE, P., ed., *Lettres de la Marquise du Deffand à Horace Walpole (1766–80)* (3 vols., London, 1912)

VOLTAIRE, *Œuvres complètes*, I (Paris, 1883); XLVII (Paris, 1882); L (Paris, 1882)

WOLF, A., ed., *Leopold II und Marie Christine. Ihr Briefwechsel (1781–92)* (Vienna, 1867)

WOLF, G., *Josefina* (Vienna, 1890)

MEMOIRS

BORN, I., *Travels Through the Bannat of Temesvar, Transylvania, and Hungary, in the Year 1770* (translated from the German by R. E. Raspe; London, 1777)

BOUILLÉ *Mémoires du Marquis de*, in *B.B.M.* (Paris, 1890)

BRISSOT, *Mémoires de*, in *B.B.M.* (Paris, 1877)

CAMPAN, *Mémoires sur la vie de Marie-Antoinette Reine de France et de Navarre*, in *B.B.M.* (Paris, 1886)

DOHM, C. W., *Denkwürdigkeiten meiner Zeit, oder Beiträge zur Geschichte vom letzten Viertel des achtzehnten und von Anfang des neunzehnten Jahrhunderts. 1778 bis 1806* (Lemgo and Hanover, 1814–17)

GEORGEL, ABBÉ, *Mémoires pour servir à l'histoire des évènemens de la fin du dix-huitième siècle depuis 1760 jusqu'en 1806–10*, I (Paris, 1817)

GOETHE, W., *Dichtung und Wahrheit*, I, in *Sämmtliche Werke*, XX (Jubiläums-Ausgaben, Stuttgart and Berlin, n.d.)

LIGNE, *Pensées et lettres du Maréchal Prince de*, in *B.B.M.* (Paris, 1890)

MARMONTEL, *Mémoires de*, in *B.B.M.* (Paris, 1891)

PICHLER, C., *Denkwürdigkeiten aus meinem Leben* (2 vols., Munich, 1914)

RICHELIEU, *Mémoires du Maréchal duc de*, in *B.B.M.* (Paris, 1889)

SÉGUR, *Mémoires, souvenirs et anecdotes par M. le Comte de*, in *B.B.M.* (Paris, 1890)

TILLY, *Souvenirs du Comte Alexandre de*, in *B.B.M.* (Paris 1882)

*Wahl und Krönung Joseph des Zweyten zum römischen Könige* (An anonymous contemporary account; n.p., n.d.)

WEBER, *Mémoires de (frère de lait de Marie Antoinette)*, in *B.B.M.* (Paris, 1885)

WHEATLEY, H. B., ed., *The Historical and the Posthumous Memoirs of Sir Nathaniel William Wraxall, 1772–84* (London, 1884)

WORMELEY, K. P., ed., *The Prince de Ligne, His Memoirs, Letters, and Miscellaneous Papers* (2 vols., Boston, 1902)

WRAXALL, N. W., *Memoirs of the Courts of Berlin, Dresden, Warsaw, and Vienna, In the Years 1777, 1778, and 1779* (2 vols., London, 1799)

BIOGRAPHIES

ARNETH, A., '*Biographie des Fürsten Kaunitz. Ein Fragment*', in *A.O.G.*, LXXXVIII (1900), pp. 1–95

ARNETH, A., *Geschichte Maria Theresia's* (10 vols., Vienna, 1863–79)

ARNETH, A., '*Graf Philipp Cobenzl und seine Memoiren*,' in *A.O.G.*, LCVII (1886), pp. 1–177

BEER, A., 'Joseph II', in Gottschall's *Der Neue Plutarch*, IX (Leipzig, 1882), pp. 111–204

BRIGHT, J. F., *Joseph II* (London, 1897)

BRIGHT, J. F., *Maria Theresa* (London, 1897)

BRICKNER, A., *Katharina II* (Berlin, 1883)

BRUNNER, S., *Joseph II. Charakteristik seines Lebens, seiner Regierung und seiner Kirchenreform* (Freiburg i.B., 1885)

CARACCIOLI, MARQUIS DE, *La vie de Joseph II, Empereur d'Allemagne, Roi de Hongrie et de Bohème* (Amsterdam and Utrecht, 1790)

GROSS-HOFFINGER, A. J., *Geschichte Josephs des Zweiten* (Leipzig, 1847)

HOLMES, E., *Life of Mozart, Including his Correspondence* (London and New York, 1868)

HORMAYR, J., 'Wenzel Anton Fürst von Kaunitz', in *Oesterreichischer Plutarch*, XII, ch. XXV (Vienna, 1807)

JÄGER, A., *Kaiser Joseph II und Leopold II. Reform und Gegenreform 1780–92* (Vienna, 1867)

KÜNTZEL, G., *Fürst Kaunitz-Rittberg als Staatsman* (Frankfort a.M., 1923)

MITROFANOV, P. P., *Joseph II; seine politische und kulturelle Tätigkeit* (2 vols., Vienna and Leipzig, 1910)

NISSEN, G. N., *Biographie W. A. Mozart's* (Leipzig, 1828)

PADOVER, S. K., *The Life and Death of Louis XVI* (New York and London, 1939 and 1965)

PAGANEL, C., *Histoire de Joseph II, Empereur d'Allemagne* (Paris, 1845)

RAMSHORN, C., *Kaiser Joseph II und seine Zeit* (Leipzig, 1845)

RIOUST, M., *Joseph II, Empereur d'Allemagne, peint par lui-même* (Brussels, 1823)

WENDRINSKY, J., *Kaiser Josef II* (Vienna, 1880)

WOLF, A., *Fürstin Eleonore Liechtenstein 1745–1812, nach Briefen und Memoiren ihrer Zeit* (Vienna, 1875)

WOLF, A., *Marie Christine, Erzherzogin von Oesterreich* (2 vols., Vienna, 1863)

ZWIEDINECK-SÜDENHORST, H., *Maria Theresa* (Bielefeld and Leipzig, 1905)


REFORM AND ADMINISTRATION

BEIDTEL, I., *Geschichte der österreichischen Staatsverwaltung 1740–1848*; I, *1740–92* (ed. A. Huber; Innsbruck, 1896)

FOURNIER, A., *Historische Studien und Skizzen*, II (Vienna and Leipzig, 1908)

GRÜNBERG, K., *Die Bauernbefreiung und die Auflösung des gutsherrlich-bäuerlichen Verhältnisses in Böhmen, Mähren und Schlesien* (2 vols., Leipzig, 1893–4)

HOCK, C. and BIDERMANN, H. I., *Der österreichische Staatsrath* (1760–1848) (Vienna, 1879)

HOUBEN, H. H., 'Kaiser Josephs II Zensurreform', in *Z.B.*, neue Folge, x¹ (1918), pp. 85–93

KELLE, J., 'Die Jesuiten Gymnasien in Österreich', in *H.Z.*, xxxv (1876), pp. 230–345

REICHARD, 'Der in den deutschen Provinzen de österreichischen Monarchie bestehende Behörden-Organismus für die Justiz und Verwaltung', in *Zeitschrift für die Gesammte Staatswissenschaft* (1847), pp. 479–522

## THE CHURCH

FEBRONIUS, J., *Buch von Zustand der Kirche und der rechtmässigen Gewalt des Römischen Papsts, die in der Religion widriggesinnten Christen zu vereinigen* (Translated from the Latin; Wardingen, 1764)

DUBNOW, S., *Die neueste Geschichte des jüdischen Volkes*, viii (Berlin, 1928)

GEIER, F., *Die Durchführung der kirchlichen Reformen Joseph's II in vorderösterreichischen Breisgau*, in *K.A.* (Stuttgart, 1905). See also the review in *Revue d'histoire ecclésiastique*, vii (1906), pp. 123–5

GRAETZ, H., *History of the Jews*, v (Philadelphia, 1895)

GUGLIA, E., 'Zur Geschichte der Bischofswahlen in den deutschen Reichstiftern unter Joseph II', in *Mitteilungen des Instituts für öosterreichische Geschichtsforschung*, xxxiv (1913), pp. 296–314

KUSEJ, J. R., *Joseph II und die Aussere Kirchenverfassung Innerösterreichs*, in *K.A.* (Stuttgart, 1908)

MICHIELS, A., *Secret History of the Austrian Government and of its Systematic Persecution of Protestants* (London, 1859)

SCHLITTER, H., *Die Reise des Papstes Pius VI nach Wien und sein Aufenthalt daselbst*, in *F.R.A.*, xlvii, sec. 1, pt. ii, pp. 1–222 (Vienna, 1892)

ZILLICH, H., *Febronius*, in *Hallesche Abhandlungen zur neueren Geschichte*, no. 44 (Halle, 1906)

## CULTURE

BAB, J. and HANDL, W., *Wien und Berlin. Vergleichendes zur Kulturgeschichte der beiden Hauptstädte Mitteleuropas* (Berlin, 1918)

LANSDALE, M. H., *Vienna and the Viennese* (Philadelphia, 1902)

LUSTKANDI, W., *Die Josefinischen Ideen und Ihr Erfolg. Festrede zur hundertjährigen Gedenkfeier des Regierungsantrittes Kaiser Joseph des Zweiten, gehalten in der Aula der Universität zu Wien am 29 November 1880* (Vienna, 1881)

MARX, A. B., *Gluck und die Oper* (2 vols., Berlin, 1863)

SALOMON, L., *Geschichte des Deutschen Zeitungswesens*, I (Oldenburg and Leipzig, 1906)

SCHIEL, A., *Ignaz von Felbiter und Ferdinand Kindermann, Ihr Leben und Ihre Schriften* (Halle, 1902)

THURN, R. P., ed., *Joseph II als Theaterdirektor. Ungedruckte Briefe und Aktenstücke aus den Kinderjahren des Burgtheaters* (Vienna and Leipzig, 1920)

TIETZE, H., *Wien* (Leipzig, 1918)

TULLA, A., 'Kleine Bausteine zur Bibliographie des Wiener deutschen Theaters im 18 Jahrhunderts', II, in *Z.B.*, neue Folge, XI[1] (1919), pp. 83–87

WOLKAN, R., ed., *Wiener Volkslieder aus fünf Jahrhunderten*, I (Vienna, 1926)

FOREIGN POLICY

ANGEBERG. *See* CHODŹKO.

ARNAUD-BOUTELOUP, J., *Le rôle politique de Marie-Antoinette* (Paris, 1924)

ASKENAZY, S., *Die letzte polnische Königswahl* (Göttingen, 1894)

BEER, A., 'Zur Geschichte des bayerischen Erbfolgkrieges', in *H.Z.*, XXXV (1876), pp. 88–152

BEER, A., *Die Erste Theilung Polens* (2 vols. and one volume entitled *Documente*; Vienna, 1873)

BEER, A., 'Die Zusammenkünfte Josefs II und Friedrichs II zu Neisse und Neustadt', in *A.O.G.*, XLVII (1871), pp. 383–527

BOUTARIC, M. E., ed., *Correspondance secrète inédite de Louis XV sur la politique étrangère avec le Comte de Broglie, Tercier, etc.* (2 vols., Paris, 1866)

BROGLIE, DUC DE, *Le secret du Roi, correspondance secrète de Louis XV avec ses agents diplomatiques* (1752–74) (Paris, 1879). *See* the review in *Journal des Savants*, September 1879, pp. 550–60, 581–9

BROWNING, O., 'The Triple Alliance of 1788', in *Transactions of the Royal Historical Society*, new series, pp. 77–96 (London, 1885)

BRUNNER, S., *Der Humor in der Diplomatie und Regierungskunde des 18 Jahrhunderts. Hof- Adels- und diplomatische Kreise Deutschlands, geschildert aus geheiman Gesandschaftsberichten und anderen ebenfalls durchwegs archivalischen bisher unedirten Quellen* (2 vols. in one; Vienna, 1872)

CHODŹKO, L., *Recueil des traités, conventions, et actes diplomatiques concernant la Pologne, 1762–1862, par le Comte d'Angeberg* (Paris, 1862)

DUNCKER, M., *Aus der Zeit Friedrich des Grossen und Friedrich Wilhelms III* (Leipzig, 1876)

FLASSAN, M., *Histoire générale et raisonnée de la diplomatique française, ou de la politique de la France, depuis la fondation de la monarchie, jusqu'à la fin du règne de Louis XVI*, VI and VII (Paris, 1811)

GOERTZ, E., ed., *Mémoires et actes authentiques relatifs aux négociations, qui ont précédé le partage de la Pologne* (Weimar, 1810)

HAMMER, J., *Geschichte des osmanischen Reiches*, IV (Pest, 1836)

HANFSTAENGEL, E. F. S., *Von Marlborough bis Mirabeau. Die weltpolitische Bedeutung des belgisch-bairischen Tauschprojekts im Rahmen der hydro-geographischen Donau-Rhein-Scheldepolitik und der österreichisch-amerikanischen Handelspläne Kaiser Josephs II und John Adams*, etc. (Munich, 1930)

JORGA, N., *Geschichte des osmanischen Reiches, nach den Quellen dargestellt*, IV (Gotha, 1911)

LOEBL, A. H., 'Österreich und Preussen. 1766–68', in *A.O.G.*, XCII (1903), pp. 365–482

MILLER, W., 'Europe and the Ottoman Power before the Nineteenth Century', in *English Historical Review*, XVI (1901), pp. 452–71

MARSANGY, L. B., *Le Chevalier de Vergennes, son ambassade à Constantinople*, II (Paris, 1894)

PADOVER, S. K., *Prince Kaunitz and the First Partition of Poland* (Ph.D. Dissertation, MS. in the University of Chicago Library, 1932)

PADOVER, S. K., 'Prince Kaunitz' Résumé of his Eastern Policy, 1763–71', in *The Journal of Modern History*, V (1933), pp. 352–65

RANKE, L., *Die deutschen Mächte und der Fürstenbund* (Leipzig, 1875)

RUTKOWSKI, J., *Histoire économique de la Pologne avant les partages* (Paris, 1927)

SEIFARTH, L., *Die auswärtige Politik Friedrichs des Grossen von 1772 bis 1774* (Leipzig, 1918)

SMOLENSKI, W., *Dzieje narodu Polskiego* (Cracow, 1921)

SOREL, A., *The Eastern Questions in the Eighteenth Century, the Partition of Poland and the Treaty of Kainardji* (Translated by F. C. Bramwell; London, 1898)

TEMPERLEY, H. W. V., *Frederic the Great and Kaiser Joseph, an Episode of War and Diplomacy in the Eighteenth Century* (London, 1915)

TRATSCHEWSKY, A., 'Das russisch-österreichische Bündniss vom Jahre 1781', in *H.Z.*, XXXIV (1875), pp. 361–96

WOLF, G., *Oesterreich und Preussen 1780–90* (Vienna, 1880). See the review in *H.Z.*, XLV (1881), pp. 115–25

ZINKEISEN, J. W., *Geschichte des osmanischen Reiches in Europa*, V (Gotha, 1857)

## THE LOW COUNTRIES

DE BOOM, *Les ministres plénipotentiaires dans les Pays-Bas Autrichiens, principalement Cobenzl*, in *M.C.* (Brussels, 1932)

HUBERT, E., *Les finances des Pays-Bas à l'avènement de Joseph II* (1780–81) (Brussels, 1899)

HUBERT, E., *Le voyage de l'Empereur Joseph II dans les Pays-Bas (31 Mai 1781 – 27 Juillet 1781)*, in *M.C.*, LVIII, pp. 1–468 (Brussels, 1899–1900)

LINDEN, H., VANDER, *Belgium, The Making of a Nation* (Translated by S. Jane; Oxford, 1920)

LORENZ, O., *Joseph II und die Belgische Revolution nach den Papieren des General-Gouverneurs Grafen Murray. 1787* (Vienna, 1862)

LORENZ, O., *Joseph II und die Niederlände* (Vienna, 1862)

MAGNETTE, F., *Joseph et la liberté de l'Escaut*, in *M.C.* (Brussels, 1896–8)


## THE AUSTRIAN LANDS

ANONYMOUS, 'The Wallachs in Transylvania', in *Fraser's Magazine*, XLII (1850), pp. 552–60

FINKEL, L., 'Memoryal Antoniego hr. Pergena, pierwszego gubernatora Galicyi, o stanie kraju' [Memoir of Count Anton Pergen, First Governor of Galicia, concerning the condition of the land], in *K.H.*, XIV (1900), pp. 24–43

GRAGGER, R., *Preussen, Weimar und die ungarische Königskrone. Mit dem Faksimile eines Goethe-Briefes* (Berlin and Leipzig, 1923)

HORVATH, E., *Modern Hungary, 1660–1920* (Budapest, 1922)

KAINDL, R. F., *Geschichte der deutschen in den Karpathenländern* (3 vols., Gotha, 1907–11)

KERNER, R. J., *Bohemia in the Eighteenth Century. A Study in Political, Economic, and Social History, With Special Reference to the Reign of Leopold II, 1790–92* (New York, 1932)

KNATCHBULL-HUGESSEN, C. M., *The Political Evolution of the Hungarian Nation* (2 vols., London, 1908)

LOZINSKI, B., 'Poczatki ery józefinskiej w Galicyi' [Beginnings of the Josephan Era in Galicia], in *K.H.*, XXIV (1910), pp. 163–206

LOZINSKI, B., 'Z czasów józefinskich' [From the Josephan Times], in *K.H.*, XIX (1905), pp. 42–64

LÜTZIW, COUNT, *Bohemia, An Historical Sketch* (London and New York, n.d.)

MARCZALI, H., *Hungary in the Eighteenth Century, With an Introductory Essay on the Earlier History of Hungary by H. W. V. Temperley* (Cambridge, 1910)

ZIEGLAUER, F., *Die politische Reformbewegung in Siebenbürgen zur Zeit Josef's II and Leopold's II* (Vienna, 1885)

### GENERAL HISTORIES

ATKINSON, C. T., *A History of Germany, 1715–1815* (London, 1908)

BEER, A., *Geschichte des Welthandels im neunzehnten Jahrhundert* (2 vols. in one; Vienna, 1884). Ch. vii in vol. II discusses Austria under Joseph

BIEDERMANN, K., *Deutschland im achzehnten Jahrhundert*, II (Leipzig, 1880)

*The Cambridge History of Modern Europe:* VI, *The Eighteenth Century* (London and New York, 1909)

COXE, W., *History of the House of Austria, From the Foundation of the Monarchy by Rhodolph of Hapsburgh to the Death of Leopold the Second, 1218 to 1792*, III (London, 1889)

GOTTSCHALK, L. R., *The Era of the French Revolution (1715–1815)* (Boston, New York, 1929)

IMMICH, M., *Geschichte des Europäischen Staatensystems von 1660 bis 1789* (Munich and Berlin, 1905)

KRONES, F., *Handbuch der Geschichte oesterreichs von ältesten bis zur neuesten Zeit*, IV (Berlin, 1879)

ONCKEN, W., *Das Zeitalter Friedrichs des Grossen* (Berlin, 1881–2)

PALMER, R. R., *The Age of the Democratic Revolution* (Princeton, N.J., 1964)

RENARD, G. and WEULERSSE, G., *Life and Work in Modern Europe* (Translated by M. Richards; New York, 1926)

SCHLOSSER, F. C., *Weltgeschichte für das deutsche Volk*, XIV (Berlin, 1886)

SOREL, A., *L'Europe et la Révolution Française*, I (Paris, 1893)

STRYIENSKI, C., *The Eighteenth Century* (Translated by H. N. Dickinson; London and New York)

TUTTLE, H., *History of Prussia under Frederick the Great* (New York, 1888)

VEHSE, E., *Geschichte der deutschen Höfe*, XII–XV (Hamburg, 1852)

WARD, A. W. and GOOCH, G. P., *The Cambridge History of British Foreign Policy, 1783–1919*, I (London and New York, 1922)

WOLF, A., *Geschichtliche Bilder aus Oesterreich*, I (Vienna, 1878)

WOLF, A., *Oesterreich unter Maria Theresia, Josef II und Leopold II, 1740–92* (Berlin, 1884)

# Index

# INDEX